SHORT STORIES IN THE MAKING

A WRITERS' AND STUDENTS' INTRODUCTION
TO THE TECHNIQUE AND PRACTICAL COM-
POSITION OF SHORT STORIES, INCLUDING
AN ADAPTATION OF THE PRINCIPLES OF
THE STAGE PLOT TO SHORT STORY WRITING

BY

ROBERT WILSON NEAL, A.M.

Whitworth College
Spokane, Wn.

NEW YORK

OXFORD UNIVERSITY PRESS

AMERICAN BRANCH: 35 WEST 32ND STREET

LONDON, TORONTO, MELBOURNE, AND BOMBAY
HUMPHREY MILFORD

1914

To
My Wife

FOREWORD

WHAT is wanting in this book, critics, teachers, and students will all too readily discover without my help. Let me rather point out, then, what it is meant to do.

First. It deals with short stories (contes) in the making. Therefore it is intended for the writer. And because many of the readers most interested in such a book are beginners, it is intended in large part for the inexperienced. Yet it is intended for the advanced undertaker of story-telling too; for no one can stake the border between elementary theory and expert application of it, and even the experienced writer may find surety and improved method in a study of technique. Yet the book is for the non-writer also—for him who wishes in compact form a reasonably complete and concrete explanation of the short story and its nature.

Second. The book does not profess to be scholarly— certainly not to be scholarly in the academic sense. It has avoided the historical entirely; it attempts no comparative studies in development and types, no evaluating estimates; it is not a research volume, and the reader will seek through it from end to end without finding a single formal citation of authorities, the proof that the writer knows the conventional doctrine, dares not depart from it, and is ready with marshaled knowledge to protect himself from any who may accuse him of betraying the gentle trusting reader by novelty or new departure. Not that this book can pretend to either of these. At most (and even this it does not profess), it adds a trifle of discussion at a place or two. But it does undertake to make its own approach and use its own plan in summarizing what is our present knowledge of the theory and technique of the short story.

Third. The book is written, not from the critic's but from the practicing author's viewpoint—from the standing-ground and outlook of the man to whom the abstract theory, although interesting and valuable, is less interesting and valuable than the concrete management and application of it. It is written to meet the needs of the man who, for practical and utilitarian reasons no less than from abstract intellectual interest, desires to know the what, the how, and the why of the short story. I have written good, bad, and indifferent short stories, and hope to keep on writing; and this interest in the mechanics, the artisanry and art, the technique of the work, has caused me to treat the subject from the viewpoint of the active worker rather than from that of the esthetic theorist or the literary investigator. Throughout, I have been concerned to learn the governing rule, and then to state it in such form that my statement may make it available to other practitioners, especially to apprentice workers striving to extend their workman's knowledge and develop their artisan skill. (The author expects to publish soon a companion volume, *To-day's Short Stories Analyzed,* in which the practice of modern writers of short stories will be fully illustrated and exemplified.)

Fourth. Most of the principles stated are drawn as much from reading and observation of the ordinary mill run of short fiction, in book collections and in magazines, for the last twenty years, as they are from the recognized authorities on short story writing. He who reads and runs away sometimes carries with him well-defined ideas that are usable another day; and I have felt that such readers' observations and conclusions are as valuable in checking up the statements of the authorities, as the statements of the authorities are in checking up one's own observations and conclusions. I owe (as any one can see from this book) a great debt to some of these authorities—especially to Pitkin, Albright, and Esenwein, if I must discriminate —and I here acknowledge it, with gratitude. But even so I have endeavored to remain independent in reaching and stating my conclusions; and in this I have been frequently aided by personal experience of success or failure in handling problems of like sort in my own writing.

Fifth. The book attempts to define terms with especial precision; with tedious over-precision, some may think. It tries, too, not to employ the same term with two meanings in any position where confusion may result. Probably it fails sometimes in this attempt to avoid ambiguity and confusion; but on the whole I trust that it succeeds enough to lessen for its readers the difficulties of this sort that occasionally I have met in my own reference to treatises upon fiction.

Sixth. Plot being indispensable to the true short story, or conte, and the short story being in effect a narrative drama, the book undertakes to re-present the familiar theory of the stage play, but to present it adapted and applied to the nature and needs of the short story. This fact calls for mention only because so outright an application of formal stage plot theory to short story narration has not been made elsewhere—not, at least, in English. A satisfactory treatment of the theory of the specialized short story (conte) plot has yet to be produced; but lacking it, the student will find in a re-statement of the theory of stage plot like that given in this book, a helpful presentation of essential principles. . . .

Need of a specialized term by which to indicate the specialized form of short fiction sometimes awkwardly called the true short story, has long been felt. Professor Canby's suggestion of the term *conte* has not been bettered; and as without undue violence to historical descent or to strict meanings *conte* can be applied to this particular type of short prose fiction, I have ventured to employ it interchangeably with the term "short story," in order that students using this book may at least become familiar with this possible synonym.

Those who complain of the fullness and, possibly, redundancy of the treatment given very simple matters, I would ask to remember that the book is largely for beginners in short story writing and readers of ordinary education seeking instruction or an increase in literary understanding and appreciation, who can find these things in study of short story principles. Those who mislike the occasional discussion of remote or special problems, will please remind themselves that I am writing for persons also who have more than a tyro's interest in the technicalities of the subject. Those who blame me for omitting an explanation of narration itself, are referred to the numerous excellent treatises already in print upon the general principles of narrative writing, with the suggestion that even in writing about the short story, one must begin somewhere, assuming some preparation at least for study of the special type. And those who wonder why matters so important to literary art as style and

esthetic qualities are not discussed, are told—in the strictest confidence, please—that style and literary art are quite
another story.

A last word—to those who scoff at " attempts to manufacture writers." This book is written to guide and help
persons who wish to write short stories. But it is not
written with the belief that short story writing, or any
other form of literary composition, can be taught. It
cannot. Literature is art, and art is incommunicable.
Theories of its methods and success can be inferred and
explained; its practical technique can frequently be explained and acquired. But neither theory nor technique
makes art; the living spirit is not in them. Moreover,
many a person who aspires to write lacks ability to achieve
even technique. Books such as this are not written with
any other belief. They can aid intellectual expansion;
they can enable the competent to acquire technique; but
more than this they cannot do unless the student bring to
them an equipment of capacity, ability, and natural gift
approaching talent or genius. Technique can produce
well conceived, well planned, well constructed, and often
salable stories, but it cannot produce living literature.
Let no prospective student think otherwise.

ROBERT W. NEAL.

TABLE OF CONTENTS

CHAPTER I

THEORY OF THE SHORT STORY TYPE, OR CONTE

I. Fiction Aims at the Interpretation of Life and the Diversion of the Reader, by Means of Concrete Presentation

1. When we ask, what is the purpose of fiction? we find that a complete answer must include two assertions. True, in many discussions concerning fiction, its structure, its methods, and the like, sometimes one of these assertions, sometimes the other, is disregarded. But a complete understanding—one that is philosophically sound—nevertheless cannot be had without including both in the answer.

2. These two purposes of fiction when fiction is typical and at its best, are:

A. To interpret human life, and

B. To interest (amuse, divert, entertain) the reader. "Interpret" must here be understood to mean, produce in the reader a clearer understanding of or a sense of having experienced human life. But much good fiction is produced in which emphasis is laid mainly and even solely on entertainment. This does not, however, mean that such fiction is without interpretive value.

3. We must understand, however, that this interpretive aim is not an immediate, but rather an ultimate and sub-

conscious aim.   The author is, at the moment of writing, not engaged expressly in producing an interpretation, but in giving *a clear account of certain persons and acts as he sees them.* Yet as a serious man, given to observing and pondering life, he feels himself responsible for *a sincere, accurate report.   Such an author would not be satisfied with his work unless, under all its artistry, wit, humor, incident, plot, and amusement, there were to be found a definite view of existence;* and though he may not aim first of all directly at interpreting humanity, yet—in the end —this often is his great purpose.

4. With the best writers, this need of showing forth mankind " as in itself it truly is," constitutes the great and often the all-sufficient compulsion to writing.   His very nature compels the true fiction-writer to interpret life.   Nevertheless, much diverting or merely entertaining fiction is written in which the emphasis is laid on the amusement, not on the interpretation.   But with the steady advancement made by the reading public in the appreciation of technique and the power to comprehend human motives, even the writer who aims only to amuse must in our day base his tale upon conceptions that are true to the world as clear-sighted men know it to be.   The best fiction of its very nature does and must have both these aims.   Interest and interpretation are so combined by the best art that no one but persons of limited mentality or education can fail to profit from and appreciate each of the twain.

5. Fiction, we have said, must interpret life.   But to interpret life, it must first *present* life.   Frequently—indeed, more frequently than many authors realize—*this is all it needs to do to interpret life.*   A true, vivid, stirring

presentation is enough to compel us to sense, think about, and understand more fully this human world. Seeking the shortest expression of the purpose of fiction, we therefore may say that *fiction aims to present life.* Now let us see how fiction may effect this presentation.

6. To present life, fiction must embody some truth or truths of human life; for only truths, only abstract conclusions, more or less completely perceived and appreciated, make up what we call our understanding of life. But in dealing with these truths, fiction does not much discuss them, expound them, or argue about them. Neither does it seek to deal with them as abstract truths at all. On the contrary, it seeks to avoid, not only the abstract form of the truth, but also the explanatory methods essential in dealing with truths as abstract thoughts. It prefers instead to show forth concrete facts in concrete forms, letting the abstract truth that underlies these facts be expressed in the facts themselves. That is, *fiction seeks as its final result to embody, or body forth, some truth or truths of human life, but seeks to bring about this result in a particular way; namely, by embodying, or bodying forth, in concrete form specific and concrete facts wherein the truths of life are exemplified.* We must, however, note this: Fiction does not necessarily *begin* its presentation with these truths in mind; that they are found in the work of the good artist, he could not help if he would, for they are embodied there as a result of that process of concrete presentation which fiction must employ. *Fiction has, as its* **immediate** *purpose, to body forth, not truths, but concrete facts, of human life.*

7. What " concrete " means a few illustrations will show. Anger is one of the facts of human life—an

unpleasant truth in our existence. Yet no one ever saw, tasted, smelt, touched, or heard anger; he merely has seen and heard manifestations of it. Anger as we know it is an abstraction. But a scowl, a blow, a curse—these are concrete things that manifest anger. Again, charity does not take on a concrete form until some individual act of charity is done—a shilling passed to a ragged beggar, or a wearied laborer given a lift in our automobile. Such acts are concrete manifestations of a thing which is merely an idea bearing the name "charity."

8. So is the great engine in the ship's depths a concrete embodiment of power, as is likewise the stroke of a hammer that drives in a nail. Affectionate devotion is concretely embodied in the acts of Mr. Peggotty, wandering throughout southern Europe in search of his wayward Little Em'ly. It is embodied equally as much in a wife's act when she writes a letter of forgiveness to the husband who has wronged her.

9. In short, *by " concrete " we here mean an individual instance; for in such an instance, we can always discover bodied forth, or manifested, a truth of human nature and life*. Moreover (although this fact is not necessary to our essential understanding of the term), *the concrete manifestation always comes to us embodied in acts or facts that in part at least we can perceive by means of our physical senses*. Only, in fiction we are not in the presence of the *actual* fact; the fact is presented to us, *not in actuality, but in an imagined form,* by means of words.

10. This presence of *imagined instead of actual fact* is vital to fiction; for the very term " fiction " carries the idea of things made up by the mind. Fiction deals, not with pure fact, which is only something actual, but with

imagined fact conceived to embody truth; and truth, though not actual, is something better than actual—that is, real. *Actual fact can—let us realize it now—be less true than fiction.* A few years ago, a community near New York was shocked by the act of a father who burned his children's tender hands with match flames as a means of "teaching" them. The report was true; he did just that. But what he did was terribly untrue to human life. The truth of human life is, that most parents love their children and undergo suffering and death to save the little ones. This is a reality of parental nature, a truth of life, not a mere fact, which may be quite untrue to life. The less effective forms of fiction are those that come closer to actual fact; they present truths which are of a less general nature, and hence are more nearly like actual facts and less like universal principles. Melodrama, for illustration, imagines what might happen sometimes, but is unlike the general course of life; it deals with the exceptional fact, not the general truth.

11. We can now sum up in a final statement the aim of fiction. Fiction deals with the truths of human life; it aims to present these truths embodied in concrete forms, or instances; and it deals with imagined facts, not with the actual. We say therefore that *the aim of fiction is, to present some truth or truths of human life manifested concretely in a body of imagined fact.*

12. Before we close this section, however, a few words will be worth while about imagination. Imagination is the power or operation of the mind that builds up new conceptions, ideas, or pictures out of those already in its possession—that is, out of experience. *Experience is made up of all the knowledge—physical, mental, moral, spiritual*

—that has come to us in any way, by any means, at any time.

13. There are three degrees of imagination. The most ordinary imagination is that which merely reproduces in its possessor's mind a body of imagined fact entirely similar to the actual fact from which the imagination has drawn its originals. It does little more than reproduce in the mind incidents and scenes already experienced. Evidently this degree of imagination (if imagination indeed it be) is not much better than good memory. It is reproductive imagination, or *imaginative memory*.

14. The second degree of imagination does more than merely reproduce a sort of combined memory-picture of past experiences. Drawing on memory—as all imagination must—it nevertheless selects, rejects, recombines, and remodels until the body of facts that it produces is a new one. From past experiences, it rebuilds a new structure, using the old materials as a skilled builder might, who, selecting choice materials from many old buildings, put up a new edifice perhaps surpassing any of the old. This selective and constructive degree of imagination we term *constructive imagination*.

15. Yet, superior as constructive imagination is to mere imaginative memory, it is nevertheless inferior to imagination of the third degree. Imagination of the third degree works as does constructive imagination, and it uses past experience. But it has a greater power than has constructive imagination—a power resulting from deeper insight, stronger sympathies, more catholic taste, keener and wider observation, stronger intelligence, stronger emotions, and whatever else contributes to artistic genius. *Hence its material is not old material reworked, but rather new*

material, originally discovered and got out by the writer through his deeper insight and understanding, and handled in a way original with and possible to him alone.

16. The consequence is, that what it produces is not merely something put together, but something created— something we are likely to call real, with the feeling that it springs direct from nature—something convincing, true-seeming, alive, capable of making one feel it as if it were an actual, a primal fact, not merely an output of the mind. Such products of the imagination of genius are creations,[1] not constructions. *This highest degree or power of imagination we call creative imagination;* and when it bodies forth a series of fact for us, we feel as if we stood in the presence of the truth of human life itself.

17. But no matter what be the degree of imagination possessed by the fiction-writer, the object of fiction is always the same: to body forth concretely in imagined fact some truth or truths of human life. This does not mean that fiction ought always to be heavy or even serious. Few things could be worse for the beginner than to think so. Indeed, the quality of the writer's imagination will, if high, make his treatment even of trivial themes creative (consider many fairy stories); and on the other hand, a lack of creative power will result in dead writing, no matter how serious and high the theme. While realizing, therefore, that fiction aims to body forth some truth of human life, the young writer should at the same time realize that *this aim will be attained by him only after he has mastered the art and methods of fiction.* Nor will it

[1] Dickens created Sam Weller; Thackeray created Becky Sharp and Colonel Newcome; Shakspere created the scenes of Ophelia's madness and Lear's passion; Mark Twain created Tom Sawyer.

be attained even then unless he knows also the human heart and human life. *He will best serve his ambition by developing his intellectual and spiritual gifts, by studying men and man, and by mastering his craft—by learning to see facts, to understand people, and to tell a story well.*

II.　The Short Story, or Conte, is a Type in Itself

1. By "short story" we do not nowadays mean any short piece of narrative fiction. The term has come to mean a particular kind of writing, having its own characteristics. Loosely, we speak of all the shorter pieces of fiction appearing in the magazines or in books as short stories. *But in fact a large number of such writings belong to some other class. They may be character sketches, tales, scenarios or outlines, novelets, anecdotes, episodes, incidents, or what not;* but many of them are in no strict sense contes.

2. All these types of fiction are closely related in some way to the short story (conte); but they are not identical with it. They are worth writing; they call for skill; they have their own place in fiction; practice in them aids one in writing the conte. But they lack, one and all, something that the conte has, and consequently some of them are, and any of them may be, inferior to it both in final effectiveness and in artistic quality. The conte—although perhaps it can never, being short, be absolutely as *great* as a great novel—at its best is at the present time *the most finished, artistic, and closely wrought form of narrative fiction.* It manifests a higher art and perfection of technique than the novel has attained, and it equals the best drama in constructional excellence.

3. Although the student cannot, before he has mastered the definition of the short story given in section III, completely grasp the differences between this form and other types, these differences are here enumerated. They should be reviewed and studied by the student after he has learned what the conte is.

(a) Character or other sketch.—Lacks dramatic plot; lacks dramatic action; may be descriptive, not narrative. When having dramatic plot and dramatic action, thoroughly unified to produce a single predominant effect, it becomes a conte.

(b) Tale.—Lacks dramatic plot; may lack dramatic action; may leave the reader with several distinct and equally strong impressions, instead of the one impression that is the final result of the short story. Like the character sketch, passes over into the conte if given dramatic plot and action producing a single predominant impression.

(c) Scenario or outline.—The scenario is merely a skeletonized outline of the action, plot, scenery, etc., of a play, a story, or a moving picture film. It gives the substance merely, not the effect, and it may be concerned with any form of drama or narrative. Further, it may be so condensed that it is nothing more than a catalogue of essential personages, action, setting, and " business." (When it outlines merely plot and action, it is technically known as action-plot rather than as scenario.)

(d) Novelet.—Merely a short novel; subject to the same looseness of structure, content, method, and treatment as the novel may and frequently does show (no similar looseness is permissible in the conte).

(e) Anecdote, episode, incident.—Usually very brief,

and therefore do not permit development of dramatic plot; often involve no more than a single isolated act or speech; do not necessarily aim at single effect, although on account of their brevity they frequently produce it; and frequently do not aim at dramatic effect.

(f) Allegory, fable.—From the narrative viewpoint the fable is little more than an anecdote, episode, or incident, except that it frequently makes not men, but beasts, its persons. Allegory is a method of symbolic presentation, not a type of narrative. Therefore it should not be compared with or contrasted to the conte. The conte may be allegorical; an allegory may be given the form of a conte.

III. THE CONTE IS A DRAMA IN NARRATIVE

1. The short story is a drama in narrative form. "Drama" is here used in a strict sense to mean a play, the plot of which is closely wrought. By "plot" we commonly mean a series of acts, events, or incidents that runs through a play or a story, giving it framework and carrying it on to its end. Plots may be *loose,* or they may be *close-wrought;* and the close-wrought plot may further be *dramatic.*

2. The loose plot is nothing more than a chance succession of incidents, without necessary relation to one another or to the outcome of the story. If I say, "I have had a day of disappointments," and outline it thus: Burned toast at breakfast; missed my usual train to the city; lost a good customer; crushed my straw hat against a low beam; and found I had no cigars at home for an after-supper smoke—I outline a loose plot. The series of incidents is wholly chance and accidental. *Moreover, there is*

no final, climactic act or situation to which all these precedent incidents have led up and which they make the natural
or inevitable outcome.

3. Now let us *turn this loose plot into a more closely-
wrought plot; we accomplish this by introducing the relations of cause and effect.* Waiting for new toast at
breakfast causes me to miss my train; missing my train,
I reach my office so late that my customer, disgusted, has
gone, leaving word that he withdraws his trade; this
worries me all day, and so takes up my mind on the way
home that I do not notice the beam against which I smash
my hat; and stopping to get a new hat causes me to forget
to buy cigars to take home; hence after supper I miss my
accustomed smoke.

4. Evidently our plot has become more close-wrought,
because each incident in the series leads up to and is the
cause of the next. But even yet these incidents do not
interweave and interlock; they merely follow each other as
single causes and effects, not as an <u>interacting body</u> of
cause and effect. Moreover, the story is still without a
climax; it is *a succession,* but not *a progression and ascent
to a conclusive outcome.* If the plot is to be close-wrought
to the full, *something must happen at the end that is more
important and more impressive than anything that has
gone before (or at least fully as impressive and important),
and this something must be the direct and combined outcome of all the incidents together that have gone before,*
not merely the last event of a string of events, each of
which is merely the cause of the next one in the chain.

5. Let us therefore make our plot still more close-
wrought, and thus bring about this final achievement of
artistic plotting. We will start again. Let us assume

that we mean to show through our story how ordinary, everyday events may create a tragic situation. The final event, or scene, will be the combined result of all the others taken together, and will be that in which the tragic situation is completely revealed.

6. Now for simplicity we will omit the incident of the cigars; and to prepare for the final situation, we will assume at the outset that I have been guilty of a murder, but have escaped capture and established myself prosperously in a respected business in this distant city. I am an irritable, quick-tempered man. The burned toast, the missed train, and the lost customer gradually rouse my anger. It is on the point of boiling over already; and when I strike the beam and crush my hat, it gets beyond control. I break into profanity. When a policeman cautions me, I swear at him. He arrests me. I am taken to the station—and recognized. As I am led away to prison, I realize that I am going to the scaffold.

7. Step by step our plot has led forward, simply and naturally, to a point of crisis when, standing in the police station, I am recognized and realize my ruin. Incident has interlocked with incident, my character has affected my acts and my acts have reacted on events, until all together have produced a culminating situation that suddenly is perceived to be tragic. *Not only do the incidents constitute a progression; they constitute an interwoven body of influences so closely related, every one with the others, that each is felt to have a part in the final outcome*—to be a part of the total motivation and result. Here manifestly we have a plot that can fairly be called close-wrought.

IV. The Plot of the Conte Must be Dramatic

1. Now we come to the plot which is dramatic. A dramatic plot is always a close-wrought plot; it can never be (in the strictest sense) a loose plot. But it not only is a close-wrought plot; it also is *a close-wrought plot that depends upon and grows out of the traits of character of the persons involved in it, and in turn produces some after-effect in or upon these persons.* What this means, a few illustrations may make clear.

2. Assume yet again that the appearance of burned toast is an incident of the plot. In dramatic plot, this *incident must in some way grow out of something in my own character, and must also in some manifest way affect me or my future*—either establish my course in life more firmly, or change it, or confirm or alter my character, or leave me in some pleasant or unpleasant situation, or influence my fortunes for good or ill—in short, *in some way make itself felt as a determining element* in my existence.[2]

3. Now, how may the incident of the burned toast grow out of some trait of character in me? Suppose me to be a domineering sort of man, given to enforcing services from others regardless of circumstances. It is my way to demand help of the cook without considering her convenience; and I have shouted to her this morning for shaving water, then for clean towels, then for the shoe-brush. Knowing my disposition, she has hurried to wait on me, leaving the breakfast to its fate. Hence the charred toast.

[2] The student is cautioned that *this influence need not be felt in a serious direction*. It may result in nothing more than making me ridiculous for the moment. Thus, in a humorous story, the mock-hero is made laughable.

The burning of the toast is therefore the result in fact of this imperious element in my character;[3] and to this extent the incident may be regarded as constituting part of a dramatic plot.

4. But *the incident must not only spring from some element of character in me; it also must have some effect upon me, my character, or my after life.* Again let us assume that I am ill-tempered. We will also assume that my wife and I have quarreled frequently, the consequence being that we are almost at the point of separation. The blackened toast stirs my black temper; I fling some insult at her; and because of it she refuses longer to live with me. Plainly my future will be different as a result of this incident. It may indeed be different in various ways or to various degrees. My wife may have been my good angel, and lacking her influence, I go to the dogs (character development). Or it may be that, deeply loving my wife, I am horrified at my own behavior, and thereafter live a different life, conquering my temper and transforming my ill disposition (another instance of character development). Or again (a weaker outcome), my wife may have been my banker; so that withdrawal of her money deprives me of the capital necessary to carry through my industrial plans, and I go to pieces upon financial reefs.

5. If in any manner the incidents, growing out of some trait of character in me or in other persons of the story, thus affect me or the other persons, our future life or character, they make the plot which they constitute a *dramatic plot—one in which character shapes event and incident,*

[3] Let the student observe that, by shifting the character emphasis, he can make the burning of the toast result from the weak or subservient character of the cook.

and event and incident react on person, character, or life.

6. What we have just been considering is known technically as *motivation—making every act or result spring from a clearly perceivable and adequate cause in the nature of the person and the situation, and making every cause produce a logical consequence affecting the person, character, or situation.* A dramatic plot, therefore, may be described as one that is adequately motivated throughout—it being always understood that character enters into motive. We must not suppose, however, that the incidents or outcome of a dramatic plot must always be serious. Both may, on the contrary, be light, even within bounds frivolous; and a plot can be farcical and burlesque, yet observe this principle of dramatic motiving, or motivation.

V. The Short Story Requires Persons in Action in a Time of Crisis

1. Our understanding of the essential nature of the conte may be made clearer by stating the requirements of this form of fiction anew. The essence of the short story is this: *persons in conclusive action, each according to his own character, in a time of crisis.* To understand this crisis, we must perceive that it has grown out of incidents which these persons, each according to his own character, have helped to make, and that it will inevitably affect the present or the future of one or more of these same persons.[4]

[4] Stories occasionally appear in which the dominant character is that of some one not introduced at all as a person acting *in* the story. For practical purposes, however, we may regard this person as one of the persons of the story.

2. For the moment, let us regard the idea of *crisis* as most important in this description, or definition. By this time we must have realized that, *rightly understood plot before everything else is the essential element of the short story (conte)*. The consequence of this importance is, that the construction of the plot demands exceedingly careful procedure. *Our plot must not only be close-wrought, it must be close-wrought according to the strict dramatic requirements of motivation;* and we are now to see further, that *this dramatic plot must virtually consist, not so much of a long series of incidents terminating in a climactic scene, incident, or situation, as of this climactic scene, incident, or situation itself, with the preliminary incidents and complications of which it is the culmination, subordinated to it, or even suppressed when suppression be possible without rendering the climactic situation obscure or lessening the total impressiveness of the story. For the conte is written to show forth character in conclusive action at some moment or in some period of crisis.*

3. Hence *the plot of the conte always tends to cover:*

(a) So much preliminary incident as—and no more than—may be necessary to make clear the essential aspects of the crisis with which it deals; and then—

(b) The situation, incident, character-play, or action that creates and constitutes the crisis. This situation, incident, character-play, or action it develops particularly, carrying it through a climax [5] *to its logical conclusion.* [6]

---

[5] See Sec. XV., on the Rising Action stage of the plot, and especially the paragraphs concerning decisive moment and climactic moment.

[6] The conclusion must be merely *logical;* it need not be (as some say it must) *inevitable* from the first. It becomes inevitable only at the decisive moment.

4. This fact—that the characters acting dramatically to a logical conclusion in a crisis are the main object of attention in the conte—must be borne constantly in mind. In application, the principle permits a wide latitude; in the hands of some writers, it may even seem to be disregarded without interfering with the success of the story; but it is nevertheless fundamental, and examination will show no successful story in which it has not been respected. *For the conte exists for the sake of an effect that cannot be produced except with the aid of conclusive action taking place in a time of crisis; whatever does not help to cause this action, or to create the critical situation or free it of obscurity, has no place in the plot development;* [7] *and matters that help to rid the situation of obscurity, or to create the crisis, or to cause the action, belong in the plot, but belong there only in so far as they do actually thus contribute to the crisis.*

5. Let us emphasize the fact that *the short story tends to present only the incidents and elements of the crisis at its height, subordinating or suppressing all unessential preliminary matters.* [8] How characteristic this method is of the short story (conte)—as it is in fact of the short drama also—is shown by the assertion of excellent critics that the true short story is produced only when the crisis alone

---

[7] To say that it has no place in the development of the plot is not to say that it has no place in the story. It may have uses as an aid to characterization, theme emphasis, atmosphere creation, etc. So used, it does, however, contribute at least indirectly to the plot development.

[8] The student is cautioned to bear in mind that we are now speaking of action, incident, and plot only. We shall see later that for its total effect a story may require the introduction of material that is not essential to the plot when considered by itself.

is presented.   Rightly understood, the assertion is true; but without explanation it is likely to mislead.   For the term "crisis" is ambiguous.   In our discussion *crisis refers to a critical situation of affairs at a certain time, and this time may be either the briefest space of time or a long period.*   Sometimes, it is true, the plot permits the almost complete suppression of preliminary explanatory incident; it is merely hinted at—suggested through some speech or act belonging to the critical situation itself.   Moreover, this suppression is characteristic of the theoretically ideal plot.   But many things theoretically ideal are not practically ideal, and *the preliminary incident may be so inwrought with the crisis that it will demand full narration.*   Thus, in De Maupassant's *The Necklace* we are carried by the preliminary plot-matter through a period of ten years, through all which time the grand climax, the height of the crisis, is preparing.   Moreover, the climactic moment, the height of the crisis, occupies but a minute or so of time; it is put before us in a single short speech, and of itself, without the preparation given by the preliminary matter, it would be forceless and artistically unintelligible. Throughout the story, the persons are acting in a time of crisis; the critical period, in truth, extends over ten years; yet De Maupassant's story is as thoroughly a short story as any wherein all preliminary matter is suppressed and the climactic moment alone presented.   A study of *The Necklace* will make this plain.   (Incidentally, too, it will show the student that in stories of this type *the plot is likely to include several preliminary or preparatory climactic points, each bringing nearer the grand climax or height of the main crisis.*)

VI. Singleness of Effect is Necessary to the Short Story

1. The artistic success of a conte, like that of the one-act play, is to be judged by the singleness of the effect or impression that it produces. An impression so strictly single is demanded of no other type of fiction except the play. Few novels or romances, even purpose novels, yet approach the conte in concentrated singleness of effect; and in some respects such effectiveness is beyond attainment by the longer forms of fiction. In poetry, only the lyric can be compared with the conte with reference to concentrated impression; for the purpose of the lyric is, to convey to the hearer a single poignant emotion. The tale may produce several effects and still not fail of its purpose; *Rip Van Winkle,* for instance, at one point leaves the reader impressed with Rip's good-natured vagabondage, at another with the mystery of his adventure, at another with the pathos of his return. It has no single impression on which readers would at once agree. But *the true short story (conte) must produce just such an effect.*

2. To define " single effect " is less easy than to feel the singleness of the effect when it is present. No one can miss the one overwhelming effect in the situation here outlined:

The scene is laid in the poorly-furnished room of an employee of the Paris Electric Light Company. In one corner is a little bed, on which the child of the workman and his patient wife lies very ill. The mother tells the father that the doctor, who has been to see the child a short while before, has said that the crisis will come in about three days.

The man tells his wife that he ought to go to a meeting of the labor union to which he belongs, as important matters are to be decided; but says that he does not feel like going out, because of their baby's condition. His wife, however, urges him to do so. "Nothing can happen," she reassures him, "because the doctor said three days."

Meanwhile, their friend, Mme. Marchaud, will stay with the wife. The women sit and talk. Madame tries to pacify the wife's wrought-up feelings by telling her of the sickness of her own youngsters.

Suddenly a sound is heard from the bed. The mother springs up, hurries to the bed, looks at her baby, and screams.

The baby is strangling.

The friend rushes for the doctor.

"May I ask you to leave the room?" he says to the mother. "You will only suffer, and your presence will disturb me. There is no reason to worry. The crisis has simply come earlier than I expected. It is better as it is. Just a slight operation—I give you my word of honor that all will be well! Go!"

The mother leaves the room. Reaching for the single electric light that illuminates the room, the doctor moves it next to the bed and, taking out his instruments, begins hastily to sterilize them, Mme. Marchaud standing by his side ready to help him. Quickly he bends over the bed and makes an incision. Another. Then another.

Suddenly—darkness!

The lone light has gone out.

"Great good God!" he shouts wildly to the woman. "Why did you turn out the light?"

" I didn't turn it out," comes from the darkness.

" Then quick, quick! " literally screams the man.   " On with it again! "

A pause.

" But it won't light! " from the woman.

In the black room the doctor pulls at the switch; but the light will not come.   The mother rushes in.

At last—it seems hours—a candle is found.   They light it with quivering fingers.   They bend over the bed.

Too late!   The baby is dead.

A noise.   The sound of marchers is heard in the street below.   It comes nearer; it grows louder.   They are singing the Marseillaise.

The door of the room bursts open and the husband, his face aflush with triumph, stands in the entrance.

" Victory! "   he   cries.   " Victory!   We've   won! There's not an electric light burning in all Paris to-night! " [9]

3. We feel this effect, but what is it?   It is just one thing—the shock of horrified sympathy for the man who, through the very victory over which he is triumphing, finds himself the means of his child's death.   And here we have a good practical test for singleness of impression.   It is this.   *A single effect is susceptible of statement in a single sentence, not unreasonably long, which itself fulfills the requirements of rhetorical unity.*   To state it still more simply: A sentence is the expression of a single, complete thought.   If the effect of the story can be summarized in such a sentence, it may fairly be regarded as unified.   We

[9] From " Trained Nurses of the Thrill " (George Jean Nathan), *Associated Sunday Magazine*, May 25, 1913.   By permission.

may further test the effect by condensing the *plot* into a sentence in the same way. If the plot can be stated in a single unified sentence, then the story, if well constructed, should itself be unified and result in a single effect.

4. While speaking of singleness of effect, we should consider the word " short " in the term " short story." Why short? Many contes contain only 1,000, 1,500, or 2,000 words (the shorter stories often lack in literary quality). But, on the other hand, stories as long as 8,000 and 10,000 words, and even more, are accepted by some editors. Indeed, fiction running to 40,000 words or more (10,000 or 15,000 words longer than some novelets, and only 20,000 words under the length of writings sometimes classified as novel) is properly deemed short story, provided that it otherwise meets the requirements imposed on this form of writing.

5. The fact is, that the conte does not *have* to be notably short. Usually it *is* short, however, because it seeks the singleness of effect described above. Comparison with the drama is here useful again. We have already seen that the short story and the one-act play are especially near akin. We know, too, that even the most intense and closely-wrought drama is hard to watch for three hours; the tendency is, to keep the time down to two hours or thereabout, because a longer time is likely to dull the spectators' impression. The play is planned to make its impression within the time for which the close attention of the spectators can be held. The one-act play ordinarily takes still less time than does the two- or three-act play, and it is found to produce a correspondingly more unified impression (not invariably a *deeper* impression, however).

6. In this fact we have also the reason for the shortness of the short story. It is planned to be " taken in " at a single sitting—to be read through without interruption; to be grasped, understood, and felt as a whole. If the reading of it be interrupted, the impression, the " spell " of the narrative, is broken. The powerful effect of the conte depends in no small degree upon this fact: the narrative is *not too long to be completed in one absorbed reading.*

7. The wide range between the longest and the shortest contes commonly accepted by editors—from 800 words to 8,000, 10,000, and occasionally 15,000—is to be accounted for by two things. First, many readers are not capable of concentrated attention and continued understanding beyond a few hundred words; a story of 5,000 or 8,000 words is beyond their powers. Second, the adequate development of some plots, or the adequate presentation of the full story material, requires in some instances only 1,500, 2,000, or 2,500 words; in others, adequate presentation demands eight or ten times as many. The student should not be misled by any insistence upon the need of *compression* in the short story (and compression is needed) into thinking that absolute brevity, too, is essential. *Adequate presentation is essential; brevity is not,* provided that singleness of effect is preserved. And as a matter of fact, an educated reader can read a close-wrought story of 40,000 or 50,000 words at a sitting, and get from it its single dominant impression. But few single critical situations involve an amount of essential facts so great as this for their adequate understanding and conclusion, or call for such amplified development as a means of producing their effect.

VII. THE CONTE MAY AIM AT DIFFERENT KINDS OF EFFECT

1. We have been insisting strongly upon the supreme importance of the plot. Lest that insistence result in a serious misapprehension, we must now insist also on a vital distinction. *Plot is of supreme importance to the* STRUCTURE AND OUTCOME *of the story, but the plot may be of minor importance in producing the* EFFECT *of the story.*

2. We will examine this assertion more closely. It depends on this fact: the conte involves *two chief factors toward final effectiveness—an outcome and an impression.* The outcome belongs to plot only; *the impression is the result of plot combined with various other elements, and these other elements may in their importance as* IMPRESSION-PRODUCERS *quite overshadow plot.* Let us make this still clearer by restating once more.

3. The plot is the logical summary of that body of incident and event which creates and constitutes the dramatic crisis. The essence of the short story is people acting dramatically in a time of crisis. In order to produce a single crisis that shall be single and unified in effect, the plot must be close-wrought, single, and unified. *But this crisis does not have to be itself the most important thing in the story.* It may exist either for its own sake, or merely for the sake of affording effective presentation of other impression-producing elements. But however this be, we shall ultimately perceive that underlying this total effect of the story, the most important element contributing to the outcome through which the effect must at least in part always be reached,—are persons acting, each according to his character, in a crisis brought

about by a dramatic plot. Without persons, and without certain things done by these persons in the course of a crisis, there can be no outcome of the dramatic sort—and therefore no short story (conte).

4. Now these persons, doing what they thus do in the surroundings and under the conditions determined by the dramatic crisis, may, according to the management of the story, thus produce in us any one of four predominant impressions; namely—

(a) Impress us with a *theme* (thematic story);

(b) Impress us with the qualities of their own *character* (character story);

(c) Impress us mainly with the *incident and action* of the plot (plot story); or

(d) Impress us most distinctly with *a feeling;* perhaps merely of the conditions and environment surrounding them, and of which they are a part, during the time in which they are in action, and perhaps of a deeper emotional or spiritual quality (subjective coloring) belonging to them and their deeds (atmosphere story).

5. We see, then, that the materials and essential elements of a story, gathering round and depending on the persons-in-action and governed by the plot, can be so managed as to produce stories of different classes; and these classes can be discriminated one from another according to a clear, logical principle. Neither plot, nor substance or subject-matter, affords such a principle. Plot especially does not, for plot is essential in every conte. But in the effect produced by the different possible ways of managing the materials and elements (including the persons-in-action) which are found in the short story, we have a safe classification by which to distribute contes into

groups. According to this principle, *every short story will fall into one or another of four classes, as the emphasis may be placed on one or another of its four elements; namely, (1) theme; (2) character; (3) plot, incident, and action; (4) atmosphere (total conditions and environment; subjective coloring).*

VIII. SOME SHORT STORIES EMPHASIZE THEME

1. The conte that emphasizes theme is either among the easiest to write, or among the hardest. If it attempt nothing more than to present a " moral "—that is, if it is nothing more than a piece of didactic writing in narrative form—it is comparatively easy of composition; it has only to announce its theme, or moral, group a set of incidents together that make the moral idea, or lesson, that it presents obvious to the reader, and so end. But the short story that does not aim at bald didacticism is a far different and more difficult achievement.

2. The baldly didactic narrative scarcely deserves the name story, for in desire to make its moral obvious, it is ready to sacrifice all the literary qualities. It amounts to little more than argumentation masquerading as narration. But the literary story that concerns itself with the effective presentation of a theme is, on the other hand, thoroughly artistic. It strives for *impression,* not for *conviction or conversion.* Therefore it is careful to characterize, to find adequate motiving and true-seeming incident for its plot, and to create a setting and environment equal to their task of giving atmosphere.

3. Thus to work into a consistent artistic whole significant traits of character; true human motives resulting

in convincing acts that illustrate and develop the theme; and a coherent body of incident that likewise demonstrates a central thought;—and withal to keep this central theme itself clear, prominent, and dominant—this demands great power of imaginative conception and high skill in literary construction. We will therefore drop out of consideration the merely didactic narrative and, in further mention of the thematic story, understand that it is the true short story emphasizing theme to which we refer.

4. The thematic conte, so limited, may be either a purpose or a problem story, or a pure-theme story (see par. 13). The PURPOSE story is the literary parallel of the unliterary didactic narrative. It differs from the didactic narrative by giving adequate attention to those elements of fictional material which we found the didactic narrative neglecting: character, atmosphere, and well-motived plot. It *establishes its theme by means of an impression depending upon artistic method*. Character, plot, incident, and atmosphere are used to emphasize the theme, and the theme is emphasized in order that the reader may be persuaded to espouse some theory or belief. The purpose story aims at conversion, it is true; but *it aims at conversion through artistic effect*.

5. We must observe here that excellent authorities maintain the impossibility of an effective purpose short story. They urge that conversion cannot be the aim of the conte; that the presentation of arguments is not consistent with literary effect; that short stories do not afford scope or room for marshaling facts and debating a proposition; and that any theme about which there is a division of opinion is unsuited to the short story, because the short story must immediately appeal to each of its many classes of readers.

6. Now it is true that no great number of true contes
aim at convincing or converting the reader, and that those
which have this aim often fail in it. But one reason for
these facts is, the difficulty of constructing an artistic
purpose story—one that does not drop into the merely
didactic class; and perhaps another is, the feeling which
writers have—brought about by commercial necessity—
that stories seriously attacking a disputed theme will have
less chance of a market with editors. That such stories
will sell less readily is true, not because the conte cannot
be a purpose story, but because editors are fearful of
offending readers who may not agree with the theme
advanced, and of wearying that not inconsiderable class
whose mental energies faint in presence of any effort
greater than that necessary to wrestle with the impressive
moral truth of " See the man! " and " This is a cat."

7. But inherent reason there is none why a narrative
built upon a dramatic plot and producing a single effect
should not aim, *through this effect,* to persuade or convert
the reader to a definite theory or belief. That such short
fiction is influential is indicated by the little whirlwinds
of discussion that occasionally arise over stories thus advocating a cause by embodying its appeal in the impression created by well-managed narrative. Only the
editors who get the letters of approval and protest know
how impressive such an appeal may be.[10]

[10] American drama has in recent years supplied some interesting
examples of purpose plays—naturally analogous to purpose short
stories. Study of *The Lure* and *The Fight*, each presented
in New York City at the beginning of the season of 1913-14, will
be suggestive. So will consideration of their fate, illustrative of
the grotesque unwillingness of certain classes of people to let either
drama or literature offer an interpretation of life by presenting it

8. We are therefore compelled to conclude that the short story *may* be written "with a purpose," but that the artistic success of the story so written will depend mostly upon the literary gift and skill of the author. If he present his theme artistically embodied in concrete facts that are truly significant of human nature and life, so managed that they produce a single, dramatic effect, we

as different from what it conventionally is supposed to be. The attacks upon these plays will give the writer an idea of the reception likely to be met at any time by problem or purpose stories; although, to be sure, a story may escape much of the prominence that a play has which becomes the subject of public discussion.

Probably the writer's conclusions will not be much changed by considering what explains but does not alter the situation; namely, that the fate of the plays mentioned seems to have been largely the result of a newspaper raid carried on by editors and reporters with the zest which most people feel when they have got hold of "a good thing" and have succeeded in persuading their conscience that it is their duty to make the most of it. Having observed the methods of several such campaigns—that, for instance, against Shaw's *Mrs. Warren's Profession*—the present writer cannot convince himself that they represent any "popular uprising" until the "revolt" has been stirred up. An admirer of New York City journalism, he nevertheless feels that the methods employed in some of these instances are a reproach to the profession. The news "stories" and the headlines over them were alike "editorial" and "colored" in character—full of expressions of opinion and inflammatory in tone; yet the highest ideal of good newspaper work is that of giving the facts, and giving them *uncolored*.

However, that (whether sincerely or insincerely) the papers thus at times descend to sensationalism, and that their power is sufficient to stir up prejudice that neutralizes the artist's aim and wrecks his reasonable expectation of earnings, puts the author face to face with a serious personal problem. Shall he present life as he sees it, running the risk of vilification and probably business ruin, or shall he conventionalize and popularize his work, consenting to take the artistic "Easiest Way"?

have no right to quarrel with him because the facts thus presented carry a logical corollary that convinces us.

9. Unlike the purpose story, the PROBLEM story does not try to convince the reader that its solution of the problem is the right solution; it endeavors merely to lay before him a clear proposal of the problem involved by the situation, whatever that be. To understand " problem," we must, however, consider the term " crisis."

10. The conte requires a crisis. Crisis exists when the character of the persons and the nature of the incidents are such that a *conflict* of interests, desires, or duties is brought about—that is, when the plot has developed what is called a *complication*. If the person decides or acts in one way, a certain set of consequences will follow; if he decides or acts in another way, an altogether different and probably quite opposite set of consequences will follow; and it is immaterial whether at the moment of his deciding or acting he know that he is doing something to bring on such consequences, or not. The critical moment, now, is that in which he makes the decision or performs the decisive act. (This is not necessarily the moment of supreme impression, i.e., the climactic height.)

11. Now the purpose story and the problem story (like all other short stories, or contes) have each a crisis, which—technically—is ended with the decisive moment. Moreover, each presents a problem, some question of right or wrong, or better or worse, out of which its crisis grows. Still further, they center the interest on this problem; they lay it before us with the implied question, What is best to do in such a situation? In which way ought this person to decide, or in which way will it be more fortunate for him to act?

12.   We now come to the difference between the purpose and the problem story.   Having once laid its problem before us, the purpose story does one thing, the problem story another.   The purpose story not only solves the problem, but solves it in the way that, it would persuade us, is the only true or right way.   But the problem story either does not solve the problem at all *(The Lady or the Tiger?)*, or it solves it so impartially as to convey no opinion of its own concerning the expediency or rightness of the solution.

13.   In other words, the purpose story answers for us the question, What is best? and intends this answer to satisfy and convince us.   But the problem story (although of course it usually solves the *complication of the plot*) does not attempt at all, notwithstanding this solution, to answer the question, Which is right or what is best? It aims only to lay the problem clearly before us, leaving us, uninfluenced by the plot outcome, to decide on the answer for ourselves.   In such stories (we must be sure to remember) *the outcome is an artistic or dramatic outcome, not an ethical inference;* it works out the plot to one of its possible conclusions, but this conclusion does not answer, and is not meant to answer, the question of right or wrong, or better or worse.   Notwithstanding the plot outcome, the problem is left with us still unanswered.

14.   The third kind of thematic story we have not yet discussed.   This we called the PURE-THEME STORY.   In fact, however, purpose stories, problem stories, and all other contes of the thematic class, are pure-theme stories; for *by theme we signify the central topic or proposition, the ultimate working-thought.*[11]   If the writer's intention be

[11] See paragraphs 19 and 20.

to convince and convert, he nevertheless must reach his end by dramatically developing his theme. If his intention be to propound a problem, this very problem is the sum and substance of his theme.

15. But besides the two sorts already discussed there remain the great majority of thematic stories. In these, the author's immediate intention is neither to convert nor yet to propound problems as such. Instead, starting with some central thought or proposition, he strives to build this up and amplify it in a course of dramatic narrative, until he has transformed it from a bare logical proposition into a coherent body of action, character, and setting, making of it a portrayal which can leave but one main impression. *By employing dramatic narrative, he gradually enlarges on and develops his proposition until it reaches the reader as an impression, unified, whole, and artistic, realized through the imagination and emotions rather than through the reason or the intellect.* This dramatic bodying forth of a proposition or a theme it is— whether the theme be bodied forth solely for its own sake or with a purpose also to convince or to propound a problem—that makes the thematic story effective; and it is emphasis laid especially upon the theme that produces the thematic story.

16. Before closing this section we should make note of one further fact about the theme. In one sense, every story has a theme. Yet many stories have no immediate theme; their " theme " is an exceedingly general proposition, perhaps even nebulous in its universality.[12]   In

[12] The theme is virtually the " masterplot "—a conception, or rather a proposition, of so general a character that it can be bodied forth in a large number of distinct plots and stories. See *plot germ, working-plot*, etc.

stories of this kind, the *working-plot* is likely to be mistaken by the careless thinker for the theme itself. But the plot is not the theme; it merely outlines the body of incident which, combined with character-portrayal and atmosphere, will body forth the theme. Concrete examples will enable us to realize the nature of the general, remote theme in contrast with the specific, prominent theme characteristic of the thematic story.

17. In " Nine Assists and Two Errors " (Charles E. Van Loan, *Saturday Evening Post,* May 31, 1913) the theme is: A winning personality overcomes prejudice and commands friendship. A thousand plots might be built up to present this theme. It is so general that, in a story of much incident, characterization, or atmosphere, it is likely to be overlooked entirely—not a bad thing for artistic effect, provided only that the reader *feel* the theme, even though he is not consciously aware of it. And in fact some thought is required to determine the ultimate theme of this story. But its plot is easily stated. A young man, ambitious to be a baseball pitcher, but quite without ability, through his pleasing personality overcomes the prejudice of a manager, gets on the team, and actually persuades the " old man " to " throw " an unimportant game in order to help him win his lady-love, an admirer of ball-players (a surprise element is introduced by making the lady-love the manager's daughter). The story is a character, atmosphere, and humor story, not a story of theme; and only upon consideration can we determine the underlying conception which the plot embodies.

18. But in " Nerve " (by William Slavins, *Collier's,* September 20, 1913) the theme is intentionally made prominent by the writer. In this story (which is taken

merely at random as an example) there is a philosophical introduction, mainly dialogue, wherein different views of the same question are presented; and in the course of the dialogue the man who presently tells the story that exemplifies the theme, says: "To my way o' thinkin' a man shows clean game when he does the thing that's *hardest* for *him,* whereas the same thing might be just like eatin' a meal to me." Here we have the theme stated in exact words—thought out and shaped up for the reader's attention before any element of the plot has been introduced. In fact, the introduction is no true part of the actual plot and story; it is merely the author's device in this instance for making certain that the theme is emphasized so plainly that no reader, in the interest of the story itself, shall overlook it.

19. In the two stories here cited, we have therefore excellent though haphazardly chosen examples of extremes in theme importance. But the fact that in Mr. Van Loan's story we really do not need at all to know the theme, and yet with a little thought can readily find it, illustrates this truth: *Every conte embodies a theme, no matter how general or remote this theme may be; for no reasonable plot can be stated, based on the realities of life, that does not exemplify or contain in the concrete some truth of human existence.* Were it otherwise, the story would be untrue.

20. *The thematic story,* we may here remark, *is exceedingly adaptable to purposes of direct interpretation.* We have already noted that the best fiction does more than merely interest; it contributes to the better comprehension of life itself. It brings before the reader, in coherent inter-relationships, motives, influences, deeds, ideals, char-

acter; and when he comprehends these relationships, he comes into possession of *a theory, a view, or a principle of human nature and its workings* as the author conceives it to be. This conception on the part of the reader is identical (at least theoretically) with the conception on which the author built up his story; that is, with the theme itself. Therefore, the writer who wishes particularly to interpret life—to give the reader an explanation and simplification of life as it appears under certain definite conditions—has an effective means in the thematic story; for *in the theme he summarizes his interpretation, and in the development of his story constantly emphasizes and illustrates this theme.*

21. From these explanations, one important conclusion follows. Unless one is writing a thematic story, he need not worry about finding a theme with which to begin. *If the plot be well built and the action truly motivated in character, they will inevitably embody a theme. The beginner, therefore, will do as the experienced writer oftenest does: first seek a plot,* or at least the " germ " of a plot. When the plot idea, or germ, is discovered, it will develop into a story if rightly managed; and behind the story there will always be a theme.

22. Unless the presentation of an *emphasized* theme be the writer's main object (let us repeat), he need not worry about anything at first but the creation of a plot, with its developing material. True, he cannot build a plot without realizing that in it is embodied some central idea or proposition. But the gift of art is, to present things in the concrete; and its value is, that as it sees deeply and truly, that which it presents concretely is itself, by reason of this grasp and insight, an illustration

of or a commentary upon life or character. A clearly visioned, truly motived story, therefore, always contains some inevitably embodied theme; fit matter for reflection. But it is reflection on the part of the reader. To him the writer had better leave the discovery and weighing of the theme, provided only that the story as the writer creates it, incarnates this controlling conception in a body of coherent fact and action, true to human nature and to life.

IX. SOME SHORT STORIES EMPHASIZE PLOT

1. We have already seen that the final effectiveness of the conte involves two chief factors: an outcome, and an impression. "Outcome" we are to understand somewhat narrowly. The incidents and action of the story bring forth a final deed, incident, or situation—the outcome; something done or happening that puts a close to the series in such a way as to be the conclusion of the whole matter—the consequence and end of what precedes.

2. Some outcome is necessary to the conclusion of every short story, but this must not be thought to mean that the outcome itself is always the principal source of the impression. *"Impression" indicates the sum total of the effect worked on the reader by the story—aroused interest, stirred emotions, character appreciation, etc.—united and merged in one definite, single, predominant effect.*[13] In making this impression, theme, character, atmosphere, and plot have each a part; but in one type of conte, that which emphasizes plot, the plot of course is the leading impression-maker. In the plot story, the total effect must

[13] Inasmuch as this effect is worked by stimulating fancy, imagination, and emotion, the impression is predominantly emotional in nature. See Sec. XI., 14.

mainly depend on the two plot parts; namely, the incidents and action that produce the outcome, and the final situation and outcome itself.

3. *The plot story therefore must have much quick action, stirring incident, adventure, surprise, mystery; complicated situations, romantic situations, etc.* Not that all of these are likely to be found in any one story, but that every one of them is likely to supply the material for a plot story or to constitute an important element in its effectiveness.

4. For the sake of simplicity we may include all of these characteristics, and any others belonging to the plot story as such, in three categories. We shall then see that the plot story is a story in which the effect is produced through (a) lively action, (b) abundant incident, and (c) abundant activity. Roughly defined, *an incident* is one of the single coherent events included in the story as being either essential to the action or as otherwise clearly contributing to the total effect. *Action* is the combination and advance of incident and events toward a definite outcome in accordance with the scheme provided by the plot. *Activity* is the behavior, acts, deeds, and " business " (stage meaning) of the persons singly or together. Quick action, abundant incident, and much activity, are the characteristics of the plot story.[14]

5. Classification of plot stories into sub-groups is difficult. We may, however, further indicate the nature of

[14] Somewhat more loosely, " action " carries the idea of " all that's doing " or " whatever is doing." It then indicates all that we have classified separately above.—A story may include several groups of incident; incident groups may then be termed " events," the term " incident " being reserved for the single coherent event of smaller compass.

the plot story by mentioning various sub-types, provided that we do not regard these sub-types as clearly delimited and mutually exclusive. With this understanding, we may say that plot stories fall into two classes. They are either stories of *ingenious complication* or else stories of *lively action*. In the one case, the interest lies in the ingenuity of fancy, incident, entanglement, and solution. In the other, it lies in the excitement of the rapid movement, the quick passing from deed to deed, incident to incident, and event to event, up through a stirring climax to a stirring outcome. Usually, of course, rapid action and ingenious plot-complication go together.

6. In stories of the ingenious-plot type, the attention is held, not primarily by the persons who act, nor by the surroundings or atmosphere in which the action takes place, nor by the theme embodied in the story; first and mainly it is held by the body of incident itself. What interests the reader is, the single incidents and successive events as they are wrought together, one by one, and the situation or situations [15] brought about by these incidents as they succeed and combine with one another, and so draw on toward the grand climax.

6A. The more ingeniously these are wrought together, to arouse interest and yet to keep the outcome seemingly uncertain, the more concentrated will the reader be in

[15] " Situation " indicates the state of affairs existing at any particular moment by reason of the development of the story up to that point; especially, the critical state of affairs existing at climactic moments in the progress of the action, usually those produced by the culmination of a definite stage (" movement ") of plot development. In the theater, for instance, the curtain is not allowed to fall except when a " situation " has been developed to bring it down, thus marking the close of a scene or an act.

his pursuit of the plot to its conclusion. For it is the skill—indeed the ingenuity—with which detail is woven in with detail and incident with incident, moving steadily toward an outcome the more eagerly anticipated because its nature cannot be accurately guessed—it is this that gives the ingenious-plot story its fascination.

7. Various kinds of story are of the ingenious-plot type. The "surprise-plot" story is a good example. In this, the plot is skillfully shaped to lead the reader into anticipating a certain outcome, or to keep him from guessing the outcome that is intended; then at the last— and always suddenly if the best effect is attained—an unexpected outcome leaves him gasping with surprise. The surprise-plot story, well done, unquestionably is effective; and occasionally an editor is found who regards it as the chief among short stories, if not indeed the only sort worth printing. But this is an extreme opinion. Even the ingenious-plot conte can exist without a surprise outcome; and a large amount of exceedingly valuable material could not be utilized at all by the short story if it had to be presented through a surprise plot. Imagine the rendering by surprise outcome of such a tragic procession of events as that of Mrs. Wharton's *Ethan Frome!* Yet *Ethan Frome*—testing by ultimate standards—is worth dozens of the ordinary surprise-plot story.[16]

[16] The purpose of this book being the explanation of the method, or constructional principles, of the conte, the author has but seldom introduced comment depending upon those larger esthetic principles by which final worth in literature must be estimated. In other words, he has for the most part refrained from judgments in which an attempt is made to evaluate stories, types, forms, or points of view. The few exceptions will (he trusts) explain and justify themselves.

8. Again, the surprise ending itself is subject to abuse —as in stories made to end with a surprise that shocks the sensibilities, or does illogical violence to the sympathies of the reader, or to his liking for the personages of the story. Indeed, the surprise ending can quickly grow into tyranny over its employer, becoming an offensive and a fatal trick. When it has thus established domination over a writer, he will use it in place and out of place, emphasizing trivialities, subjecting his plots to mechanical and artificial manipulations, and at the end introducing impertinent incongruities to the exclusion of serious conclusions. In a word, abuse of the surprise plot is easy, and may result in flippancy, artificiality, and a general cheapening of effect.

9. Mystery stories are another interesting and favorite sort of ingenious-plot story (the surprise ending is frequent in them). As mystery stories we may classify all stories of which the chief purpose is, to solve some problem of explanation, means, or discovery. Such for example are detective stories; ghost stories and other tales of the weird, horrible, or occult, when the interest lies in the explanation, not the phenomena; [17] and many stories of crime or vengeance.

10. Commonly, mystery stories assume a state of affairs such as seems well-nigh inexplicable, together with an apparently quite inadequate body of fact from which to solve the problem of explanation or discovery. From the facts thus assumed, with the discovery and introduction from time to time of additional facts, they proceed by

[17] When the effect depends on merely the *presence* of mystery, not on the explanation of it, we have an atmosphere conte, not a plot conte.

reasoning (both inductive and deductive) through stages of advancement and renewed complication toward the final solution; and at last, by a sudden decisive piece of logic—usually accompanied with action—bring forth the true conclusion. The stages (" movements ") by which the dénouement, or final untangling, is approached, do not, however, always seem stages of progress. On the contrary, the facts, as the narrative proceeds, appear now to point to one conclusion, now to another, and are all the time baffling; and their total effect prior to the completion of the disentangling is, to keep the reader excitedly puzzled about the outcome and eagerly interested to know it.

11. To the beginner, one caution must be emphatically given about the plot in the plot story. It must not be overcrowded with either incident or action. True, it will be complicated; but all plots are that. This means no more than that it includes some element that checks, or stops, or changes, the otherwise plain course of the action. Without such an obstacle, there could be no conflict, no crisis, no uncertainty about outcome and result. In the short story that emphasizes plot, the number of such complicating influences tends to increase rapidly. But at their most numerous, they must not be so many that they congest the story, cramp the action, interfere with the just development of characterization, or require a total amount of setting out of proportion to the other narrative elements. Nor must ancillary incident overflow either the plot it supplements or the other bounds of proportion. In other words, *even the plot story must not be all plot and incident; there must be an adequate proportion of the other fiction elements.*

12. The reason for all this is very practical. The

conte must be short enough for reading at a single sitting; excessive incident or action, with a due proportion of staging and characterization, would extend the story beyond the time limit in which the necessary single effect can be attained. Since in the market few stories longer than 8,000 or at most 10,000 words find a welcome, the practical inadvisability of including copious incident or requiring unstinted action is evident. But except for this, no limitations need be observed so long as the incident and action continue to contribute to the single effect desired.

13. Turn now from the type of plot story in which ingenuity in construction and the creation and combining of incident is the leading characteristic, to the type in which action rather than ingenuity is emphasized. In the action type of plot story, the leading position probably is occupied by the adventure story. In company with this should be mentioned the stories that are built largely upon romantic elements other than adventure; for the two are difficultly separable. "Adventure" as just used has the older sense of physical adventure—that involving physical courage and endeavor, daring in the face of bodily danger, and the like. Naturally the story of intrigue (when active behavior instead of ingenious plot dominates it) associates itself with the story of adventure and romance.

14. The word "adventure" is however rapidly taking on a broader meaning, in which the merely physical connotation is much less; and this meaning is showing itself in recent literature, especially in fiction. We have had, for example, *Adventures in Contentment* (not cited, of course, as an example of fiction); and of late years fiction has

been rich in narratives that deal with industrial, business, and sociological emprise. To many of the incidents in such narratives, the term "adventure" is to be applied quite as justly as it was originally to the other kind of adventuring. These stories, we should note, have, however, a natural relationship with realism through dealing with matters that are so closely associated with ordinary life; hence they not infrequently develop a tendency to realistic treatment. The natural outcome is an effective if not a novel blending of romantic with realistic elements, producing work of no little value in interpreting life in its daily aspects. But as the realistic elements increase, the plot naturally ceases to occupy so prominent a place; hence realistic stories of this sort (like most other realistic stories) soon pass out of the plot story class.

X. SOME CONTES EMPHASIZE CHARACTER

1. "The proper study of mankind is man." This is the underlying conviction of all good literature and indeed of all art. Whatever else finds a place in fiction, finds its place there because in some way it is associated with man and the life he lives. Nature, for illustration, enters into fiction because it forms so much of man's environment, stirring his love of beauty, terrifying him by the relentless power it exerts, stimulating him to effort in order to conquer and dominate it, exalting him to awe and reverence by its sublimity. Plot and incident find a place in fiction because they show men in action under the manifold impulses and influences that shape human destiny. Theme is important in fiction because it supplies a means of sum-

marizing conclusions about man and his destiny, or of stating human problems in a suitable form for concrete observation, analysis, or demonstration.

2. Accordingly, whatever material yields itself to fiction is material found in man's relationships with the universe; whatever mood or tone or method is employed in treating this material, is employed because it is a mood or tone or method that springs from these relationships. From the most serious novel to the lightest skit, the final concern of the writer and of the reader is man and his existence, seen, of course, in the character and behavior of individual men and women; for fiction, being a form of art, deals as we saw with concrete instances rather than with general conceptions.

3. These relations of man with the universe are three. He deals and struggles with, influences and is influenced by, the physical world; deals and struggles with, influences and is influenced by, other men; and deals and struggles with, influences [18] and is influenced by, the moral and spiritual world—the forces for good and evil that lie (or seem to lie) largely in himself. In all this dealing, struggling, and influencing, it is the character of the individual that is principally involved. We may therefore say that character manifests itself—

(a) In the dealings of men with the physical world.

(b) In the dealings of men with one another.

(c) In the dealings of men with their own moral or spiritual nature, and the forces that influence it.

4. When therefore the writer creates a story that emphasizes character, and emphasizes it successfully, he creates a story that, in its appropriate class of light or

[18] For instance, he establishes his own codes of morals.

serious, is exceedingly vital and worthy. For in a character we read, writ small and in a fragmentary monument,
the nature and destiny of man. To the portrayal of sta-
tionary character, and still more to the presentation of
character in process of growth or deterioration, all the
utility of plot, theme, and atmosphere, and of all other
literary accessories of narration, may rightly be directed.
Especially effective is a combination of characterization
with theme emphasis; for the theme embodies the central
thought concerning life, and the characterization clothes on
this thought with all the vraisemblance, all the true-seeming, of actual human life itself.

5. Yet the beginning writer should not be led to
suppose that he ought to turn his prentice hand to the
character story only. Quite the contrary is true. He
should first accustom himself to the management of plot;
for in the conte the most indispensable element is plot—
even when the plot is wholly subordinate. And although
the tyro in writing may soon begin to practice on character
sketching, and even on characterization in dramatic narrative, he must not expect in any sudden burst of development to blossom into the master's skill of character treatment.

6. There is too another reason for delaying besides
that of making thoroughly ready before attempting the
work of characterization in dramatic narrative. It is this:
although as a type the character story probably is superior
to any other of the individual types of conte, it is not by any
means a universal favorite. A lamentably large proportion
of readers cannot (if the truth must be told) appreciate
or even comprehend it; it commands a more limited public,
perhaps, than any other type commands, unless it be the

atmosphere story. This assertion, of course, will not always hold of the best short stories; but that is because *the best short stories do not emphasize any one element at the expense of another, but emphasize proportionately theme, plot, atmosphere, and character;* and they are, moreover, often so simple, so human, so " universal " in their appeal (as the cant phrase runs), that readers even of comparatively limited culture can enjoy them, even though unable to appreciate them. Saying this is but re-saying what is so well known already, that many of the true masterpieces of literature are—within limits—for all sorts and conditions of men.

7. And yet even the tyro, delaying in order to make sure preparation before attempting the character story, will have the character story always before him as part of his ideal. For the plot story that is also a character story is doubly excellent; the atmosphere story that is also a character story is doubly excellent, and the theme story that is not also a character story is doubly in danger of failure even as a theme story. To study human nature, to study men and their ways, to observe the thousand-and-one manifestations through which the temperament and the human nature of every individual may reveal itself, to perceive the innumerable influences that affect men, shape their character, and help to determine their destiny, and to strive always and unceasingly to body forth in story form the facts learned in the course of this never-ceasing study—this must always be the aspiration and aim of the true artist in fiction, unsubdued and unsubduable in him because it is the very essence and spirit of his genius.

8. We should now define clearly to ourselves WHAT

character is.   All animal creatures may be said to have character.   That is, they have a set of fundamental or primary instincts, or natural tendencies or habits of re-action which have been developed by an age-long course of existence under particular conditions.   These instincts, tendencies, and habits are common to all members of the family, and by virtue of them, all members of the family respond in the same way to the same stimuli and motives to action.

9. But in each individual, especially in the higher forms of life, these instinctive, nature-given tendencies have been more or less modified by particular influences affecting the individual only, whereby the moods and acts of this individual are caused to vary from the family or racial standard, or norm.   To illustrate: All horses have the same primary, fundamental, or nature-given instincts and tendencies (we will not confuse ourselves by consider-ing how domestication has modified these as they exist in the wild horse).   Yet, notwithstanding these identical in-stincts and characteristics, one horse is affectionate and another fierce; one is patient, another nervous and im-patient; one trustworthy, another treacherous, and so on. Even different colts of the same mare and sire may have notably variant characteristics.   *This basic nature in the creature, modified or shaped into individual traits and tendencies, is the character of that creature.*   It is manifested through the creature's behavior and con-duct.

10. We may pause here to remark that there is one immense difference between the behavior and conduct of mankind and that of other animals.   *The action of man is reasoned; that of beasts is based upon no reflective*

foresight. This fact is what makes drama and fiction possible, for it is what makes possible motive and therefore conflict—the conscious struggle between man and the physical world, between man and man, between man and his own spiritual nature. The uncertainty, the variety, the comedy, the tragedy, all the interest of human life, spring mainly from this ability of man to perceive and consider alternatives, to weigh consequences, to pick and choose or predetermine (or at least attempt to predetermine) results. *Fiction is interesting largely because it thus shows us man employing—or failing to employ—this faculty of reflective foresight; and motivation and plot are possible only because there exists this reasoning faculty in man.*

11. We return now to our consideration of character. Men as a genus, family, or class, have their distinctive nature, their peculiar set of instincts, nature-bestowed tendencies, and habits and emotional reactions so long kept up that they have practically established themselves as instincts. *This is human nature—the whole set of instincts, tendencies, emotions, and motives common to mankind. And human nature is the basis of human character.*

12. But in character there is always a second element; for *character is the basic human nature shaped and modified into individual traits and tendencies that are manifested in the conduct of the individual. This second element in human character we may say is temperament, the quality or disposition peculiar to the individual.* This temperament, or *temper* of the individual (to adopt an Elizabethan term signifying quality as it results from a particular and successful admixture of ingredients), may

be the consequence of any of an indefinite number of modifying influences. Thus, it depends often upon constitution, upon nervous organization, or upon physiological conditions. Congeniality of surroundings or of occupation affects it wholesomely. Indeed, its healthiness largely depends upon the proper gratification of individual tastes and appetites. It is also partly determined by the individual's amount of will-power, enabling him to adapt himself to his surroundings; and intellectual or spiritual discipline, resulting from either education or experience, will always result in an increased control of environment by the individual, and thus by controlling one of the most important shaping influences indirectly determine temperament itself.

13. Again, habits affect temperament, whether they be developed through natural inclination or through constraint. Years of study will unfit for active pursuits a man originally of the most active tendency. Teachers of composition afford another example. Required by their business to maintain constant watchfulness for small errors, they not infrequently find themselves developing querulousness and a tendency to petty fault-finding. However, exhaustive enumeration of the influences that determine temperament is impossible; for *anything and everything, even interplaying qualities of human nature itself, may react on the individual to modify into variant aspects the elemental traits and qualities of our common human nature, and thus determine temperament.*

14. So much for the two constituents of human character. What then is character itself? *Character is the sum of the moral, intellectual, and physical instincts, tendencies, qualities, and habits of the individual, resulting from*

the union of human nature and temperament,[19] and manifesting itself in what he thinks and does. This manifestation may be internal, appearing merely in the thoughts and imaginings of the man, or external, appearing in action—his speech, acts, behavior, outward conduct.

15. For purposes of dramatic presentation, only external manifestations of character are available. Pure psychological analysis, or narration of psychological experience—recounting the events in the march of consciousness, or picturing forth in its flow the so-called stream of consciousness—is not *dramatic.* Hence it is expedient, even though arbitrary, to exclude fiction that is developed by this method from the class of the conte. This is not to say, however, that there are no true psychological short stories. *The true psychological conte, however, is that in which the mental state and action are not narrated, described, or analyzed directly, but are instead made clear through the truly dramatic—i.e., actional—means of external manifestation.* What is said and done in the course of the plot development reveals (but does not relate) what the person is thinking and feeling. The psychological story that presents these mental states otherwise than by this truly actional method of speech and act, possibly should be regarded as in fact a peculiar class. We may call it psychological description, or psychological narration, or name its product the psychological-analytical narrative, etc.; we may even argue that there is a dramatic quality

[19] The student of men in the mass will find various *divisions and subdivisions between the race and the individual.* Each of these will have its own distinctive characteristics—those of nationality, for example. Each social rank, each profession, etc., has its peculiar *class* characteristics. It follows, therefore, that *characterization must take note* of individual, of class, and of race traits.

in many psychological situations or operations. But the
fact remains, that psychological analysis does not present
persons acting; and therefore it is doubtfully dramatic in
the sense required by the short story. However (although
it has seemed well to discuss the matter rather fully here),
*the problem of presenting psychological phenomena is in
truth more a problem how to portray a person during his
passage through a psychological experience than it is a
question of character and its manifestation.*

16. We return therefore briefly to direct consideration
of the short story that emphasizes character. The means
whereby character can be dramatically presented in narrative will be discussed in some detail in a later chapter;
consequently we need here only repeat that *speech and
acts are the main, if not the sole, dependence of the author
in showing forth to the reader through his imagination the character of the persons of whom he is writing.*
Therefore, in the story written to emphasize character,
speech and act will be prominent. They will not, however,
be prominent for their own sake, or for the thrill they
may be able to communicate through directly exciting the
reader, as they are in the story that emphasizes plot. *They
will be prominent because in and through them the reader
beholds character;* they are the index, the outward symbol,
the key, the manifestation, the effect of which character is
the cause. And as the reader, in order to interpret them,
must be able to translate the symbol into terms of the
thing symbolized, to judge accurately what the cause is
from seeing only its results, so the writer on his side must
be able to translate character into suitable symbols (words
and acts); to perceive what the true and natural results
of any well-defined character, taken as the cause, would be,

and by depicting it through such results, or symbols,—the acts and speech of the persons,—make it apparent to the reader.

17. The first task, therefore, for the writer of character stories, is the conceiving of a consistent, and, of course, true-to-nature character for each person in his story. By consistent, we do not mean a character in which are no conflicting elements, but a character in which (whatever the elements of conflict) there is no self-contradiction. How far the conflict between character elements may go without rendering the character self-contradictory, is shown by Dr. Jekyll and Mr. Hyde. Perhaps we should be safer were we to say merely that the conception must not seem to be inconsistent, or self-contradictory—that it shall stand the test of a sound plausibility based upon knowledge of man and men, and a strict observance of the possibilities of character as thus discovered. Characters so conceived will be true to life, and will accordingly stand every test. We have, therefore, arrived at the point, to which we shall always find ourselves returning, at which we must recognize the fundamental importance of observing men and the ways of men and the influences that determine these ways—in other words, the importance of being familiar with character in detail. To write good fiction, one must know man and men, human nature and temperament; and to know these, he must have been a close observer of men in their activities.

18. Moreover, this knowledge must be practical, not theoretical. This assertion needs to be emphasized. Many writers—young writers of a scholarly turn especially —think that if they read books and gain an understanding of the elements of human nature as these are revealed in

poetry, fiction, history, or the like, they have qualified
themselves for their work as writers. They are wrong.
The writer of drama and dramatic fiction narrative must
know *men*. He must have seen human life living itself
in the lives of many individual men. He must know men
so well that the human nature and the temperament in
every individual will distinctly separate themselves to his
understanding. He must know not only the types of men,
but the individual variations that occur within the type.
He must know what are the type actions that go with the
standard instincts and emotions—but he must also know
how these type actions are changed or modified in the
individual. And all these things should be so familiar to
him that, the moment he conceives a person of a certain
type, he will be aware what that type of person will do
in a given set of circumstances; and beyond that, what
this one person he has conceived—an individual having
his own character, made up of human nature modified by
temperament—would do in the same set of circumstances;
for in the action of the individual will always be some
degree of individuality, and the writer who knows men
should from his knowledge realize instinctively what this
individuality of conduct and speech will be. So intimate,
so closely accurate, so extensive, so sure, should be the
fiction writer's knowledge, not merely of man, but of men.
He can never become perfect in it, yet he should never
cease to perfect himself in it. And for this there is but
one way—that of meeting and dealing with men closely
and constantly.

19. To the writer of contes in which character is emphasized, such extreme familiarity with men is indispensable. For since he must make the words and acts of each

person clearly spring from and reveal the character of the person, he must know, even to the littlest, the words that men use, the tones in which they speak them, the gestures they employ and the occasions on which they employ each, the decisions—instinctive or reasoned—to which they come, the way they behave while coming to them, and their manner of acting (each according to his own character) in accordance with their decisions. To make the character story convincing, all such things must be set down, and set down as they would be were the story a fact and not a fiction story, For if they are not set down as they would be in life, the reader will *feel* the incongruity, even if he cannot name it; and both story and character will disappoint him. Hence *the chief study of the writer of character stories must be, how to set forth a varied body of speech and act that shall clearly reveal character, the character itself being consistent and true to life—to human nature, to class-type, and to the individual.*

XI. SOME CONTES EMPHASIZE ATMOSPHERE

1. Last of the four possible types of short story that are produced by laying emphasis especially upon a particular element, or factor, of fiction narrative, we name the type that emphasizes atmosphere. But in giving the atmosphere story the last place, we are making it neither the least nor the greatest among these types. For the conte has its masterpieces of plot story, of theme story, of character story, and of atmosphere story; and if we raise the question of comparative merit, we are likely to be forced, on consideration, to dodge it, answering that the greatest of short stories is not to be found in any one of

these special types as such, but in that conte which combines all these elements according to its needs, attaining its effect by a presentation of life through the artistic union of all the four.

2.   Nevertheless, considering as we are for the present the emphasis of particular elements in individual stories, we must in fairness set down, that the atmosphere story is often tremendously effective.   As some of the most wonderful of modern paintings are those that have caught the atmosphere of the desert, the plains, or the sea, so some of the most wonderful novels and contes of our day are those that have caught the atmosphere rather than the details of phases of life—the spirit and essence of some environment in which life is lived significantly.

3.   Of the four elements of fiction narrative that we are considering,—theme, plot, character, and atmosphere— atmosphere is the hardest exactly to define; for it is not, like the others, reducible to a process, a formula, or a method, but is that more delicately impalpable thing, a subjective quality to be sensed or an emotional impression to be received.   Therefore we can, before formulating a definition, profitably consider the thing itself somewhat.

4.   Atmosphere we may describe as the quality felt in a story or drama, through the impression created by setting, mood, character, action, theme, incident, persons, personality (either that of the author or of the persons in the story), tone, and so on.   Or we may call it *the source of the total subjective impression left by the combined influence of all the elements, accompaniments, and surroundings of viewpoint, characters, action, and scene.*   The atmosphere of a story is the encompassing medium in which the narrative exists and moves.   It is the psychological medium,

as the physical atmosphere, with all its attributes of light, warmth, translucence, rarity or density, color, stimulation or depression, clearness, heaviness, purity, etc., is the purely physical medium in which animal life exists and moves. Or it may be described as the sum total of environment, psychological and physical, as the habitat of an animal, with its peculiar set of physical, vegetable, geographic, climatic, animal, and animal-nature, conditions, constitutes the total of the environment of that animal.

5. Atmosphere is, then, *the total psychological, emotional, or tonal environment wherein character and action present themselves subjectively to the reader*,[20] to

[20] The test of atmosphere is the presence of a quality in the narrative itself, permeative and intangible rather than explicit and locable. Upon further analysis, we should find that this impression of atmosphere depends on either or both of two qualities: first, the quality of place, environment, and determining conditions; second, the quality of mood. The first gives a sense of the *milieu* and circumstances; the second gives a sense of the tone—of the emotional quality and nature—belonging to the story, its persons or events. Roughly, the one is material, physical, or social, the other immaterial and psychological—the one perceived as external fact, the other as internal fact. But almost always they exist together. The effect of either is always mainly emotional—that is, subjective. Hence our discussion of atmosphere has not attempted to separate them.—Let the student compare a mood story with a story of setting (realized best in the local-color story). Mrs. Wharton's *Ethan Frome* is pre-eminently a mood story; Harris Dickson's stories of negro life (*Saturday Evening Post*) are local color stories— almost any of the "Old Reliable" series will serve, as will most of Bret Harte's California stories, Mrs. Freeman's stories of New England, etc. Yet all such stories will reveal that (except when the setting is described merely for objective interest), the introduction of an element of *milieu* or conditioning circumstance affects mainly the mood of the reader, thus giving him the impression of subjective tone or coloring in the story. We "sense" the tone and

create which, every artistic element unites which is capable
of producing through literary means the impression of a
physical sensation or a perception of mood, or of moral,
spiritual, ethical or esthetic quality, or tone, thereby producing a sense of subjective quality. To phrase the
thought in yet another way, *atmosphere is the consequence
of bringing to bear upon the reader the full power of
subjective impression exerted through any sort of literary
or dramatic device:* its purpose being, to put him into
complete emotional understanding or *rapport* (responsive-
ness and sympathy) with the various elements of the
story. It thus enables him *both to perceive the external
quality and to feel the internal quality and spirit*—accurately and truly, because he feels not only the thing
itself, but also the conditions and surroundings which are
a part of it and of which it is a part.

6. From this preliminary description of atmosphere,
let us now formulate a working definition. *Atmosphere is
that subjective quality in a story resulting from highly
characteristic elements, or accompaniments, conditions, and
surroundings, of the setting, persons, character traits, and
action; by virtue of which the persons, incidents, character,
and action are seen in a medium of natural and significant
psychological, tonal, or emotional environment of which
they are a necessary part and which is a necessary part
of them.* Condensing this, we may say that *atmosphere is*

quality of a scene rather than perceive it merely. Stevenson's *The
Merry Men;* Hamlin Garland's early western stories (as in *Main
Traveled Roads*), Poe's *Fall of the House of Usher*—these are
merely a few of the stories that owe their subjective effect, or
emotional impression, mainly to the combined influence of environmental and mood elements. For in successful writing, the two cannot
be kept distinct.

that quality which produces its effect on the reader by means of a subjective coloring of any or all [21] *of the elements of the story.* Its impression is made almost entirely on the subjective sensibilities—on the emotions—and is made in either of two ways: first, by direct appeal, as when the material used itself is emotional and address is made outright to our subjective senses; second, by indirection, as when such aspects of objective matters are chosen for presentation as are associated with subjective experiences, these aspects being, therefore, sure to stimulate an emotional response even though doing so indirectly. [22]

---

[21] A scheme will help to show forth the fact, as follows:

Subjective coloring will be found inherent in, or can be given to—

1. Objective facts: setting, appearance of persons, costume, acts, deeds, incidents, etc.
2. Determining conditions: influences of time, place, associates, social and industrial environment, education, etc., etc., such as affect character, behavior, deed, motive, etc. These may be either (a) objective (see 1 above) or (b) subjective (see 3 below).
3. Subjective facts: the relationships, influences, and reactions that pre-eminently affect or belong to psychological experience—the inner life.

Therefore, we may have either objective atmosphere or subjective atmosphere—that productive of mood or tone. Further, the story may be so written that its mood or tone will be the result of either (a) its own materials (complete detachment on the part of the author), or (b) the author's arbitrary selection of details to produce a particular mood or tone determined by himself (author's mood, or attitude).

[22] From what has been said, the conclusion follows, that *the term subjective coloring is a full descriptive synonym for atmosphere, and perhaps even a more accurate term.*

7. Among the elements that aid in creating atmosphere, *setting* is highly important. It is not to be confounded with atmosphere, although the terms are sometimes used synonymously; neither is it equal to environment. By setting we really mean the physical surroundings—what the stage manager would classify as scenery and properties. Setting is objective and can always be indicated by some direct method of description, although, of course, direct description is not necessarily preferable to other methods of presentation. Moreover, the mere introduction of description is not enough to give atmosphere, unless the setting and the description are themselves such as to be significant and produce the artistic effect desired.

8. *Environment*—a larger term—implies not only setting, but also all other surroundings and accompanying conditions; and, therefore, it may be psychological and non-objective. Well indicated, environment is an effective producer of atmosphere—indeed, is perhaps the main dependence in most atmosphere stories. Among the elements entering into environment are time, place, occupation, moral and spiritual surroundings, and (in general) whatever accompaniments of existence influence character and life.

A. *Time:* Time may determine the atmosphere of a story. Thus, there may be stories with an atmosphere of war time or of peace; of particular historical periods; of Christmas, Memorial Day, or other holiday; an atmosphere appropriate to the night, to daytime, to spring, summer, fall, or winter, to sowing time or harvest time, etc.

B. *Place:* Place may determine the atmosphere of a story. Thus, there may be stories with an atmosphere of the streets, the theater, the church, the home, the amusement-park, the city, the country, the tropics, the school, the sea, the veldt, the plains, the jungle, the air (aëronautical stories), etc.

C. *Occupation:* Occupation may determine the atmosphere of a story. Thus, there may be stories with an atmosphere appropriate to medicine, journalism, the law, the ministry; to the life of the day-laborer, the iron-worker, the weaver or mill-hand, the fisherman, the soldier or marine, the professor, the housewife, the speculator, the gambler, the prostitute, the nurse, the clerk, etc.

D. *Other Conditions:* Besides the influences such as have already been mentioned, almost innumerable items or elements of environment exist that contribute to the impression of atmosphere. Such for instance are illness in the household; educational influences; religious surroundings; the character of associates; poverty, manners, personal tastes and habits; dress; eating;—in brief, whatever can be responsible wholly or in part for the mood, tone, or other quality essential in the life itself that is portrayed. The introduction of such items as material for narration can be so affected that it will cause the persons, incidents, and action to be seen in an encompassing medium of consistent, natural, significant psychological environment; the story will, in all its parts, give evidence of the close observation, adequate comprehension, and full power of sympathetic presentation without which it will be deficient in that indispensable quality, subjective coloring.

9. By way of concrete illustration, assume now that several clergymen are gathered in a vestry room to discuss a religious crisis. If the material be well handled, the

atmosphere will be an atmosphere of deep religious earnestness, with clerical and personal manners seen in a setting of church surroundings. Now, enter to the clergymen an ex-pugilist, converted in a mission chapel but retaining all the mannerisms produced by his breeding in the slums. In the proceedings that follow, he is prominent; and inevitably his appearance, personality, speech, and behavior modify the previous atmosphere. It may be more human; it certainly will be less clerical and churchly. Further suppose that the worldly daughter of the rector, a society girl, now comes into the action. She modifies the atmosphere anew; her dress, her manners, her personality and ideals, are all felt, subtly but surely, in a changed quality in the situation. They suggest other influences in life than earnestness and religion, another outlook on life —an outlook foreign to the clergymen's and equally foreign to the crudely earnest pugilist's. Or let us assume a hospital ward, with nurses attending to their duties, and a pickle-faced martyr to her conception of duty haranguing on the subject of his soul an unfortunate nephew, occupationally a ball-player, laid up in one of the beds. Merely to suggest such a combination of time, place, persons, and character, gives an impression of atmosphere—an atmosphere individual and distinct. Then suddenly remove the maiden lady and in her place substitute a member of the invalid's team, airy, jovial, confident, and hearty. Presto! the atmosphere is vitally changed.

10. Or again, let us assume a tenement house in the city. The halls reek with the smell of cabbage, corned beef, and onion. Doors stand indecorously ajar, displaying glimpses of disordered rooms, scattered garments, old brooms, boxes, slouchy women, and dirty shouting chil-

dren. Is not here an atmosphere of shiftlessness or in-
competence? But add now some laughter and broad
repartee. An impression of the element of irresponsible
happiness supersedes the previous impression of shiftlessness. Then let the rent-collector and an officer appear, with dispossess writs against one of the tenants;
laughter gives way to grief, and neighborly merriment
to neighborly sympathy. Yet again, suppose the author to
conceive a story of village life, in which the selfish per-
sistence of one man in keeping pigs produces unsanitary
conditions from which an epidemic starts, causing the
death of several neighbors' children. The author, taking this theme seriously, turns out a story the atmosphere
of which is heavy with selfishness and tragedy. And
then suppose that he conceives his theme lightly instead
of tragically, constructing a story in which neighborhood
pigs, neighborhood rows, and simon-pure human nature
supply a farcical narrative. The atmosphere is now
quite changed. In these two instances, it is the author's
viewpoint that determined what the atmosphere—and
therefore the subjective effect on the reader—would be.
Illustration could be continued indefinitely, but the fact
is already manifest. *Anything whatever that, whether
by outright assertion or by reactive suggestion, serves to
produce a subjective impression, to create the illusion
of psychological quality, is atmosphere material.*

11. Atmosphere, we said, is hard to define. The atmosphere story is hard to write—successfully. It is the
work of the highly skilled; for *atmosphere is the fine flavor
of literary and dramatic ingredients blended by a master.*
A writer may be able to develop a theme, construct and
manage a plot, and portray a character successfully, and

yet fall short of attaining true, or natural, or satisfying atmosphere.

12. For atmosphere is the product of high artistic gift rather than of immediate effort. Before there can be atmosphere there must be sharp and deep insight, catholic sympathy, and almost universal observation; and these must be accompanied by great powers of accurate literary expression. Without this observation, this knowledge of one's material in all its aspects, this understanding and sympathy, or without the literary gift that enables one to give to others, through words, a realization of things as they have revealed themselves to him,—without these, there can be no fine exhalation of the inner nature of personality, surroundings, incident, and action into the illuminating, clarifying, softening, individualizing, naturalizing, humanizing quality that we term atmosphere.

13. Of which comment, the moral is this: Before attacking the atmosphere story, master theme, plot, and characterization; learn nature, human nature, and men; acquire the habit of observing with all the minute care of the scientist and all the sympathetic understanding of the artist; and develop a master's skill in exact words. When this has been done—*when you can report the thing as in itself it really is—you will not have to strive for atmosphere. The atmosphere will create itself for you, secured surely and accurately through the truthfulness of your report.*

14. The student may feel some confusion about the relationship between atmosphere, as here defined, and the emotional appeal, frequently spoken of in discussions of fiction. The terms merely name different aspects of the

same thing. Atmosphere is a quality possessed by and permeating the story, and inherent in its parts and materials. Then, having atmosphere, it has emotional appeal—is able to set up in the reader a subjective, or emotional, response to its own subjective, or emotional, quality. The one is cause; the other is effect. As we have noted, any and every element of the narrative may and usually does have, in some degree, subjective coloring, or emotional quality. It follows that every part and portion of the narrative may have emotional appeal (subjective stimulus). One well-chosen word, expressing a clearly-sensed feeling of the author for some inherent quality or mood of the situation, the person, the character, the scene, the environment, the act, may tinge or dye all the story with this same quality or mood. Emotional appeal (or subjective stimulus), therefore, depends upon subjective coloring, i.e., atmosphere; and *atmosphere depends upon the fineness of sense with which the writer feels the manifold qualities of his materials and the effectiveness with which he is able to translate these qualities into the words with which he reports the story.*

15. Ultimately, then, atmosphere and subjective effect depend upon the author—first, upon the fineness, the sympathy, the comprehending power of his understanding and interpreting imagination, enabling him to put himself in every situation and in the place of every person in every situation, sensing deeply and truly the essential qualities inherent in them; and second, upon his well-considered selection of the particular qualities to be emphasized and intensified for the purposes of the story. We shall see (XVIII. 3) that the story may be told from either of three main angles of view—as if it were nar-

rated by (a) an actor in it, (b) an observer merely, or
(c) a person completely dissociated from its events in
every way—and that the author cannot get far in plan-
ning his story until he has decided which of these angles
of view he will adopt for his narration. We must now
note also that *his attitude of sympathy and emotion as
well as his angle of narration will mightily affect the
quality discernible in his story.* It determines the inherent quality by determining the particular aspects of
the materials which he shall select and the particular
qualities in these aspects that he shall, by means of his
treatment and expression, intensify and make dominant
in the narrative. He may elect to be sentimental in attitude; in which case he will select incidents, settings,
acts, character traits, speeches, and situations, that are
predominantly sentimental. He may elect to be pathetic;
in which case it will be the quality of pathos that he will
seek in his selection of materials and his manner of treatment and expression. Or he may elect to intensify pathos
into tragedy, or to assume a humorous [23] attitude; his
choice of materials, of treatment, and of expression always
varying according to the requirements of this attitude.

16. The attitude, therefore, or subjective point of
view, assumed by the author toward his story, is what
determines its emotional appeal, or subjective quality;

[23] The effect of the conte always tending to be in the main
emotional, humor is suitable to it, but wit less so; wit being less
emotional than intellectual in quality. The guises in which humor
appear are: (a) permeative—dispersed throughout the story, regardless of its particular form or type; (b) comedy; (c) farce
comedy; (d) burlesque. The presence of wit in dominating quantity
tends to produce rather comedy of satire and irony than comedy of
humor.

and it determines this by determining the selection of materials to be incorporated in the story as a means of provoking in the reader a subjective response to the feeling of the author—of putting him into a subjective attitude corresponding to that assumed by the author. A word more, then, may be worth while about *the means available for communicating this feeling, and provoking this attitude. The sense of the subjective coloring, of the emotional quality, is communicated, first, by the materials themselves, and second, by the language chosen with which to report them.* The two means are of course always co-workers. But in the work of the inexperienced and the artificial writer, too much dependence on words and too little upon materials are often found; they depend on words, not facts, for effect. Yet *the words can produce their effect only when they are fully adapted to the thought and emotion—only when they adequately and truly report the facts to express which they have been assembled.* Hence words merely, unbacked by feeling, are futile. The subjective quality must exist in the materials before words can be chosen fitly to embody, express, and communicate it. Yet the number of writers who depend on words instead of materials for subjective effect, is legion.

17. *The selection of materials, therefore, wherein the subjective quality is inherent—of materials that are significant of subjective quality and mood—is imperative.* This selection well made, the adapting of the language to the material may call for either of two procedures: cutting down the number of words, or increasing the number of words, i.e., using more words with a view to the full communication of a sense of the subjective quality. *Words*

are to be increased when the facts themselves, less fully reported, will not sufficiently or certainly carry the effect of emotional quality. The author then employs epithets, descriptive phrases, and other quality- or mood-suggesting expressions—either denotative or connotative—in order that an adequate sense of the particular subjective quality may be aroused in the reader. Words are so used in the sentence, " Her vestal mannerisms and her too knowledgeable manner, as if she were overripe from manifold experiences of the world. . . ."

18. On the other hand, *some facts and situations are so great and fundamental as to imply, without comment or addition, the quality or mood inherent in them.* They make their emotional appeal simply, directly, and unaided. The power and adequacy of the simple assertion, " Jesus wept," has been noted endlessly as an example. In dealing with such self-interpreting facts and situations, the superb economy of speech often characteristic of the Bible is advisable. To be sure, every situation is a new situation, and therefore a rule unto itself; but *no situation that is intrinsically emotional calls for much verbal exploitation. Such situations are those that most depend upon the primal, basic instincts and emotions of man;* whereas those that depend upon less universal facts for their subjective quality may need interpretation. When, therefore, subjective effects are involved that depend upon acquired emotions, ideals, or points of view,[24] fuller characterization is necessary; for the quality of these is at once more diverse and less familiar to general

---

[24] Such emotions, ideals, and points of view, for instance, as result from education; from sophistication; from economic and social status; from the refining influences of culture, etc.

experience. Comparatively few words (for instance) are likely to be needed in conveying the emotional quality of a scene in which father and mother stand by the death-bed of their first-born; the situation carries and communicates its own emotion. But writers have not unhappily expended pages in bodying forth the feelings of Penrod the grammar-school boy in some of the juvenile crises of life. The less obvious, the less familiar to general experience, the less an outcome of universal fact, the subjective quality is, the more likely it is to require fuller word-portrayal; the more it depends on universal fact, the more familiar it is to general experience, the less it will require multiplication of words to procure it comprehension and provoke response.

19. With some more general explanation, we can now close this part of our discussion. As the story must have emotional, or subjective, quality, and as the quality presented must be true, the author must, to produce the essential subjective coloring, have himself felt and comprehended the feeling that he attempts to embody in his story. The more deeply and widely he has felt, therefore, the more will he be able to find in life, and to reproduce in his work, the essential elements of emotion. To have lived, to have loved, to have laughed, to have wept, and through accumulated experience to have ripened—this seems the logical preparation for the highest effectiveness in creating stories that will have emotional appeal—especially so in stories dealing with the more serious aspects of life. True, the exuberant fancy and spirits of youth make up to some extent for unripeness and inexperience—but not when the deepest meanings of existence are to be interpreted. Youthfulness of spirit need

not end with the early years of manhood; rightly conserved, emotion strengthens and intensifies itself, not
thins and perishes; and he can best portray life who
through maturity of thought and feeling—through long
experience—has most perfected his knowledge of life.

20. But experience may produce, not ripeness, but
that false maturity, sophistication. Better the green but
vital imagination of youth than the mature but sophisticated indifference and cynicism of years. For deep,
spontaneous, and natural emotion is not to be felt in
sophistication. Neither is the sophistication belonging to
a class, society, or age, to be permitted to pass its conventions and attitudes off in the place of true emotion. These
things abound in subjective quality material, but are
never to be mistaken for or presented as true emotion, and
the author must preserve an attitude toward them that
will result in showing them forth for what they are, not
for the things they falsely assume to be. Before the deep
as well as true emotion can be portrayed, the accidental
must be stripped away,[25] and when persons who have become sophisticated, over-refined, or corrupted to a false
conception of men and life,—when such persons are to
be presented as feeling true emotion, they must first be
brought back ruthlessly to their primitive human nature.
This can be accomplished only by subjecting them to the
humanizing influence of events that strike with brutal
primal directness at the roots of their pride, pretense,

[25] In such cases, the value of the " foil "—the character or situation that offsets and contrasts with another—is great. The effect
of presenting sham, convention, and pinchbeck emotion in contrast
with the true emotion, is often tremendous. Consider the Maid of
Orleans, in her sincerity and devout unselfishness a foil to all
the court of France, and of England also.

prejudice, ignorance, and self-complacency. And to be able thus to discriminate between the true and the false, between perverted and fundamental human character, the author must devoutly have preserved himself from false culture, false refinement, false pride, and false wisdom —which is sophistication and black ignorance. To see and to understand all things in all men—this must be his aim and achievement.

21. Yet truth compels the acknowledgment that an emotional appeal is sometimes made—at least with temporary success—by artificial stimuli, not by the legitimate method of reporting with accuracy the thing together with its natural accompaniment of subjective quality. It is possible to heap up pitiful details excessively—to portray emotion where none is present—to play on the feelings falsely—to get a burst of tears or a burst of laughter under "false pretenses." Bad practice, this, bad art, and bad artistic morals, the only temptation to which will perhaps be, the chance to sell to editors whose readers have a perverted taste and small artistic judgment. Whether 'tis better thus to sell, perchance to thrive, or to withstand the darts and slings of editorial rejections, keeping thereby one's artistic self-respect—that is the question. Let him who writes solve it, remembering that such editors do not represent all the market for literary wares; remembering, too, that the conscience too long accustomed to light behavior presently loses much of its sense of differences. Literary creativeness may fly out of the window when literary charlatanism comes in at the door.

CHAPTER II

THEORY AND PRACTICE OF THE PLOT

XII. The Short Story Plot Much Resembles That of the One-Act Play

1. The conte is a one-act play narrated, not acted. On the whole, this is so nearly true that we can take the play, especially the one-act play, as a guide to most of the short story principles that are dramatic, not narrative, in their essentials. The principles of dramatic plot are especially available. If not all of them can be appropriated bodily by short story art, those that cannot be appropriated can nevertheless be profitably studied by it.

2. What then are the essentials of a dramatic plot? They are:

A. Persons acting.

B. Persons acting in accordance with, or else (under the stress of conflict and situation) contrary to their previous character.

C. Things happening or done (acts and incidents), these things constituting an interlocking series ending in a conclusive outcome.

D. The things that are done resulting from the character of the persons plus the situation (the sense of the word here is both general and specific).

E. These things reacting on the persons in some such way as to seem likely to affect their future (especially as determined by their character. This will be shown in the outcome, in which the character will be seen either to persist unchanged after passage through a crisis, or else to have been altered in some respect as the result of passing through the crisis).

F. A set of conditions or influences, whether the result of character or of circumstances, that affect the persons and are in opposition some to the others; this contrary pull or push of influences rendering the outcome uncertain and thereby constituting the *complication* in the plot, this in turn creating the *conflict* and consequently the *crisis*.

3. Again, regarding the plot as an interlocking series of events culminating in a definite outcome, we shall find in it these fundamental elements, or constructional materials:

A. Motive, motivation: The reason, or causes, of the things happening or done. These causes will lie in character, or in the circumstances, or (usually) in character and the circumstances reacting on each other.

B. Action: The things that happen or are done— acts and incidents (see Sec. IX, 4) proceeding toward the outcome.

C. Outcome: The fulfillment, or issue of the action under the influence of the motivating causes.[1]

4. Every plot must have a beginning, a middle, and an end; that is, the matters that precipitate the action, the progress and development of the action and situation, and the conclusive outcome of the action as this action is in-

[1] The technical term *catastrophe* is so often associated merely with tragedy and tragic outcome that it becomes confusing when used to designate outcomes that are not tragic. *Dénouement* likewise is confusing and ambiguous. Therefore, the simpler term *outcome* is employed.

fluenced by the attendant circumstances. The *beginning* is that portion of the plot-facts which makes plain to us enough of the character traits and circumstances involved to enable us to understand the action. The *ending* is that part which brings the outcome and its consequences. The *middle* includes all the plot-facts not belonging to the beginning or the end—the main course of action, the main body of incident and event, the main part of the characterization, and (usually) the main portion of the atmosphere effects.

5. At this point we should make note of the difference between the order of events and incidents *in the plot,* as the plot is conceived to support the action and outcome (that is, as an abstract, or outline, of motivating causes and events), and the order of events and incidents as they may present themselves in the completed drama or story. In the plot abstract, everything must come in the natural order—cause before effect and motive before deed. Unless this order were followed, logical plotting would not be possible. But in the play or story that is built on the plot so conceived, this order is subject to free manipulation. The deed may be shown before its motive is revealed, the effect become apparent before its cause. This is here equivalent to saying that the *opening* of a play or story does not of necessity contain the material that actually constitutes the beginning of the plot, and that other variations also of the natural sequence may occur. This fact is mentioned at this time merely that the student shall not be left to think that the beginning of the story necessarily is identical in content with the beginning of the plot. Let us therefore return to consideration of the plot.

6. Technically, the plot consists of several divisions, representing stages of progress, namely:

A. The EXPOSITION, or stage of introductory explanation. This ends with the *exciting moment, or inciting impulse*—the moment at which the complicating influences first appear and the conflict begins to reveal itself.

B. The RISING ACTION, or critical period. This begins with the inciting impulse, or moment, and continues, often by successive stages of increasing power or intensity, to the *decisive moment*. This point—that at which the outcome is, by the progress of events, made now sure—should when possible coincide with the so-called grand climax, height, or climactic moment. The *climactic moment,* as usually defined, is the moment when the suspense is greatest, and therefore the interest most tense; it is frequently, though confusingly, termed the climax. But in truth the decisive moment, not the so-called height or grand climax, marks the end of the development and the beginning of the falling action; for this moment is that at which one certain outcome at last is made sure by the combined effect of events already past. Evidently, therefore, *the most skillful plotting will be that in which the decisive moment, or height of the plot, likewise is the climactic moment, or height of the action—the point, that is, of greatest suspense and tensest interest.* This does not, however, always happen; the height of the plot *may* not coincide with the height of the action, and therefore the grand climax may precede or follow the decisive moment. It is more likely to follow than to precede.[2]

---

[2] In tragedy, the decisive moment is also known as the tragic moment. With the decisive moment (when recognized immediately), "anticipatory delay" begins; this continues until the outcome is

C. The FALLING ACTION. This part is that which follows the decisive moment. It can be regarded as the beginning and approach of the end. Frequent names for it are *dénouement,* untangling, or resolution of the plot. We shall, however, be accurate enough and more comprehensible if we call it merely that part which carries us on, as rapidly as may be, from the decisive moment to the outcome. It may contain the climactic situation; but when it does so, the interest of this situation will not infrequently be found to depend on intensifying influences other than those of the bare plot.

D. The OUTCOME (also called by some *dénouement* or *catastrophe*). In modern plotting, the tendency is more and more to telescope falling action and *dénouement* into outcome, ending the action as quickly as possible after the decisive moment and the grand climax. Indeed, *in the conte and the short play, " falling action" is often scarcely to be found. Instead, the decisive moment and the moment of grand climax practically include the outcome,* or at least bring it immediately after them. Conclusions following the outcome are no longer found.

7. For a good many pages now our attention will be occupied by discussion of plotting and the plot. In considering this discussion, the student should bear in mind this caution: the word " plot " may and often does cover everything from a bare statement of the central thought, theme, or germ-idea of the plot, up to the completed story embodying the plot in its final and most finished form.

reached. Within it comes often a point of " final suspense," at which the outcome, before assured, seems again to hang in the balance. In fact, the anticipatory delay may include a number of points of balanced suspense.

Perhaps this will be clearer if we say that *the plot may present itself in various degrees of fullness.* These degrees of amplitude, or stages of amplification, may be listed roughly as follows:

A. *Plot germ* (or "master plot"). A more or less general conception, or thought; the first undeveloped form of an idea out of which may grow a true plot. In effect, it is a theme; and if the figure of speech be continued, we can say that the first stage of development from the plot germ produces the *plot embryo* (see B here following); the material is no longer in plasmic form, but has been organized and limited enough to have its own distinct form and characteristics, and its own natural tendency to grow or develop in a certain definite direction. That is, the plot germ turned into a plot embryo produces the working-plot. The embryo is more commonly the first form in which the plot occurs to the writer's mind. (See Hawthorne's notebooks for many examples of germ and embryo.)

B. *Working-plot, or plot embryo.* In the working-plot, the germ thought has been developed enough so that it affords a clear epitome, or miniature, of the full plot as it will be when developed. It is the complete plot compacted into the fewest possible words. The working-plot represents the first stage in the evolution that is enough advanced to present the plot definitely as a whole, although only in miniature.

C. *Plot abstract or synopsis.* The plot abstract gives us the working-plot enlarged into a skeletonized summary of the leading incidents and action. In the plot abstract the writer provides for the solution of all his serious problems of motivation.

D. *Scenario.* A plot abstract amplified further, and rearranged to bring incidents, scenes, etc., into the order they will have in the completed story. Here the writer must adjust anything he finds amiss in the previous motivation; provide for the auxiliary and supplemental incident and situation and for any atmosphere materials not involved in his motivation of incident, action, and character; and in general, reconstruct and amplify until he has a very definite forecast of the story in its completed form. The scenario may be regarded as a thoroughgoing abstract of the story in its completed form. A scenario confined solely to plot elements (amplified synopsis) is known as an *action-plot.*

E. *Fulfilled plot.* This is merely the amplified scenario, or completed story.

8. The evolution of a plot, therefore, begins with the plot embryo (or the germ). Plot abstract and scenario represent the workman's devices for managing and subjecting his materials to his purpose. The fulfilled plot, or completed story, represents his skill as a workman in handling his materials and employing the devices of his trade, *plus* his innate literary ability. In reading the discussion that follows, the student will be helped by keeping these distinctions in mind, although the references are usually to plot abstract, and action-plot—the most important stages of plot construction.

9. *Examples of plot germ, working-plot, and plot abstract* are here given:

(1) Germ: Dishonorable conduct on the part of a son who lacks a sense of honor may crush a highly honorable father.

(2) Working-plot, or embryo (the germ idea developed

into a more concrete conception) : Billings, lacking a sense of honor, by mispresenting facts induces his father to become surety on a bond for construction work that Billings fails to complete; and his father, scrupulously discharging the obligation, is ruined. [Another: Billings, lacking a sense of honor, basely betrays an innocent girl, and his disgraceful conduct breaks his father's heart.]

(3) Plot abstract: Billings, an unscrupulous man, is a contractor, and bids upon an important piece of construction. To make certain of winning, he names too low a price and specifies terms obscurely under which he expects to "catch" the employing firm and recoup himself. But this firm is doubtful of him, and requires an iron-clad bond, which he cannot procure. In desperation he deceives his father about the facts and gets his signature to the bond. But Billings has to perform his contract under a competent and incorruptible inspector, and is therefore unable to work the tricks by which he expected to make his profits; so that he finds himself without funds to complete the work and is ruined. His father, refusing to take advantage of technical defenses against his responsibility, sacrifices his own fortune in meeting his obligations under the bond, and is completely ruined.

(4) Action-plot: This again would amplify the plot abstract, working out in detail the general action indicated in the abstract, and making any transpositions or inversions that seem desirable in the order of events.

(5) Scenario: Would be the action-plot with the addition of the other necessary elements of the story indicated in compact form.

XIII. The Exposition is the Introducing Part of the Plot

1. Every plot has an outcome. This implies that there has, in the course of the action, been either a change or an imminent likelihood of change, from one state of things to another; the change either took place, or else it was averted. This in turn implies that, to understand this change and the manner in which it came about or was averted, we must know what the state of things was at the time when the action began. The purpose of the exposition in plot is, to make known this state of affairs from which there is to be a change, or in which (after a period of struggle or critical uncertainty) change is to be averted. That is, *the function of the exposition is, to make the story clear by putting before us the facts that belong to the beginning of the plot.*

2. No one should take the term " exposition " to mean what is known technically in rhetoric as exposition, or infer that exposition, in the rhetorical sense, is the means finally to be employed in making the situation clear out of which the action has its rise. Formal exposition has no prominent part in any stage of dramatic or narrative writing. This part of the plot is expository only in the sense that through it is clearly explained the beginning state of affairs. But even in the plot abstract, its methods are not the methods of rhetorical exposition, and like the completed story, it depends, even in its condensed form, mainly on narration, dramatic action, and description. Certainly when the time comes to embody the introductory facts of the exposition in the story itself, they are to be presented as far as possible through the words

and deeds of persons belonging to the story, and not through any formal explanation.

3. In the exposition, great compression and economy of detail are to be observed. By economy of detail is meant the introduction of no more facts than are necessary to serve the purpose. This implies the careful inspection of all the pertinent facts, to determine which are most serviceable and which can be set aside. For some facts will prove unnecessary, either because they indicate matters that are already sufficiently shown, or because they indicate matters that are not essential to a clear following of the story. *The principle of economy of detail is important throughout narration, but it is especially important in the exposition.* For the exposition does not exist for its own sake, but merely as an aid to the understanding—an introduction to and initiation of the action; and its usefulness and interest cease as soon as it has brought the reader to the point where he can begin to follow the movement of the plot for himself.

4. In the fulfilled plot, or completed story, distribution of the detail closely follows economy of detail in importance. By distribution we refer to the gradual introduction of preliminary information as the narration proceeds. That all the information ultimately demanded by adequate exposition be introduced immediately when the story begins, is not necessary. The best results are likely to come from distributing this information through the story, some here and some there, as circumstances permit or demand. Nevertheless, in general principle, it should come as early as possible. Here it is necessary again to distinguish the order of the facts in the completed story from their order in the plot abstract. In

the plot abstract, the facts necessary to the exposition of course come at the first, and it is not until we begin the amplification of the plot abstract into scenario form that we face the problems of distribution.

5. As the information constituting the exposition can be presented in various ways, such a distribution is more easy than it would be otherwise. The information can be given in direct statement by the author; it can be embodied in descriptive passages; it can be presented in the course of conversation between persons in the story; and it can be suggested by acts and incidents forming part of the action itself. Therefore, when he has the expository information clearly in mind, the writer finds many opportunities of distributing it, as needed, through the narrative. That this method, when it is practicable, is the better, is obvious. *An exhaustive outline of the situation as a whole (whether this outline be introduced at the opening of the story or injected later on) is usually more mechanical and less pleasing than is an exposition skillfully scattered in inconspicuous places through the narrative.* The distributed exposition does not attract attention to itself as such, but merges itself in the more important development of the story as a whole; nor does it interrupt or delay the action as the undistributed exposition nearly always does. The explanation is realized without being perceived, and it so becomes more homogeneously a part of the plot itself.

6. We well may emphasize the superiority of the distributed exposition in bringing on the action more promptly. So far as narrative or dramatic interest is concerned, the story does not really begin until the development, or " movement," of the plot begins; all before

this is nothing but prelude and make-ready. *To hold back the reader longer than is necessary from the course of events in which his interest will find its source if he become interested at all, is poor artistry.* To bring him as quickly as possible to the real stuff and business of the story is the aim of the skilled artist. A large proportion of the most successful stories open therefore with something vital to the plot itself, leaving the expository matter for introduction later on. Frequently the necessary exposition can be embodied naturally in the early speeches of the persons. This method is especially dramatic and effective. That by thus distributing this information the writer can usually clear the way for an immediate plunge into the business of the story itself, is sufficient evidence of the value of the distributed exposition.

7. Yet the general superiority of the distributed exposition does not imply that the distributed exposition is always to be preferred. A massed exposition may be better in particular instances. The nature of the material to be handled, the purpose of the author in telling the story, the mood or tone which he decides upon for the narrative, and the method of development which he adopts —any of these may make the massed exposition preferable or necessary. An illustration is afforded by one type of structure in the contrast story, namely, that in which the effect aimed at is produced by the difference between conditions as they are at the beginning of the story and as they are at the time of the outcome. True, distribution of the expository matter may prove as advantageous in the contrast story as in any other kind, for the introduction of the successive portions serves constantly to renew the suggestion of contrast. But the writer may

prefer to set off the contrasted facts in two distinct groups, one balancing the other. He then unhesitatingly employs the massed exposition.

8. Somewhat of this type is Richard Harding Davis's "A Question of Latitude" (in *Once Upon a Time,* Scribner). In this story, the influence of tropical African life is shown upon the morals and tastes of a Boston gentleman. The larger part of the story is consumed in making evident the nature, the savage brutality and vileness of barbarian tropical existence; against which portrayal is balanced that part of the story in which the Boston gentleman is seen succumbing to these debasing influences. If we wish, we may object that part of this exposition is not exposition at all, but development, intensification, and atmosphere creation. Even so, however, the utility and effect of the massed exposition when used fitly can be plainly seen in Mr. Davis's story.

9. A review of these considerations reveals the following chief facts about exposition as a plot factor: First, it is essential to an understanding of the outcome in all instances except those in which character, motive, and action completely explain themselves without preliminary exposition (that is, it gives us the beginnings). Second, the greatest compression and economy of detail are necessary in presenting the exposition, for the sole justification of the exposition is its service in making clear the story proper, and it must not usurp space or interest. Third, severe testing of all the information admitted is necessary, to avoid the introduction of matter that is impertinent or redundant. Fourth, in the fulfilled plot, distribution of expository matter through the story is usually preferable, because this enables the writer to enter quickly on the

action of the story itself, and causes the exposition to merge more homogeneously in the narration; but the question of preferring the distributed to the massed exposition must be answered by considering the nature of the material, the general plan of presentation, and the purpose of the writer. Finally, the test of a good exposition is, sufficient but not superfluous explanation of conditions, especially at the beginning of the action, and thorough merging of this material into the story itself.

10. A list of the matters, some or all of which must be known in order to follow the plot understandingly, would be useful, but detailed enumeration is impossible. No one can foresee all the combinations open to the writer when his imagination begins to deal with the limitless mass of material at his command. Some suggestions, nevertheless, are given. It will be noticed that *all the items in such a list will be peculiar items—that is, they will name details peculiar to the one particular plot, theme, character, or atmosphere. Such matters as are common to all situations or are naturally assumed because they are characteristic accompaniments of the situation developed by the story, call for no explanation.* Information that is general property needs no exposition.

11. Expository information that the writer may need to mention includes:—

A. Particular character traits that affect the plot (e.g., that a man is a woman-hater; that a perfectly honest wife has the habit of flirting, etc.).

B. Particular situations that affect the plot (e.g., that a broker is bankrupt, although his wife does not suspect it; that the maid is in love with the master; that the convict is an innocent man; that the girl has inclosed the wrong letters in writing to her two lovers at the same time, etc.).

C. Names of the persons, with or without further information at the moment (but at least a swift characterizing touch is desirable).

D. Occupation or station in life (is the hero a blacksmith, a lawyer, a book-keeper? rich or poor? etc.).

E. Personal facts—peculiarities, mannerisms, age, tastes, etc., as far as these things are necessary to the characterization or important to the action, theme, or atmosphere.

F. Time, place, setting, and other elements of environment.

G. Any other items necessary to the comprehension of motive, complication, character, theme, action, atmosphere, situation, outcome, or to the final effect.

XIV. The Exciting Moment, or Inciting Impulse, Begins the Development

1. The exposition represents the *status quo,* the existing state of things, at the beginning of the action.[3] The moment this existing state of affairs, this *status quo,* is threatened with change, that moment the action—the movement, or development—of the plot begins. Something has happened or been done that threatens to produce, or actually produces, change;[4] matters are not as they were; a new condition or influence has thrust itself in, and this

[3] The reader is cautioned to remember that the order of events in the plot abstract may not be their order in the completed story. We may now assume ourselves to be dealing with the action-plot.

[4] This something we may call the *generating circumstance.*

new element must either be overcome and got rid of, or else must be accepted and permitted to work its natural results.

2.   From this moment, therefore, a struggle will be going on—light or serious, tragic or humorous—between this new influence and things as they were.   Presently this contest will rise, through a period of climax, to a moment of crisis; then it will reach an outcome; and with this the story ends.   Until this influence appeared, there was no complication, no uncertainty, no question of outcome.   In the colloquial phrase, " everything was perfectly simple," quite plain.   But the appearance of the complicating, or opposing, or change-threatening influence, the *complication,* brought on uncertainty, debate, struggle— that is, the *conflict.*

3.   Now the moment at which the *status quo* in which affairs were shown to us by the exposition, was brought to an end by the appearance of this *complication,* is known as the *exciting moment;* and the complicating influence, no matter what it be, is known as the *inciting* or *exciting force* or *impulse.   Evidently no action, and therefore no dramatic effect, is possible before the inciting force is introduced.*   When the exciting impulse shows itself—again using the popular phrase—things begin to move; and *with the beginning of movement in the plot begins the true development of the story.*

4.   We may now ask, what sort of thing can supply this inciting force, thus complicating a simple situation and commencing a conflict?   Theoretically, anything which in the experience of man has shown itself able to produce change in his affairs, either directly or indirectly, immediately or remotely, is available as a means of

complication.   But *technical, artistic, and practical con-siderations limit this range of choice of complicating influence.*

5. *It is desirable,* for instance, *that the conflict seem to spring from causes that are natural and even inevitable, and that the complicating facts fit the situation, agreeing with the persons, their character, their environment.* That is, it must be natural and congruous. This is especially necessary for the generating circumstance. If either this, or the complication it introduces, be merely accidental, it is likely to seem improbable. If it be evidently manufact-ured, or be something " lugged in " or forced into the situation, it will seem artificial and untrue. To illustrate : It is not common for girls in the ranks of ordinary life to meet young noblemen; therefore when Annie, the daughter of the shoestore man, engaged to John the young, thriving, but, of course, bourgeois grocer, meets the prince of Schwindlermgut, who immediately begins to crowd John in the rivalry for her hand, we feel that the complica-tion is unnatural and forced. As a consequence, all the story seems untrue. But if instead of its being a prince who attracts Annie, it is Mike, the young plumber and hardware dealer, we do not have to gulp very hard to swallow the complication. Things like that do happen; they are natural; and there is no incongruity about them such as there is in the courtship of a common and com-monplace girl by a prince.

6. Accidental complication is of two sorts : those com-plications arising from the ordinary chances and mis-chances of existence, and those arising from accident in the stronger sense of the term—a happening that is unusual and extreme. Extreme accident is illustrated by the

following: The wife of a paper manufacturer, happening to pick up, when visiting his mill, a sheet of paper from the waste about to be ground up for new pulp, finds it to be a love letter written to her, but never mailed, by her husband's trusted friend. By this she is led to fall in love with this friend. Now such a discovery as that of the letter is *possible, but so extremely accidental as to seem improbable.* Only the remotest chance is involved; and if we accept the rest of the story, we can do so only by agreeing with ourselves to overlook the improbability that underlies the motivation at the outset. And this is hard to do; for the complication is vital to the story, and the generating circumstance must be convincing. It must seem natural and true to life. *The inciting impulse and generating circumstance must seem more than merely adequate to produce the result that follows; they must seem true to the prevailing (not the exceptional) facts of human experience.*

7. The other sort of accident is that which constitutes the class of merely ordinary haps and mishaps—the kind common to everyday experience, occurring all the year round. Such occurrences seem probable rather than improbable, they commonly bring no particularly significant consequences, and we instinctively class them with the ordinary events of existence; they soon cease to have meaning or distinction for us. Hence they are likely, when introduced as the inciting force or motivation, or the generating circumstance, to seem inadequate or to fail in impressiveness. This is why complications introduced by such accidents as sprained ankles, swimming mishaps, capsized boats, broken legs, runaways, fires, railway wrecks, sudden illnesses, and the like, usually lack the

quality of "convincingness" and make the stories fall flat. It is perfectly true that any one of such accidents may, *if properly managed,* constitute a thoroughly good complication.[5] Such is the complicating event in De Maupassant's *A Piece of String.* A pocket-book has been lost, a miserly old man picking up a bit of string alongside the path is believed to have found it, and from these simple happenings develops a series of incidents realistically tragic in their outcome.

8. From what precedes, it is evident that exciting [6] moment, or inciting impulse, involves two things: the complication itself, and the discovery of the complication. "Discovery," like "exciting force," is a technical term. It indicates the revelation of the existence of a complicating influence, the discovery taking place at the moment when the reader (not necessarily the person or persons affected by it in the story) becomes aware that this complicating influence exists.[7] So far as the impression is concerned which the story, at least for the moment, will make upon the reader, the discovery is as important as is the complication revealed by it. And both are subject to the same requirements.

[5] This is much more the case in realistic than in romantic treatment. Unfortunately, the novice in writing usually attempts to use these accidents as motivating incidents in—supposedly—romantic stories.

[6] The student will have observed that "exciting" has the sense of "being the causal force that arouses to action." In this sense, tickling excites laughter. Excitement, in the sense of tumultuous or highly-wrought feelings, may be quite absent at the moment when the exciting force begins to act.

[7] "Discovery" is like many other technical terms in having two meanings. Thus, it often means the revelation of a hidden identity, or similar plot fact, at some crisis in the drama or story.

9. These requirements we may sum up in the word *plausibility*. Discovery and complication must each strike us with belief; and complete plausibility exists only when we accept them without any shade of feeling that they may be open to doubt. Yet plausibility is possible without truth, and our *complications (even more than the discovery of them) should be able to stand the closest critical examination* if the reader chance to question them. The writer, of course, makes a thorough test of them in deciding upon his plot.

10. Plausibility of the sort that can stand a thorough test is the result of *consistency*. Consistency, however, must not be regarded as essential merely at the moment when the complication is revealed. *It is essential in every part of the plot, in every incident, every person, every act, every motive, and every particular of environment.*[8] Inconsistency in any part or element of the completed story, no matter how small the part or subordinate the element, is a blemish and a fault. And *as the complication is one of the most important elements of the plot, inconsistency in the complication is fatal;* it falsifies the basic conception and therefore falsifies the story as a whole.

11. Wherein, then, does plausibility lie? We have already seen. First, *the generating circumstance, the discovery, and the complication (like all other elements of the story) must be consistent with the prevailing experience of the race.* That is, they must reasonably be believable when considered (a) in the light of human nature and mind, and (b) in the light of the laws of nature and the conditions of social existence. Anything that violates

---

[8] The assertions about consistency are just as applicable concerning congruity. Congruity is, indeed, one element of consistency.

human experience concerning the way in which the mind works, or the motives from which men act, or the laws of nature by which the material world in which they live is governed, or the social conditions surrounding them, is an inconsistency so serious as to invalidate any plot and any story.

12. This does not mean that myth, legend, fairy story, burlesque, are illegitimate forms of narrative. For it is quite consistent with the working of the human mind to create such conceptions, and even the grossly impossible is allowable when it is presented, not as factual truth, but (as in the fairy tale) as an idealization of or a recognized departure from the truth, or (as in the burlesque) a commentary on the truth.

13. This fact brings us to *a secondary form of consistency,* the principle of which may be thus stated: The main conception having been decided on, and being a conception that is consistent with human experience and human viewpoint, *we must in working out the story itself introduce no element that is inconsistent with our main conception.* Hard fact is likely to violate the consistency of the fairy tale; episodes of romantic adventure but poorly fit the realistic story; a complication arising from some high ethical ideal assumed to exist in the mind of a jungle warrior is untrue to human experience; the cook lady who discards her footman lover because he eats with his knife, is in obvious disagreement with the standards of manners in her class. The scholar does not say " ain't," the gunman seldom discourses philosophically, the back-woods girl does not wear high-heeled pumps or pannier skirts except upon the stage, the machine-gun is not good material for a story of black art, and florid language does

not agree with a simple, heartfelt theme. There is a seemliness of minor consistency as important as is consistency in the basic conception.

14. It is evident, therefore, that the generating circumstance, the complication, and the discovery—the plot-facts belonging to the exciting moment—*must be consistent with experience and with the rest of the story;* that they must be thus consistent in order that they and the story of which they are a part shall be *plausible;* and that plausibility is necessary in order that the story shall have *the vitally important quality of true-seeming, or verisimilitude.* Without verisimilitude, the story had better not exist; and verisimilitude is produced only by the *consistency that results from fundamental truthfulness in the presentation of man and nature, and the exclusion of all incongruous detail.*

XV. The Rising Action Develops the Plot to its Decisive Moment

1. The moment the discovery has advanced far enough so that the reader senses a complication, even though this complication be as yet incompletely revealed, *that moment the story begins to move; the action is on. And from that moment, it must advance.* If there are lulls, they must be but temporary, and must end with a new and considerable advance. Moreover, the plot, the action —indeed, all the story—must not merely advance; it must *advance with rising interest.* Onward and upward is the motto: onward for the development, upward for the interest. Until the climactic moment, or height of intensity is reached, this rule is imperative. And *interest in*

the thoroughly effective story, continues and may even in-crease after the plot-action, having reached its decisive point, begins to drop off to the conclusion.

2. The rising action, then, includes all the development of the plot that begins with the first hint of the complication and continues until it completes itself in the decisive moment.   (We have seen that the climactic moment is usually found at the close of the development, or rising action, included in or closely associated with the decisive moment.)   The importance of the decisive moment calls now for consideration.

3. Plot depends upon conflict—the push and pull of opposing influences that threaten to change, and attempt to thwart the threatened change, in the state of things as in the exposition they were shown to be.   Out of this conflict springs the action; in the end, the action brings the outcome; and, *therefore, somewhere in the course of the action, a moment has to come when one set of influences gains such an advantage over the other set that the prevailing set cannot fail, in the long run, to triumph.* This is the decisive moment.

4. True, the struggle does not necessarily end at this moment; for a while at least it is likely to continue.   Indeed, there may come another time (perhaps even a second, found in the falling action) when the outcome *seems* again uncertain.   Moreover, the reader may, at the time, not realize that the decisive moment has been reached (see " His Bubble Reputation," *Adventure,* December, 1913). But when the action is complete—when the height has been passed and the outcome at last is known—then he can look back and say, " It was *there* that the outcome was settled; after that, no other result was possible.   There was the

moment in which was decided all that followed." (The
most obvious examples are the surprise stories.)

5. Now let us draw our conclusions from these facts.
The decisive moment is the turning point of the plot (we
are to remember that it had best coincide with, or at least
closely precede, the climactic height). *All that precedes it,
leads up to it and makes it possible; all that follows it
flows from it directly toward the outcome. Therefore, the
construction of the plot throughout the stage of rising
action—the choice of incidents, the characterization, the
indication of environment, the motiving, all in short that
is involved in developing the story to a point where its
outcome is made inevitable—must be managed with a
view to creating this decisive confluence of causes.* This
moment, this concurrence of character, motive, environment, and act, is the first main goal of the constructive
mind in the process of building up the plot.[9] *The aim
of the writer must be, throughout the developing stage, to
make all the elements of his plot so converge that this
moment shall be in truth and necessity decisive. Success
in plotting lies much, if not mainly, in this subordination
of the story materials to the production of this moment.*
Upon this will depend the plausibility and strength of
the climactic height.

6. We naturally ask now how to proceed in order thus
to subordinate the material of the story to the production
of a decisive moment; but the question is of that sort
which can scarcely be answered in full.   To do so would
involve a complete exposition of the management of
description,   incident,   and   action,   atmosphere,   and

[9] But *in building up the complete story, the climactic height
is the goal.*

characterization, for all these may happen to be employed in creating a state of affairs to which there can be but one outcome. Our discussion of plot development (rising action) leads to frequent incidental mention of all these, as accessories and aids to plot growth, but only one of them is primarily important to plot development. This one is incident. For *the plot, as the necessary framework of every conte, is a group of acts, incidents, or events, springing out of and leading up to one another, and collectively producing the outcome. So far as the theory of plot is concerned, therefore, the developing element of chief importance is incident*—the acts and events constituting the true plot-action. Hence at this point our study must concern principally the management of incident.

7. *Plot development, then, consists in the management of a set of acts, incidents, or events, in such a way that presently they will make one particular result sure* and, consequently, another contrary result impossible. But what do we mean by management?

8. First and most important, we mean *combining the acts, incidents, and events, into an interlocking group or series; so that each shall depend on one, several, or if possible all of the others, and so that a certain result shall flow from them, dependent upon them all collectively. The art of plot-building lies in this combining of incidents to produce sound motivation, leading to a conclusive outcome.* After this, " management " means the successful presentation—by narration or other means—of the incidents individually; for much that is gained by good workmanship in plot-building may be offset by inartistic or incapable presentation.

9. In the combining of incidents so that they shall converge to a decisive moment—so that (putting it another way) their accumulating effects shall unify themselves in creating a situation which naturally terminates everything in a single definite outcome—the writer must attend with no small care to motiving and motivation. The two terms are coupled here because the attempt is sometimes made to employ them with distinct meanings, although it is not always clearly successful.

10. Except in music, the word motive means, " exciting (or inciting), or responsible cause." In music, motive, or *motif,* is the theme and purpose of the composition. The word—preferably in its foreign form, *motif*—has been brought over into literary criticism with this specialized meaning; so that to speak of the motif of a story is to speak of its basic theme and purpose, taken together. But motive in its common acceptation—not that of motif —means either, (a) the reason or object which leads *a person* to do a certain thing (" What was *his* motive for the murder ? "), or (b) the set of causes out of which *an act* springs (" What was *the* motive for the murder ? ")

11. The only difference, however, between (a) and (b) is this: in (a) the attention is fixed on the person who acts; in (b) attention is fixed on the act itself. In the one, we consider the responsible cause as it involves character; in the other, we consider the responsible cause as it affects the result. This difference indicates the distinction—if any can be drawn—between *motiving* and *motivating. Motiving consists in providing good and sufficient cause for the behavior of the person; motivating consists in providing good and sufficient cause for conse-*

quences found in act and deed and in event. We motive acts in character. We motive incident and action by means of plausible causes of any sort.

12. Adequate motivation, therefore, includes the consideration of motive and character, *plus* such other influences as likewise determine action or create incident. The term is a technical term indicating the process by which the literary artisan builds action and incident out of the materials of environment, character, and situation. As a matter of fact, however, the student is as likely to find the process indicated by the more limited term "motive" as by this more precise designation; for motive is always very prominent in motivation. The important thing for him to remember is, that *character, act, and incident—each and all—must be rooted deeply in adequate cause.*

13. How he shall motivate the incident of his plot is a matter that must be left to the story-teller to work out anew with every story; for every plot is a new conception, and brings its own problems of construction and management. Its characters, its atmosphere, its incident, its action, and the detail wherein each of these is embodied, are distinct from those of every other plot. They are peculiar to this one conception, and the combining of them consistently and effectively is a work that depends for its success solely upon the constructive ability of the writer and the skill he has acquired through practice.

14. Yet a few hints can be given. For instance, the "row-of-bricks" ordering of incidents is usually less natural and less satisfying in results than is the "dissected picture" method of combination. By "row-of-bricks" is meant the plotting of the *incidents in a series,* the first

of which results in the second, the second producing the
third, the third the fourth, and so on, as one brick in a
row, falling, knocks down the one next it, and so begins
a movement that knocks down all the row one by one.
But by " dissected picture " method is meant the *dove-
tailing, or interlocking,* of each incident with various
others, until all are fitted into place and at last—and only
then, with the completion of the most skillful combination
—the problem of the conflict shows itself solved.

15. An example of the chain-of-sausages, or row-of-
bricks, plot will be found among those given in Section
III. The weakness of this style of plot is twofold. In the
first place, it is not as consistent with the usual order of
events as is the plot of interdependent incident, because
in the natural order of things, especially in human activities, many separate influences co-operate at the same time
in the production of any particular result. Act and deed
and event are not the result of a mere *succession,* a
single *string,* of causes. They are *the result of an interwoven and interoperative* **group** *of causes.* These indeed
are often so intricate and complex in their influence upon
one another, and so inextricably interactive in producing
any definite outcome, that the writer has to pick and
choose among them in order that his plot shall not itself be
inextricably complex and confused. The bringing on of
a decisive moment depends upon this selection, or choice
and rejection, of possible material. *Good workmanship
in motivating, therefore, springs from (a) the skill with
which a sufficient group of adequate interacting causes is
chosen to produce a decisive set of conditions, but also
from (b) the skill with which influences and causes that
are not necessary to the production of this particular set*

of decisive conditions are discriminated from the necessary causes and resolutely excluded from the plot. In the light of these facts, the row-of bricks plot is seen clearly not to conform to the usual conditions of cause-and-effect in the actual world.

16. The second weakness of string-of-beads motivation is, that it does not result in closely-woven plot—the essential requisite of the conte. This form of plot is that which belongs rather to the tale than to the story intended to produce a single and dramatic effect. A mere succession of incidents *can* lead up to and terminate in a climactic incident capable of producing the single dramatic effect; but except in the most skillful hands it is much more likely to prove only what it is—a string of events. Even when the series closes with an incident greater in interest than is any of those that precede it, it is likely, nevertheless, not to prove a close-wrought plot. *In the close-wrought plot, the decisive moment and the climactic height consequent upon it, depend on all the preceding incidents taken collectively, not successively.* Altogether, therefore, the plot of interacting and interlocking incident is that which involves the most effective motivation; and that it therefore calls for a higher constructive skill is nothing to its disparagement.

17. Yet in one sense the incidents that are chosen because of their fitness collectively to produce a decisive moment resulting in an outcome of single dramatic effect, must, nevertheless, constitute a series. *Their effect, it is true, is collective; but it is built up cumulatively. Therefore, they must succeed one another in a series of "movements" that produce constantly intensifying sub-effects.* Incident B ought not to fall below incident A in

individual interest, and at least in theory should surpass it. Incident C must carry to a higher point the interest of incident A + incident B; and incident D must not only be as interesting in itself as incidents A, B, and C individually, but must also, in combination with them, carry on the interest to a still higher point. Figuratively, the incidents resemble the ingredients of gunpowder; taken separately, they have merely their individual efficacy and force, but *combined they have a force far in excess of the mere sum of their individual potencies.*

18. *So from incident to incident (whatever the order be in which the events are ultimately introduced), the uncertainty of the conflict, the force of the situation, the charm of the atmosphere, the power or attraction of the character traits, must not only continue, but grow.* Unless in this sense the incidents constitute a series, the holding power of the plot itself will fail. No reader reads a story that " drops off " as the action proceeds. The very terms " rising action," " development," " growth," used to describe this stage of the plot, imply rising interest, developing interest, growing interest, advancing interest. This result is essentially the object sought in dramatic plotting. The very aim and purpose of the close-wrought plot is, to produce and fulfill a rising interest.

19. Yet in the struggle to make each incident of higher interest than the one before it, the inexperienced writer may easily fall into a serious fault—that of exaggerating, of over-straining for effect. Nor is the student to understand that the term " interest " is an absolute term, or that interest is synonymous with excitement, " strenuous " action or situation, or sensationalism in any form. It does not imply that, if incident A kills off a man for us,

incident B must kill off two or else fail of interest; the increased interest of incident B may lie in its showing us the murderer happily eating breakfast in the bosom of his admiring family.   This mistake about the nature and quality of interest leads the writer to strive at any cost for increasing effect, and is as fatal as it is common. It produces an artificiality of plot and treatment that recklessly deserts nature and truth.   Rather, *interest must be measured by considering* [10] *the kind of story, the kind of situation, the sort of persons, the manner of incident employed, and the kind of outcome—all these together.* The interest of the arrow-pierced target legs in Kipling's *Cupid's Arrows* is *relatively* as great as the interest of poor little Bisesa's chopped-off hands in the same author's *Beyond the Pale,* but it is of an entirely different kind and quality, and neither incident would for a moment be usable in the other of these two stories.

20.   All this amounts to saying that *interest is a relative fact only, and is to be measured, so far as the sequence of incidents is concerned, solely by the standards established by the particular story* that is in the making.   The most powerful incident in De Maupassant's *The Necklace* is practically nothing more than the brief sentence of dialogue in which Mme. Loisel learns that she has slaved ten years to replace a lost necklace the gems of which were nothing but paste.   Further, the interest of any incident does not lie solely in itself.   *The plot interest of any incident lies in the significance of this incident in association with all its companion incidents* (as in that just cited from *The Necklace*).   *The incident is interesting either because (a) it carries forward to a new stage what has*

[10] For suspense and interest, see XVIII.

*already occurred, or (b) introduces new elements of com-
plication, or (c) adds significant information to what we
already have, or (d) introduces action that seems to offset
preceding events, thus renewing or increasing uncertainty.*

21. This being true, we see that *the most trivial happening, the most commonplace act or remark, may become,
as an element of plot, vitally important and vitally
interesting. From the point of view of plot, therefore,
interest lies not so much in what the incident itself is as
in what it stands for in the development of the plot.*
Thus, in *Moonlight* (De Maupassant) we are not deeply
concerned in the beauty of the night as the woman-hating
Abbé Marignan sees it; tens of thousands of men and
women have seen and reveled in nights as fair. What
makes it interesting is not this, but its effect upon the
Abbé; for it touches an unsuspected spring of sympathy
in him, reveals what to him is a new element in human
life; and thus, transforming his conception of God and
man, remodels his character. Moreover, through the story,
De Maupassant presents a theme that cannot fail to interest many thoughtful persons, and from the theme too, the
incident derives interest.

22. Plainly, then, *interest in any incident lies largely
in its significance as a plot element* [11]—*in what it stands
for or brings about in developing the action toward the
outcome.* But because, for plot purposes, the interest
lies in the result more than in the incident, we are not to

---

[11] This assertion is somewhat lopsided. In character stories,
interest will lie largely in the characterizing value the incident has;
in atmosphere stories, in its power to suggest atmosphere; and
so on, according to the purpose of the story. This fact should
be carefully noted. See concentrative incident, etc., ¶¶ 30-42.

suppose that incidents which in themselves are uninteresting, can be safely used. Quite the contrary. No material that is inherently tedious will become less tedious for serving as an exemplum or an argument. True, *incidents that are not, of themselves, of any particular significance, can be effectively employed—but only when they become positively interesting through their relation to the rest of the plot events,* and the best results are those that follow when incidents themselves of positive interest are employed to carry forward a plot that itself is interesting. In thus attempting, however, to estimate the positive or intrinsic interest of any plot material, we are on very dangerous ground; for to one who has eyes to see, ears to hear, and power to understand, nothing is without significance, and what is trivial, trite, jejune or commonplace in the hands of the incompetent is not so in the hands of a master. *So long as any incident or act is true to the nature of things and is so used as in some way to advance the presentation of a conception that likewise is true to the nature of things, and that is important enough to deserve development, so long will that act or incident be interesting within the story.*

23. Reviewing, we recall that interlocking incident produces more effective plot than does row-of-bricks incident; that interest must increase with the progressive appearance of the various incidents essential to the plot; that incidents are interesting, in their plot relations, not for intrinsic qualities, but for their significance as developing elements in the action; and that, with masterly insight and skillful handling, even the most commonplace matters become significant. We are now to see that the principle which prescribes a steady rise in interest with the develop-

ment of the plot, is subject to qualification. But this qualification, let the student note at once, is in no degree a modification of the fundamental rule that we have just been considering.

24. The qualification mentioned is, indeed, nothing more than an explanation of conditions that arise when a more or less full or complex plot is to be carried to its decisive moment; for in such a plot there may be several interlocking groups of incident (movements; events), the groups having perhaps little plots, or chains of development, of their own. But here we must digress to say that *subplot, or any excessive complexity of incident, is dangerous in the conte.* The mere space limitation of the story often makes adequate development of such a plot impossible. Moreover, with an increase of complication and incident (involving more extensive characterization, more numerous persons and motives, more intricate motivation, a more inclusive setting—in short, a multiplicity of interest elements and materials), the one single, unified, simple effect of the dramatic story (conte) becomes increasingly difficult to produce. Often single effect becomes impossible, and the narrative passes over from conte into novelet or novel.

25. Yet the fact does remain that a certain amount of complexity of plot is possible, even to the extent of subplot. But these are occasional instances only, and development of subplot, and solution of the separate complications in them, must be possible with extreme simplicity of action and of detail. Only so will the narrative be preserved in the form of the conte. Keeping now in mind this important warning—that a complex plot, if given adequate development, may so increase the necessary amount of

fictional material as to render singleness of dramatic effect impossible—we may return to our explanation.

26. In the complex plot, we said, there may be several groups of incident. These groups fit together to make the complete plot, but each of them is developed to a considerable degree separately. Now, the requirement that interest steadily increase applies to the management of these groups in the plot when the plot is considered as a whole, just as it applies to single incidents in the simpler plot. That is, as the development passes from one *group* to another, the interest must continue steadily to rise. At the close of the development of group B, it must be higher than it was at the close of the development of group A, and so on. Indeed, every group, in its relation to the plot as a whole, is practically equivalent to a single incident in a simple plot; it produces an advance and a higher interest.

27. So much is plain. But what happens when interest, following one group of incidents, or movement, through its individual course of development to its individual climax, then finds itself suddenly at a stop unless it take up and follow through another group? Does not this pause and turning back produce a break and a letdown in the interest? It does. And this is one reason why the subplot and the plot of complex incident is dangerous for short story (conte) purposes. The breaking of continuous interest at the points where one stage of development ends and the action turns back or changes in order to develop another stage, may destroy the reader's feeling of unity, of totality, of singleness of interest, of material, and of outcome. If it do so—good-by to the true short story effect.

28. But, on the other hand, one group of incident may

be very closely wrought in with the next,[12] and the groups can perhaps be so promptly and simply developed that the break does not become serious. Then no harm is done. As one passes from one group to the next, he feels that he is actually moving forward in the story; before one group is fully developed, the development of another has been begun, and whatever gap there might be is already bridged across. In fact, the rising action may be, and often is, not an unbroken upward increase, but rather an increase by successive stages, or degrees. Interest rises through stage A to the climactic moment of that stage; then, still alert, it turns quickly to the incident of stage B. So far as this B group is concerned, it is not yet thoroughly aroused; but even at the outset it is higher than it would be had it not been already excited by following through stage A; and it continues to increase until, when the climactic height of stage B is reached, it is as high as the effect of all the incidents in group B *plus* the held-over interest of stage A can raise it. That is, we may compare the grand climax of the whole plot to a mountain peak in the further and highest range of a mountain system. To reach the final peak, we must pass over several intervening ranges, with the valleys that lie between. But every succeeding range is higher than the one

[12] Some of the technical devices for binding such groups together are: Having persons who take part in one set of incidents appear in the other set; making a happening of one set become the cause of something that happens in the other; carrying one set partly through, then breaking off to take up the other, returning later to the first once more; causing the two sets to take place at one and the same time—a fact indicated by time references as may be needed. So slight a thing as the occurrence of two events in the same place tends to bind them together.

before it, and every succeeding valley is at a higher level than the last preceding valley; until the last valley is crossed and we attain the master summit.

29. Thus from stage to stage the interest is kept alert, held over, and increased. If at the beginning of each new stage of development it drops back a little from the point where the height of the preceding stage left it, it drops back but a little, and it quickly rises higher still as the incidents of the present stage combine with those of the preceding stages. By a series of successive climaxes, therefore, each having a starting-point higher than did the one before it —by such a series of successive stages or movements, the development goes on and the interest rises. The decisive point is reached; the grand climax is completed; and the outcome either has been revealed already (at the climactic moment) or is just before us. The ranges have been crossed, the peak scaled. Interest has been conserved at every point, and has been made to grow steadily through every stage of the rising action. In the story of complex plot, as in the story of simple plot, the rule of intensifying interest has held.[13]

30. Before we pass to consideration of the next stage of the plot we must discuss, however, the function of *the plot as the carrier of non-plot material.* For *often a considerable amount of story material must be introduced that*

[13] Evidently, the opening of the different movements in such a story is a trying problem. On the one hand, these "valleys," or internodes and points of lowered interest, are plainly the place for introducing massed exposition, description, etc. But on the other hand, they are as plainly under the necessity of getting the new movement under way as promptly as possible, so that interest may not slacken. Here as elsewhere, the safer practice seems to be, to reduce accessory matter to a minimum.

*is not plot material (in the strict sense of the term
" plot "), but which is just as necessary to the success of
the conte as is the plot itself,* with its conclusive outcome.

31. The plot, we must remember, no matter how slight
or how inconspicuous it be, is always and ever the framework, the supporting skeleton of the story. The skeleton
must be filled forth into a body. Therefore, as the framework of the story, the plot must provide, in some or all
of its different divisions, opportunity for the adequate
presentation of every element that enters into the final
effect of the story. Somewhere, the plot must provide
opportunity for presenting character, atmosphere, setting,
situation, mood, emotion—all that enters into the completed narrative and helps to make it a finished creation.
Therefore, *somewhere in the plot as finally organized
there must be a place for every necessary passage of
description and of dialogue, for every scene, act, situation,
and incident essential to getting the needed story material
before the reader.*

32. The inference from this is, that in both the rising
and the falling action and either accompanied or not accompanied by other story material, *incidents may be
introduced that are not vital to the plot, but that are,
nevertheless, vital to the total effect of the presentation.*
Such incidents as are vital to the plot are known as *plot
incidents;* and it is this kind of incident with which we
are concerned throughout the present chapter. But here
we must mention the so-called developing, or amplifying,
material—a better designation for which is *intensifying* or
concentrative material. A plot incident is one that cannot
be omitted, or of which the essential character cannot be
made different, without destroying the plot itself by re-

moving its essential motivation, or else changing it so
fundamentally that its outcome is thereby changed.[14]   A
concentrative or intensifying incident, however, is one that
can be omitted without fatally crippling the plot in its
original form, or that can be changed or varied materially
without producing thereby a different outcome.

33. *The purpose of the plot incident is, to achieve
the outcome; the purpose of the intensifying, or concentrative, incident is, to center attention on significant facts
of any sort,* to concentrate in a limited space and time
as much of typical action, characteristic trait, significant
environment, and other elements of the desired effect, as it
can pack in.   By selecting elements and material that
will go furthest toward producing the desired impression,
and presenting this significant material in well-managed
incident, the writer *concentrates* its force and *intensifies*
through it the final effect of the story.

34. We here speak primarily of incident as the means
employed to present concentrative material; but we must
fix in mind that *intensifying material does not lie in act
and incident only.*   Both character (expressed in acts),
and atmosphere, in all their limitless variations, are intensifying material of the greatest value.   Nor is incident the
only means available for presenting these sources of concentrated interest and interpretative fact.   But this we
need not discuss here.

35. To distinguish or even to discriminate the plot
incident from the amplifying, or concentrative incident,
is difficult.   In the best stories, plot incidents are likely
to be the only incidents employed, the writer's gift ena-

---

[14] Such incidents will seldom occur in the plot until it has reached
the synopsis stage of development.

bling him to conceive a plot so perfect, and to develop it
with so sound judgment in the selection and command of
material, that adequate presentation of the plot itself
results in adequate presentation also of all other elements
essential to the effect desired. Yet the introduction of
incidents, and of other material, not to further the plot,
but to emphasize some element that will contribute to
the total effect, is frequent. In general, therefore, we
say that *plot incident may be (and should be) concentrative incident; that intensifying incident may be plot
incident; and that either may shade off into or merge with
incidents of the other class.* (The term " incident " may
here be interpreted to mean any material necessary to the
intended *effect* of the story.)

36. Brief illustration will show the nature of plot
incident. The germ idea of our plot is this: A son,
lacking a sense of honor, commits an act which ruins his
father, the soul of honor. Considering how to develop a
plot from this idea, we see that the ruin worked upon
the father may be either material (financial) or psychological; the son may bankrupt his father or he may break
his heart, or he may do the latter by first doing the
former. We decide upon financial ruin. To ruin his
father financially, the son must do some act or acts involving his father's fortune. Formulating a working-plot,
we will assume that he is engaged in contracting, and that
to secure an important contract he offers a bond signed by
his father under a misapprehension. Unable to carry out
his agreement (as he knew he might be), he forfeits
the bond, the payment of which ruins the old man.

37. In this transaction we have a plot incident; that
is, an incident indispensably a part of the series that brings

about the predetermined outcome.   After the working-plot has been decided on, a plot incident cannot be materially changed, since to change it would materially alter the action or the outcome.   From the plot germ stated above, various working-plots might have been developed (as is true of any master-plot or plot germ).   Billings (the son) might have forged his father's name to a crushing obligation; he might have compelled him to meet ruinous gambling debts; he might have cornered and taken advantage of him in some " deal "; and in numerous other ways, he might have brought him to bankruptcy.   In each of these working-plots, the incident employed—the forgery, the gambling payment, etc.—would have then been a plot incident, and would have been indispensable to the development of that particular working-plot.   We may, therefore, define a plot incident as *any incident that is indispensable as a motivating step toward the production of the outcome required by the working-plot adopted.*

38.   Now let us change the character of the outcome, and state another working-plot to match.   Billings is to break his father's heart, not merely his finances.   To do this, his acts must strike at the old man's sense of honor, not at his fortune.   What the son does must be of a sort so conclusively and crushingly dishonorable that the father shall feel himself and all he holds dear involved in the dishonor of the son.   The son may, for instance, betray for a price the secrets trusted to him of a great cause to which his father and his father's friends have devoted life and fortune.   This betrayal, like the bond transaction, is a plot incident—an incident that is an indispensable part of the series intended to produce the outcome.   True,

any other incident of a sort permitting it to be similarly employed to bring about the same outcome—the breaking of the father's heart—could be used as a plot incident suitable to this plot, provided it were equally forceful, vivid, and natural, and in general offered equal dramatic, theatric, and narrative advantages. Thus, base behavior on the son's part in the betrayal of an innocent woman might as completely crush the father. But the working-plot would not then be the same; a new and different working-plot would have been created.

39. Such are plot incidents—incidents indispensably a part of the particular series meant to bring about the outcome. But amplifying or intensifying materials may be selected much more freely than may strictly plot materials. Amplifying incidents are not necessarily part of the causative series indispensable to the predetermined outcome; they may only concentrate attention upon some fact, or quality, or emotion, that will directly or indirectly, but surely, contribute to the intended final *effect*. So to contribute, they must be adapted to awaken immediate response in the reader, and must be in keeping with the story as a whole; for incongruous material is always to be shunned absolutely. *Any material, therefore, that is in keeping with the plot, the setting, the tone of the narrative, and the character of the persons, may be introduced into the story for the purpose of heightening its effect; provided that this material be so managed that it do not interfere with the progress of the plot.* For, however effective it may be toward intensifying desired effects, if it, nevertheless, occupy too prominent a place or require too extended treatment in proportion to other parts of the story; if it attract attention to itself, to the obscuring of

the main theme or plot; or if it otherwise cease to be frankly and solely subordinate and contributory, usurping on the contrary the attention due only to the main theme and plot;—then it must be subdued, or if this prove impossible, must be resolutely rejected for some less stubborn material.[15]

40. Concentrative or intensifying passages abound, for intensification is freely employed to emphasize the significant facts of character, environment, atmosphere—of everything, indeed, involved in the total impression aimed at in the story. A single paragraph from *The Outcasts of Poker Flat* (Harte), although taken at random, sufficiently illustrates the nature of the concentrative incident. It reads:

". . . Mr. Oakhurst . . . had met him some months before over a ' little game,' and had with perfect equanimity won the entire fortune—amounting to some forty dollars—of the guileless youth. After the game was finished, Mr. Oakhurst drew the youthful speculator behind the door and thus addressed him : ' Tom, you're a good little man, but you can't gamble worth a cent. Don't try it over again.' He then handed him back his money, pushed him gently from the door, and so made a devoted slave of Tom Simson."

41. This incident, or episode, has nothing to do with the outcome in any way. Its sole purpose is, to concentrate attention on and emphasize the character qualities of the two persons whom chance or fate has thrown together once more, this time to be partners in the tragic outcome of a

---

[15] We must concede, however, that some thoroughly successful short fiction owes its value to its contributory, not to its essential, elements.

series of events [16] unconnected in every way with their former meeting. Yet as a concentrative episode, this incident is so in keeping with the rest of the story, is so simply and skillfully managed, so natural and well-chosen from the great number of incidents that the author might have employed to the same end, so thoroughly kept subordinate to the main facts, that the reader does not in the least feel its complete disconnectedness from the plot. As an example of skillful choice and skillful management of intensifying, or emphasizing, material, it will repay further study.

42. The student will observe that the discussion just given to concentrative, intensifying, or emphasizing, incidents is somewhat a digression. It has, however, been introduced here for several reasons. First, it is desirable that the difference between plot incidents and non-plot incidents be fixed permanently in mind. Second, it is necessary that, here or elsewhere, attention be directed to the function of the plot as the carrier of non-plot material. Third, the stage of rising action, or development, is the stage in which plot incident most prominently occupies the writer at the time when he is constructing his plot; for although plot incident will be found in every stage of the plot from the moment when the complication first appears, it is in the rising action stage that the most skillful and careful management of it is required, in order to create the decisive moment. Without forgetting the importance of intensifying incident in the story when finally completed; and realizing that this sort of incident, like plot incident, may occur in any part of the story, but is likely to be most prominent in the stage of exposition

[16] Let the student pick out the plot incidents in this story.

and of the rising action;—the beginner will, therefore, in constructing his plot, have to concern himself—prior to the scenario stage—with the creation and organization of plot incident only.

XVI. THE FALLING ACTION BRINGS THE OUTCOME AND CLOSE

1. Broadly speaking, when the outcome has been made sure through the gaining, by one set of influences, of a permanent advantage over the other set, as determined by the decisive moment, the best thing thereafter is, for the action to bring on that outcome as rapidly and impressively as possible. For suspense continued and renewed, for accumulating incident (either plot or concentrative), the place is rather before than after the decisive moment. The place for a regatta at Niagara is not in the falls, nor in the waters that have been caught in their rush. And the plot that has come to its decisive moment has been caught in the rush of the stream toward the falls. The end once determined, the outcome at last made sure, is to be reached and got over as quickly as may be; for if he wait too long, the reader loses interest. This consideration dictates the principle that is more and more showing itself in drama and dramatic narrative; namely, that *falling action shall be reduced to the least possible amount.*[17]

2. For this advice, there are two justifications: When

[17] Continuing the Niagara comparison, the decisive moment is that at which the waters are caught in the rush toward the falls, and the falling action is their sweep forward from that moment until they plunge over the precipice.

the outcome is made to coincide with the decisive moment and the climactic height, it is likely to gain greatly in effectiveness—the impression it makes is quicker, deeper, and stronger—that is, more theatric, in the best sense of the term. When their pull begins, the falls themselves— and the end of the story—are at hand. Such an ending materially strengthens the dramatic effect sought by the conte, and is nearly always characteristic of the closely-wrought plot. In addition to this, the omission of amplifying materials wherever they are unnecessary to the full development and effect, is in accordance with the general principle of compression, or economy of detail, that we have already mentioned, which prescribes: *the fewest and simplest means with which the desired effect can be fully wrought.*

3. Inclusion of the outcome in the decisive moment is particularly advisable in stories which, in the course of the rising action, have made very plain what the results are that the conflict can produce. The reader, clearly perceiving the consequences of this or that turn of events at the height of the conflict, and watching with eager interest to see what this turn will be, knows as soon as he sees it what the outcome is. When the boat is just above the falls and the rope holding it breaks, the rest is sure. When the decisive turn takes place, the problem is solved. If the decisive turn reveals itself, the end of things is already clear to him; he understands this end; he realizes in advance its grief or happiness, its comedy or tragedy. Therefore, he needs little or no falling action, untangling, or resolution, little or no separate presentation of an outcome already felt in its full force. We should have to qualify this assertion only as it affects one kind of story. *When the*

effect sought is that which springs from contemplating the steady, sure approach of fate (usually tragic, although it may be comic), the proportions are reversed. The rising action is short, the decisive moment comes early, and the falling action is long drawn out. Naturally, in this kind of story, the climactic point is more or less widely separated from the decisive moment.

4. In most stories having closely-wrought plot, therefore, the decisive moment, the climactic situation, is itself the final, the conclusive situation; and to hitch on other incident or situation is to couple on an empty trailer behind the observation car. The trailer merely interferes with or spoils the view from the observation-platform, the decisive climax. *In a story so plotted and managed that its decisive height embodies or unmistakably suggests the outcome, further scenes or situations after that of the decisive height are superfluous, and dilute and nullify the impressiveness of the plot culmination and climactic height.*

5. Nevertheless, well-built plots may not always permit this complete telescoping of decisive height and outcome. *The decisive turn of events does not always make plain to the reader* WHAT *the outcome is to be, but only* WHICH SET *of conflicting influences is to prevail.* Indeed, some stories would fail of their effect (*cf.* par. 4), and some plots would refuse to yield themselves to development, if this rule were universal. The surprise story especially is likely to require further action after the decisive point has been reached; for its essential characteristic is, the springing of an unexpected outcome brought about by a set of influences which only at the very last are seen to have combined decisively some time before.

6. In stories likewise that emphasize character, especially those that present character transformed as the result of the conflict depicted in the story, it may be necessary to carry on the action after the decisive moment; for *what determines the outcome may merely draw this outcome in its train, not include it.* The character facts may *depend* upon the influences which, at the decisive height of the plot, combine to one sure result, but *the full working out of which* may not yet have taken place. Therefore, to enable these influences fully to work out their results on the character they affect, additional incident and action may be necessary. Even the bare fact that verisimilitude often requires the impression of passage of time between cause and effect may make such additional incident and action advisable. Very often these considerations hold also when applied to the plot story.

7. We must acknowledge, therefore, that although the telescoping of outcome with decisive moment is highly effective when it can be accomplished, not all plots will yield to it. Wholly legitimate conte plots may require further action, further incident and situation, to carry them forward from the point where the outcome is made sure to the point where this outcome is actually reached. The decisive moment is not always decisive except as we look back at it; and it often is not sufficient in itself to support the outcome unless reinforced by incident, action, or situation following it. In short, *after the outcome has been made sure, it must still be brought to pass; and to bring it to pass, completely motivated, and at last to present it as conclusively the result of the whole plot, is the function of that division of the plot termed the falling action. In other words, the falling action brings forward and con-*

*summates what the rising action and decisive moment have
made sure.*

8. Illustration of these explanations will make them
clearer. In *The Pope's Mule* (Daudet), the plot has a
clearly distinguishable stage of falling action, or resolution.
The height of the *plot* [18]—that is, the decisive moment—
comes when Védène so maliciously conducts the favored
mule to the top of the great tower, thus frightening and
humiliating her greatly. From that time, but one outcome
is possible: the mule will have her revenge. But the
opportunity for it must be created, and the stage prepared
for its actual accomplishment. Hence comes the additional stage of the plot, wherein this outcome is prepared
for. Seven years she waits her opportunity. Then
Védène, returning from long service away from Avignon,
receives the appointment he has asked, and is taken to
see the beloved mule whom he pretends so to admire.
Only then has the outcome been sufficiently motivated;
only then is the famous kick—the kick that she had been
saving up for seven years—ready to be delivered—" a
kick so terrible, so terrible, that even at Pamperigouste one
could see the smoke; a cloud of yellowish smoke in which
fluttered an ibis plume, all that was left of the ill-fated
Tistet Védène."

9. For the sake now of understanding what is meant
by the uniting in one situation of decisive moment and
outcome, let us tamper a little with Daudet's plot. The
mischievous Védène gets the poor mule to the top of the
tower; she brays forth her terror; the humiliating process
of rigging her into the cradle ready for lowering back to

[18] Remember that the height of the *plot* is not necessarily the
climactic moment of the *narrative*.

earth has been completed. She stands waiting to be swung off. At this moment, not seven years later, Védène comes within reach of her heels and receives her kick. In the very moment of her humiliation, she avenges herself. The plot is now closed, the action is complete, the story ended. In every respect (perhaps) except one, this management of the outcome is more effective than is that actually used, in which a period of falling action intervenes. But that one respect is exceedingly important: it is this long waiting that makes the kick really impressive. In the story as Daudet produced it, we gain, from the long years through which she kept it burning, an idea of the intensity of the mule's hatred; in the plot of telescoped height-and-outcome, no such impression could have been created. The mule's kick in the telescoped version is the result only of sudden anger and passionate impulse. In this instance, then, the form with falling action gives us a longer and more satisfying period of suspense, a deeper realization of mule character and motive, and a higher gratification at the ultimate success of the tremendous kick.

10. Here falling action clearly has advantages; but such is not always the case. In *Markheim* (Stevenson) we have an excellent example of the story in which the turning-point and the outcome are telescoped. The turning-point is that where Markheim's conscience succeeds in making him realize exactly what he has become and what —except for a single possibility—he will always be (but increasingly worse as the years go on). This point comes almost at the close of the story, and the closing lines of the story itself are virtually the closing lines of the paragraphs in which this climactic situation is developed. Markheim in effect says, " Well, if I cannot change for

the better, I can at least prevent myself from growing worse in this terrible way "; and thereupon, going to the door, he throws it open to the servant and says, " You had better go for the police. I have killed your master." Thus his last act closes not only the decisive situation, but also the plot and the story. De Maupassant's *The Coward* presents a similar example. The decisive situation is that in which the viscount, shaken by fear and torn between impulse and reason, mechanically picking up the dueling pistol, finds it loaded. Five sentences later, " he suddenly thrust the pistol into the very bottom of his throat and pulled the trigger." Three more sentences end the story itself—and these three are not needed.

11. The question, whether to telescope or not to telescope, will therefore be answered automatically by the plot conception itself. According to the requirements of the plot as ultimately it dictates itself to the writer's constructive and artistic sense, falling action will or will not be called for. But when it is not called for, the plot and the story will be better without it.

CHAPTER III

THE COMPOSITIONAL CONSTRUCTION OF THE SHORT STORY

XVII. The Opening Seizes Interest, Introduces Action, Strikes the Keynote, and (Perhaps) Conveys Exposition

1. Up to this point we have considered, first, the distinguishing characteristics that make, and second, the theory of plot as it affects, the short story; and incidentally we have given attention to matters belonging rather to the story in the completed form than in its plot outline. Having treated these matters and emphasized the importance of dramatic plot to the true short story (conte), we can now devote our attention for a while not to questions of motivation—of cause and effect interacting through event and character toward a single impressive outcome—but to the compositional construction of the story—that assembling and manipulating of all its facts, materials, and parts which leave it (let us trust) a finished work. Our consideration will first be given to the opening of the story. The function of the opening is:

A. To seize interest. This oftenest results from (B).

B. To begin or bring on the action.

C. To strike the keynote of the story.

D. As far as may be expedient, to convey exposition.

2. In discussing plot, we noted that plot sequence is

not the same as narrative sequence, or dramatic sequence. The essential sequence of incident in the plot is, we saw, the time-sequence—cause before effect; the contributing facts before the situation and outcome they produce. But the natural sequential order may be altered and even quite reversed in the completed narrative, especially as the incident not infrequently is more important for the facts that gather round and depend upon it than it is merely for itself; so that it is managed with a view to emphasizing these accompanying facts, and not the pure incident. We may even find the outcome at the beginning of the story, which then works backward to those facts which constitute the beginning of the plot.[1] This sort of *disarrangement and relocation of incident and of other facts is often necessary for dramatic emphasis,* which is the effect sought by the conte.

3. For we are not to understand that such dislocation of facts from the natural time order is universal, nor that it is invariably necessary or expedient. The time order should in fact be varied no more than dramatic effectiveness requires. Yet this implies that the artist, in handling his materials, often must deal with them in ways that render the time order—so essential in the earlier processes of plotting—impossible in the story as it finally reaches the reader. For in that stage of composition in which the plot is transformed from a bare outline of incident into an artist's conception of the dramatic significance of

---

[1] This is in general the method of the mystery story. Beginning with a puzzling outcome, the mystery story carries the reader, but backward, through an explanation of the facts that explain this outcome. The circle is completed when the explanation brings the reader back at the close to the same outcome with its mystery removed.

these incidents together with all the facts of every sort involved in them in some significant hour of human life —in this stage of composition *that order is the most logical which best shows forth this conception with a vividness and forcefulness likely to impress it deeply on the reader.* We are to remember, therefore, that *plot se-quence and narrative sequence are different things. Both order the same body of facts, but each orders them as re-quired by its peculiar function in the creating of the com-pleted story, the one seeking to make clear the history of a certain outcome, the other seeking to make clear the signifi-cance of this outcome and impress it on the reader.*

4. From what has been said, it follows that the begin-ning of the story itself may contain matter not found in the beginning of the plot, and that it may omit matter nec-essarily included in the beginning of the plot.[2] In other words, the beginning of the story may be different from the beginning of the plot. The opening of the story may—

A. Begin the action.

B. Begin the characterization.

C. Begin the creation of atmosphere, presenting either tonal, environmental, or merely setting elements.

D. Begin the theme presentation.

That is, the beginning of the story may concern itself with material especially suited to the purpose of any one of the four fundamental types of short story. Moreover, any one of these four types of beginning is likely to be usable in any one of the four sorts of story, although not all the types of beginning are equally suited to all the types of story.

5. This means that in the whole range of the conte there are sixteen possible combinations of story emphasis

[2] Before the stage of scenario, or action-plot.

with beginning materials, although (of course) when the single story is in question the possible combinations are only four. In a character story, for example, the author can at the very opening begin his emphasis upon character, or he can open rather with materials that belong particularly to the action, or to the atmosphere, or to the theme. *The natural and usually the best procedure will be, to make prominent in the beginning that element which will be most prominent in the completed story*—a character story taking a beginning that emphasizes character, a theme story opening with emphasis on the theme, an action story with emphasis upon action, and an atmosphere story with emphasis upon atmosphere. This procedure, however, although highly useful in many instances, and especially in " striking the keynote " of the story, is by no means always obligatory.

6. Accepting the rhetorical theory that the beginning of any piece of writing is a place of great importance in the giving of emphasis, we are thus led to lay down *the rule, subject to qualification, that the beginning of a story should always emphasize that one of the story elements which the story itself is intended to emphasize*. But this is sound theory and good practice only when it is not overdone. We must not lose sight of everything but solely our intended effect; we must remember at the same time that this effect can be attained only through the skillful employment of various means, and that the organization of our story as a whole—the assembling of its materials, the ordering of its incidents, the working in and subordinating of all the sub-effects essential to the production of the final effect—may call for numerous adjustments involving modification of general principles. The rules

of art are plastic, not rigid, and its materials resemble modeling clay rather than cast iron. Any one of many considerations may, therefore, warrant the disregard of the rule as first stated. Accordingly, the more practical and general rule is this: *In the opening, use that material which will best contribute to the organization and effect of the story as a whole; remembering, however, that at the beginning it is desirable to emphasize, so far as practicable, the same elements as are to be especially emphasized in the story as a whole.*

7. We will now in a single clause emphasize the self-evident truth, that *the opening must indispensably have interest,* and turn to consider the story materials from this point of view. First of all, we observe that all four of *the types enumerated above are beginnings likely to possess interest because of their inherent qualities.* Interest, we have already seen, is something quite different from excitement or avid pursuit of sensation, being the result of internal quality and of significance to the plot, rather than of external characteristic. It is roused whenever anything is brought before the mind that by reason of its nature, its intrinsic qualities, or its relationship with other matters, has power to command attention; and the human mind is so constituted that it inclines to give attention whenever anything closely related either to human life or to the individual experience through which human life is realized, is presented to it, provided that this thing is so presented as to make its relationships and significance clear.

8. Accordingly, men instinctively attend to that wherein the acts of other men, their traits of character, the conditions surrounding and influencing their lives, or a

conclusion concerning human existence, is presented. This
is equivalent to saying that *they instinctively give attention
(or tend to do so) whenever action, character, atmosphere,
or theme is brought before them.* For these are things
that of their very nature appeal to man as affecting his
daily life, or entering into his experience of it, or throwing
light on the problem of his own nature and destiny.
Recognizing, therefore, the wide range of subject-matter
which thus possesses inherent interest quality, we see that
as a consequence each of the four types of opening is
intrinsically suitable for the beginning. À propos this
topic, more will be said in pars. 12 and 15-21.

9. We next note that another function of the beginning
is filled by these four types. *This function is, to present,
when essential to the narrative plan, and in other cases
when reasonably practicable, all or part of the facts belonging to the plot exposition.* Here we observe again that, as
acts, character, environing conditions, and recognized
truths of life are all we know of, seeming to bear upon
human life, so they are all that can be made use of in
any exposition. Accordingly, the matter of these beginnings—acts, character, theme, and atmosphere—is the
sole material out of which the exposition of any plot (or
indeed any plot itself) can be built up. Recalling then
the general principle, that the expository facts are best
presented earlier rather than later in the narrative, we can
lay down another rule of practice for the story writer:
*When the plan of narration permits it and the unified
effect sought will not suffer by it, the details introduced
at the opening of the story should be selected with a view
to presenting the necessary exposition.*

10. This brings us to a third function of the opening;

namely, *striking the keynote of the story—a function of great importance*. By "striking the keynote" we mean, creating a sense of the essential quality and tone, of the attitude, manner, and point of view, of the story. By a well-managed beginning, the reader will be put in sympathy—*en rapport*—"in touch"—with what is to follow. He will be led by it to preperceive (more or less unawaredly, it is true) the attitude of mind of the author, the spirit in which the subject is to be handled, the mood and tone of the story itself, and the nature (though, of course, scarcely the actual event itself) of the outcome. He will begin at once to receive somewhat of the subjective and emotional impression which the story as a whole is planned to produce. We will not insist that this amounts to saying that the beginning must have atmosphere; yet that is practically what it does amount to. And when we reflect that, after all, no fiction or drama is thoroughly good that does not encompass itself with an atmosphere (the product of truthfulness and naturalness in the facts themselves and the reporting of them) ; that no play or narrative can produce a perfect total effect lacking this quality ; and that the opening of the story will inevitably go far toward creating in us the impression with which we shall read the rest of the narrative ;—when we reflect on these facts, we begin to *realize the importance of striking, at the outset, the keynote of the story*.

11. The opening of every story should make the reader begin to feel at once that here is a story which has, not merely "a name," but also "a local habitation"—a story which "belongs"—which deals with persons and things, with acts, motives, emotions, and surroundings such as, no matter how fanciful or impossible they may be in

themselves, are, nevertheless, as here presented real [3] and self-consistent. The reader must be made to sense this reality, to sympathize with, to enter into the spirit of, these things, to catch the point of view, the outlook, the purpose, the individuality, tang, and tone, of the narrative that presents them. Without being thus in responsive understanding of the nature of the story, he is unlikely to read further, or if he read, to do so blindly, unsympathetically, and non-appreciatively. This function, therefore, of the opening—that of striking the keynote—is exceedingly important. *The prudent writer will so select his opening, and so present its details, as either to create at once in the reader the mental attitude and imaginative mood that he desires, or at least to prepare him for it.*

12. On the importance of the opening as a means of catching attention, so much has been said by many critics that the present writer has chosen not to dwell, in the preceding discussion, insistently on that topic. This does not mean, however, that he thinks the catching of interest by the beginning an unimportant matter, but that he is a little doubtful whether so much emphasis on particular aspects of the matter may not prove misleading. For from feeling strongly the necessity of attracting attention at the outset, to striving for it unduly, is but a step. Hence he here gives a few paragraphs of after discussion to this ticklish problem of the opening as an interest-catcher. We

---

[3] "Real" and "actual," as already noted, are not synonymous. The sensitiveness of the mind to suggestion is such that even the impossible can be made to seem real to the imagination. Poe's tales "deal with an unreal world," and accordingly have an atmosphere of unreality. But while we are under the spell of Poe's narrative, this "world of unreality" seems a *real* world of unreality, and its atmosphere an atmosphere of *real*-seeming unreality.

are now, therefore, to take up expressly consideration of *the opening as a means of getting into the narrative action and of creating the suspense essential to increasing interest.*

13. We will first stop long enough to note that *fiction materials should be chosen, not merely with regard to intrinsic interest, but also with regard to their fitness for narrative-dramatic presentation.* We have seen that interest seems inherent in anything of a sort that touches human life in general or associates itself with the experience of the individual; and as there is nothing in the known world that does not belong either in one or in both of these categories, so there is nothing which may not in some set or other of circumstances have intrinsic interest. Nothing is uninteresting in itself if presented so that its significance appear.

14. Subject to one important qualification, therefore, we may say that there is nothing which cannot be used as material in the opening (or in any other part) of a fiction narrative. The qualification is, that *no material is suitable for dramatic fiction narrative which does not submit itself to the methods of dramatic narrative.*[4] It must not only be tellable, it must be tellable in a narrative that obeys dramatic principles. It is easy to agree that philosophy and science are unsuited for short story presentation—that they do not yield readily to presentation in dramatic narrative. Yet the reason

[4] Contemporary drama shows how unsafe generalizations are concerning what is and what is not possible material. Brieux's *Damaged Goods*, for instance, stood the test of successful if not popular stage presentation, yet its material is material that has been held quite unsuited to dramatic presentation—that is, unamenable to dramatic technique.

for rejecting such material must be one of convenience and expediency, not of absolute necessity; for the master writer finds it quite possible to reduce philosophies and sciences to subjection, and to make them furnish forth, in no funeral-baked fashion, warm meats for the dramatic narrative. Consequently, IF *the writer has skill to find concrete dramatic and narrative forms through which to body forth the facts of philosophy, science, or any other subject, he need not hesitate to introduce this supposedly unfit material into his work.* On the contrary, his work will gain in clearness of understanding and breadth of view whenever it thus enriches and energizes itself from the general stores of human knowledge and experience. Crude as is the old morality play, *Everyman,* it exemplifies this truth; for it bodies forth morality and religion so well in concrete forms [5] that even in our day—wherein the form of allegory and the morality seems strange, and the religious thought perhaps remote or alien—this old dramatic allegory proves impressive. Our conclusion must be, that although the writer needs to be exceedingly cautious how he introduces difficult and impliant materials, there is no such thing as absolutely unfit material if the writer have skill and creativeness to find for it concrete forms and dramatic expression.[6]

[5] This play affords an excellent illustration of what is meant by the expression "finding concrete forms." In it, vice is actually a person; so is good works; so is death. Similarly, other abstract ideas, such as dying, are given concrete form (Everyman, a person, descends into an actual grave, etc.).

[6] "Dramatic" is here equivalent to "theatric"—suited to presentation by the methods of the theater (for instance, by dialogue). The term having sometimes been given a specialized or restricted

15. But these conclusions are perhaps less immediately important than is the one which we will now take up for brief discussion; namely, that *the principle of an-opening-to-catch-interest may easily be overworked*. We have already seen how extensive is the available material having intrinsic interest; but in the struggle to create a beginning that will at once "grip" the reader, the writer may not only slight some of the most valuable of the materials available, but also be led into adopting some form of opening that is flippant, overwrought, false in tone, sensational, or otherwise dishonest to fact, life, and art. There are ways (and often better ways) of attracting one's attention other than slapping him in the face; and there are ways (and often better ways) of arousing interest in a story other than that of "putting a punch" in it at the beginning and making that "punch" a punch in the reader's "wind."

16. In truth, the cult of the punch has been a little over-cultivated. There are, and there always will be, many readers, and readers well worth having, who appreciate the interest quality of other than the slap-in-the-face beginning, and read with pleasure openings of discursive or philosophical comment, description, and what not. The one reasonable requirement is, that *the opening shall adequately present the material with which it attempts to deal, shall closely relate itself to the story as a whole,*

meaning in this book, "theatric" ought to be used in its stead in such assertions as that in the text above, thus noting the difference between what is dramatic and what is theatric, or especially belonging to theater presentation. The author hopes that he has nowhere fallen into the unjust usage whereby "theatric" and "theatrical" are used in a derogatory sense—implying what is insincere or false, or affected rather than natural and spontaneous.

and shall with satisfying promptness bring us to the action of the plot itself. The writer, therefore, who has a subject or a plan of treament that in its best-organized form calls for description, comment, reflection, or any other such manner of opening, even though it be an opening of which the grip-the-reader extremist would not approve, need as an artist not hesitate to employ that beginning. Rather, as an artist, he should hesitate not to employ it.

17. Yet the practicing author, depending on his typewriter for an income, and the author seeking invariably that form which is best adapted to the particular story then in hand, will not despise the counsel of the impressive opening. To the natural born artist, of course, advice and caution on this matter is scarcely warrantable; he will build his stories as they should be built, and their effect will take care of itself. Yet even he should be advised of the conditions which (often at the expense of truer literature) enforce the principle on the writer who goes to market with his wares. To see the reader in the editorial office, or the literary agent whose business it is to know how to pick what the editor will choose—to see these experts in public (or is it merely editorial?) taste snatching at the beginning of a manuscript, then perhaps giving the rest of the story only a glance here and there, or no further glance at all, is to realize how much depends, from the commercial point of view, on the beginning that will " grip."

18. It is no exaggeration to say that the story which can thus " jab " the reader with its first paragraph, or even its first sentence, stands a much larger number of chances, by and large, of meeting acceptances than does the story,

even the better story, lacking such a "punch" at the first. Nor is the result of this by any means all bad. True, sensationalism and similar sins have been part of this result. But so has been also a sharper inquiry concerning the nature of interest, the kinds of material containing interest, and the best methods of handling such materials in story openings. Consequent on this has come an improvement in the technique of openings, and a closer weaving into the narrative of all the fiction materials. Unquestionably, stories on the whole begin better than they used, even when they employ old-fashioned materials and types of opening.

19. Our criticism, therefore, of the principle which directs the employment of a beginning that will immediately "grip" the reader, is partly a caution against mistakenly discarding good though old forms under the assumption that they are not able to awaken interest, and a protest against forced and sensational methods in applying a principle itself perfectly sound and thoroughly useful. Perhaps even the caution is superfluous. Art always rids itself ultimately of false conceptions and bad practice, and writers even of the day are freely employing all manner and styles of opening, many of them quite unhampered by slavish subjection to the theory of the initial "punch."

20. Through this discussion of intrinsic interest, and cautioning against subserviency to a catch phrase—the cant "slogan" of a literary school that over-emphasizes what, truly conceived, is an important principle,—we come now to a direct consideration of the opening as a means of creating suspense. A moment's reflection will show that *suspense is really the key to the effectiveness of*

the opening when the opening is considered in relation to the story as a whole. The opening is the appetizer that comes before, yet is part of, the full dinner; or if likening it to the *hors d'œuvre* seem to make it too inessential a part of the meal, we may call it the first course, which begins to satisfy our appetite and yet makes us more desirous of the courses yet to come; and what we protested against in the preceding paragraphs is the tendency to make of the opening a cocktail instead of a true part of the meal. For the beginning *is* part of the meal, and the writer of stories must keep in mind the fact that it, like every other division of the story, exists not for its own sake, but for the sake of the story as a whole of which it is a part.

21. Hence *the opening must be conceived, planned, and managed with reference to the whole story; and as the conte has but one immediate governing aim—to show us persons and action—we cannot escape the conclusion that the opening must be so conceived, planned, and managed that it cannot fail to make us desirous of going on in order to see these persons, and the events of which they are a part.* This is what we mean when we say that the beginning should " grip " the reader. It should do more than merely interest him in its own subject-matter; it should make him desire to go on in order that he may see something more important that that of which, merely by itself, the opening treats—who the persons are; what their character is; what they do and how they come to do it; why they are what they are; what truth is illustrated by them in their behavior; and what sort of world it is wherein they thus move and act. This sort of interest, this desire, it is that is commonly meant when we are

told that the opening event should have " interest " and
" seize " the reader. *From this point of view, we need
not, when we are selecting a beginning for any story,
trouble ourselves primarily with questions about the intrinsic interest of the materials used; our problem is
rather so to select and manage that the material used shall
create in the reader the desire to pass on from the opening
to the continuation of the story.*

XVIII. The Purposes of the Opening can be Served by Various Kinds of Beginning

1. We turn now to more immediately practical questions of technique affecting the opening of the story.
The opening is to seize interest, strike the keynote, begin
the action, and, when practicable, advance the exposition.
What are the means by which the writer can accomplish
these purposes? The four things which the opening can
immediately [7] present are: activity (action by or involving
a person of the story, whether forming an integral part
of the true plot-action or not); character; theme; setting.
At this point we will put aside further special emphasis
upon the opening as a means of advancing plot exposition,
and deal only with its function in striking the keynote
and creating interest; the student will, however, bear

[7] We now drop for the present consideration of atmosphere as a
story element, confining ourselves to the less extensive term " setting." Atmosphere *can* be presented directly, but usually it is
attained indirectly—mediately rather than immediately—through
truth, naturalness, and adequacy in the presentation of other essentials, with due regard to their subjective as well as their
objective quality. However, the substitution leaves us still concerned
in a large measure with what is essentially atmosphere.

in mind the general desirability of early development of the exposition unless it seem best managed by introducing it piecemeal as the action advances. We now consider, then, the topic, *how to manage the opening with a view to securing interest (anticipatory suspense) and striking the keynote*. We might perhaps omit mention of the keynote; for the striking of the keynote at the beginning is after all merely another device for getting interest by indicating in advance that tonal quality and that attitude in treatment which will have so much to do in producing the total effect. On the other hand, as the means of commanding progressive interest lies mainly in the creation of suspense, we shall now use that term largely instead of " interest."

2. For the sake of simplicity, therefore, we can say that *all the practical problems of managing the opening can be solved by attending to the requirement of suspense*. True, the opening must not be uninteresting in itself; but this it is not likely to be if it relate itself closely and organically with the rest of the story (especially perhaps with the plot and with the tone or atmosphere). Well-managed openings, then, may create suspense by:—

(a) Giving setting.
(b) Delineating character.
(c) Suggesting the tone or spirit of the story.
(d) Plunging at once into incident.
(e) Presenting some general proposition, or theme, which the story is to illustrate.
(f) Providing necessary antecedent explanation (much skill is necessary to make mere expository matter produce suspense).

(g) Flinging some merely stimulative expression or fact at us just to catch attention (an inartistic method at the best; at its worst, flippant, false, sensational, and offensive—the " flash " manner of a literary " con " game. Of course, when the story is legitimately told throughout in this manner—as it might be, for instance, in depicting character—the expression warrants itself as striking the keynote).

In well-managed openings, several of these ends are usually accomplished at one and the same time.

3. We next ask, what shall be our manner of approach to the opening? To determine this, we must first determine, among other things, who shall tell the story. Of course, the writer is always, in one sense, the narrator; he does the writing. But shall he write it as himself, or as some one else? If he tell it as himself, shall he tell it (a) with complete impersonality, keeping himself absolutely and wholly out of it, or (b) with some degree of personality, letting himself as a recognized individual show forth in the narration, indicating by direct comment or other means his own point of view concerning the theme, persons, acts, and opinions appearing in the narrative, and thus injecting himself, a sort of extraneous author-chorus? Or if, on the other hand, he tell it as if he were some one else, shall he (c) tell it in the guise of a person actually having part in the story, either as chief actor or a secondary actor or even an unimportant spectator, or shall he instead (d) tell it as one who was himself outside the story and yet is not identical with the author who chances to be the one to set down the narrative?

4. Each of these methods has disadvantages (we will not stop to discuss them here); but before he can make up his mind just how to approach the opening, the writer must have decided which of them he will use. With this decision out of the way, the ground is cleared for selection among the various forms of beginning. Experience will prove to him that *every one of these forms can be employed more or less effectively* in getting before the reader the facts implied in the catalogue given in paragraph 2; and *any good opening, moreover, will nearly always accomplish more than one of the several aims there outlined.* We will consider some of them.

5. In making choice of an opening, the writer will first (let us say) choose between THE DIALOGUE AND THE NON-DIALOGUE FORM. Dialogue (by which is here meant direct speech in the mouth of any one directly appearing at the moment as a person in the story) would seem to offer a particularly effective form of beginning, the more so as it introduces without delay persons in action. We need not, therefore, attach especial importance to statistics which indicate that only some ten per cent. of short stories actually employ this form of beginning. True, the narrative plan decided on, and the spirit in which the story is conceived, have much to do with the rejection or employment of direct quotation. In some narratives, dialogue at the beginning would be quite unsuitable.

6. On the other hand, to some stories it would be thoroughly adapted. It is, for instance, an almost invariable accompaniment of action. In stories opening with incident, therefore, the opening may take the form of speech—really part of the action, and helping it forward. Again, speech is a valuable means of character portrayal:

" Thy speech bewrayeth thee." To put significant expressions on the lips of a person when we are just meeting him in the story, is a quick and sure way to give us an impression of his character. Again, speech frequently becomes suggestive, not merely of character, mood, and act, but of the surroundings; a few words naming actual details, introduced into the dialogue, may effectually outline the setting. In short, the opening of direct speech, when the plan and nature of the story permit it, is thoroughly useful and effective.[8]

7. Yet again, then, we return to the desirability of INTEREST (SUSPENSE) IN THE OPENING, and the means of attaining it. Frankly, the most important of these means is action. There is interest in setting, character, atmosphere, and theme, but *that opening will be most effective which, in giving us these things, gives them to us embodied in or as accompaniments of action.* That this action be plot-action is highly desirable, but is not indispensable; it may be merely activity (but significant activity)— simply an introductory episode or incident of the concentrative class. But if activity there be—something moving, something doing, whether that something be or be not indispensable to the plot—by that very fact attention will

[8] Reread par. 4; observe how dialogue can at one and the same time explain situation, advance the action, indicate setting, portray character, make us feel the general tone of the situation or the mood of the speaker or the story, etc. This will impress the fact, that any good opening can accomplish several purposes at once. The more the beginning, by presenting well-related, carefully chosen detail, compresses into small compass and coherent form the various story elements at the outset, the greater its interest and effectiveness. The " compression " so often insisted on as characteristic of the conte is merely such management of detail throughout the story, whereby several ends are accomplished by single means.

be more immediately commanded, with the likelihood that
it will continue and increase.

8. *For when all is said and done, the conte exists to
show us persons acting; hence the sooner any story gets
action going, the sooner it will begin to show us that for
which it most immediately exists.* Even character delinea-
tion, unless given through action, will be less interesting
(in the more immediate sense of the word) than action.
It will show us man, but it will not show us men in action;
and it is to see men in action that we buy our ticket to
the short story show. Reasonably interpreted, therefore,
the rule which prescribes action, or at least significant
activity, as an important part of the opening of any short
story, is a rule of great importance. *The writer who,
without sacrificing other qualities, and without making
his method merely one of mannerism or sensation, shows
us always something doing from the first, thus creating
not only present attention, but also that forward-looking
eagerness that we term suspense, has successfully met one
of the most positive requirements of the art of short story
dramatics.*

9. Some further observations concerning the fiction
elements likely to enter into the opening, and their skillful
management, may be worth while. To the inexperienced
writer, it may seem, for instance, that the importance of
the SETTING to a just appreciation of the story warrants the
placing of setting at the very opening. And he may be
right, the more so as such placing helps to get this material
out of the way at once. The setting is important,
especially in atmosphere stories; yet that does not mean
that it should all be bunched and huddled into one long
initial passage, especially if this passage be direct descrip-

tion. Such was the older method, but it is not the modern practice. *Even in the novel, modern technique now usually shuns the descriptive panorama as an opening,* preferring to place description (if anywhere it describes at length) in chapters which lie buried within the narrative. In the conte, the most probable exception will be found in the story that emphasizes atmosphere. The atmosphere story is likely to draw much of its atmosphere effects from the setting, and it therefore shows some tendency to employ description more freely and to introduce it earlier than do other stories.

10. Yet if this tendency be indulged, it must be kept under control. Even in such a story as *The Merry Men,* written by Stevenson as an atmosphere story—the fictional embodiment of the spirit of a grim, rock-barriered, storm-leaguered Hebridean coast—the narrative does not begin immediately with atmosphere elements. It opens with action (indirect). Not until he wrote some 250 words narrating action and preliminary fact, and giving character forecast, did Stevenson begin description; and even then the description is given excuse for appearing through being made the setting for further indirect action (the walk by which the young man who is supposed to relate the facts and to have taken part in the incidents, makes his approach to the scene of the main action). Thus, even though all the first chapter is, broadly speaking, concerned with the description of setting, its description is mingled throughout with elements of action and exposition and with character forehints. Without further discussion, therefore, we may conclude that *lengthy descriptive passages at the beginning are likely to prove incompatible with the prompt creation of suspense.*

11. The beginning of *The Merry Men* can give us *other suggestions* if we turn aside here to take note of them. The advantages and disadvantages found in use of the distributed exposition instead of the massed have been noted. Chapter I of *The Merry Men* may be taken as a double-header illustration of the principle. Various essential bits of information about the locality, the young man, the uncle who is the central character, his old servant (another secondary actor), and the long-past events of history that later enter into the plot, are scattered through it, offsetting and enlivening the more solid descriptive parts. On the other hand, regarded as merely the beginning of the complete story, the chapter represents in a considerable degree, not the distributed but the massed exposition.

12. Digressing somewhat more, we may observe the skill with which, towards the close, this chapter makes the description that it contains bring on the narrative passage informing us of the wreck—long before—of the Spanish treasure ship of the Armada, desire to salvage which motivates the events and complication of the plot. Yet while all this preliminary information is being got before us, more immediate, although indirect, action is going on—the advance of the young man toward his uncle's house and the scene of the main action. Hence, not only with regard to the presentation of setting, but also with reference to other functions of the opening, this chapter repays study.

13. Further thus: It illustrates one form of opening in stories wherein the author writes, not as himself, but as another person—one who has been an actor in the events he reports (par. 3, C). A severe stretching of the

term dialogue might even bring this opening into the class of dialogue beginnings. But it would not belong there, for the speech of the actor-narrator is addressed now to the reader; is not speech belonging to the time of the action or entering into the original action in any way, and besides, so far as the plot is concerned, presents only indirect action. That is, though it is words from the mouth of an actor, it is not words from his mouth at any time when he is engaged in the incidents of the story. Therefore, it is not in any true sense dialogue (plot, character, or action speech forming part of the action itself). Before getting back, therefore, closer to our present topic, we can only note here the fact that, *when setting is given as part of the dialogue content, it can not often be given in detail;* for little natural and spontaneous conversation is of a sort to permit long descriptions. When landscape or other setting is touched on in ordinary converse, it is likely to have roused some emotion in the spectator which he expresses rather in exclamation than in any directly descriptive phrase; so that its nature is frequently indicated indirectly by the impression which it is seen to produce on the beholder. Moreover, even when pointing out the " features " of a scene, people nowadays seldom talk long descriptions, whatever they used to talk in an earlier period of fiction.[9] Both shorter speeches and

[9] To one who trusts that contemporary literature a little more truly answers the universal purpose of literature—the accurate portrayal of existence—than did any writings of the past, the care with which it attempts to report conversation in such language as is individually typical and characteristic, seems significant. Literature that is striving for accuracy of report even in minor matters, and is succeeding in its effort, is not retrogressive nor decadent—not even though judged by critics whose standards are

shorter and more broken sentences are characteristic of most spontaneous, natural conversation. *Although, therefore, many settings cannot be detailed at length in dialogue, their effect and their most notable characteristics can be suggested or mentioned; but for the full and detailed account we must (a) either resort to the massed passage of description or (b) depend on facts that can be introduced briefly and quickly, and distributed skillfully, among the speeches.* An extended description can seldom be introduced into a single speech, and cannot always be so introduced even in a connected series of speeches, or passage of dialogue description.

14. Our conclusion is, that *facts of setting so introduced in dialogue must be chosen for their suggestive power and high descriptive effect*—for value rather than for amount. *The same is true when they are given along with any other form of action. They must be impressively representative facts,* sure to accumulate in the reader's mind as the definite and leading characteristics of a unified set of surroundings. The reader then creates for himself, through the co-operation of his own imagination, the more complete picture of this setting.

To illustrate:

" Get back there! Get back! Keep 'em from crowding in, Bill."

conservative or reactionary—men whose taste has been formed on older models, and who lack the adaptability or the creative adjustment to orient themselves in the present and thus appreciate the work of the present. Unfortunately, our educational machine finds, in the material supplied it, many heads made of suitable wood to be polished off after the old patterns, but only now and then one that can be trained and developed in the growing state.

" Is he hurt bad ? "

" Got his, I guess.   Smashed up pretty well anyhow.
Notify the station and get in an ambulance call quick.
I can't do anything.   Did any of you fellows get the
number of that machine ? "

Here are fifty words of dialogue.   Let us put the same
facts in another form—narrative and outright description :

The policeman bent over the twisted, unconscious form,
lying without movement in the street where the automobile
had flung it.   His mate from the next corner ran up to
join him, and the quickly gathered crowd of curious or
morbid passers-by and street-frequenters pressed around,
pushing to get over one another's shoulders a sight of
human broken bones and blood.

" Get back there !   Get back !   Keep 'em from crowding
in, Bill," the officer directed.

The crowd fell back reluctantly before the second
officer, unwilling to lose anything of the free show, and
avid even of such useless prominence as standing in the
front row of the spectators of disaster and being able
to recount intimately its details to the unimportant persons
who weren't there to see it.

" He's smashed up pretty well.   Looks like he's dead.
I can't do anything.   Turn in an ambulance call quick."

The policeman slipped the man's slouch hat in a softening wad between its owner's head and the pavement, and
while his companion was at the telephone, methodically
set down names and addresses of witnesses, with such
information as he could gather about the accident and the
number and appearance of the automobile.

15. Compare now the two forms of opening. In substance, each gives the same information, either telling outright or suggesting (a) setting, (b) action, and (c) situation. The second opening is longer than the first, and may seem to present more interpretive or descriptive fact. But really it does not do so; for whatever it tells out in full is readily supplied from his own knowledge by any reader who is at all acquainted with street accidents and the crowds that attend upon them. Unless, therefore, it be desirable to picture and analyze in order to meet the needs of less imaginative or less experienced readers,[10] the dialogue form has decided superiority, because of its compactness, rapidity, and adequate suggestion of all essentials presented by the fuller opening.[11]

16. Either of the two openings given above is sufficient to enlighten the reader on two main questions in which he is always interested: what has happened or is happening (the present situation), and the place of its happening. But they do not give information on certain other matters such as are frequently presented in the opening or early in the development. They do not tell us who the injured man is, nor even give us a hint of him otherwise, except that (second opening) he wears a slouch hat. Both leave us

[10] Herein is a pointed hint to writers of juvenile stories.

[11] As a corollary, we may mention this: *The extent to which an opening—or other passage—shall interpret, analyze, narrate acts, or picture forth in detail, must be determined by (a) the degree of realizing imagination which the reader may be assumed to possess, and (b) his probable familiarity with and understanding of such places, incidents, settings, and motives as are involved; together with (c) the author's general plan and purpose in the story,* this determining the introduction or exclusion of particular material according to its usefulness in striking the keynote or laying the foundation for later emphasis.

to guess for the present whether this man is to be the central person in the story; we may find later that the man in the automobile is the central figure, or that figure may possibly be the policeman, or even some one not indicated at all yet—say another man in an automobile, who stops to make inquiries and offers to take the victim to the hospital before the ambulance arrives. Neither can we tell certainly that all the action will not work itself out in the next few minutes at this one spot in the street, although we rather think that the setting will shift. Again, this incident may be only an introductory or ancillary episode employed merely for its effectiveness as an opening. Neither can we tell whether this opening incident significantly sounds the keynote of the story; we rather think not, for it seems tuned to action rather than to tone. But all such matters will come to light fully as the narrative proceeds—and only then shall we be able to say flatly that they should have been or need not have been brought out at the beginning. For we recall that on the whole the opening performs its chief function when it so puts us in suspense that we wish to read on. Indeed, this very *failure to satisfy outright curiosity that has been piqued, may be the author's means of creating the suspense.* The effect to be thus gained by courting curiosity, or interest, and satisfying it only by degrees, shows the importance, as narrative devices, of suspense and distributed information.

17. Approximately the same comment applies to CHARACTER as applies to setting in the opening. It may be presented outright in massed statement, or it may be suggested and indicated bit by bit through significant fact presented in the advancing dialogue and action. And in

each instance, the massed and formal presentation usually proves the less successful.[12]   Indeed, the formal, massed opening, presenting any sort of preliminary or accessory fact, is virtually nothing but an " introduction "—and *introductions belong to an earlier and (so we judge) less expert literary method.*

18. In truth, not only method but also taste has changed. To depend upon the " introduction " as a form of opening, even though the introduction be made the carrier of the exposition and other essentials to an understanding of the story, is to court rejection by many editors and by a good many readers. *The modern story needs a direct or immediate form of opening rather than an indirect or mediate form.* We are at once to " get down to brass tacks." For *on the whole, that interested looking-forward which we term suspense is not to be created* [13] *by anything but action, or at least the promise of action fast approaching.* Only in exceptional instances will the intrinsic interest of the materials be sufficient to arouse anticipating eagerness—the desire to run forward with the story, not to linger (pleasantly, perhaps, but aimlessly) with the mere accessories of situation and action. Persons acting: that is what the reader desires; we cannot assert it too often.

19. This explains why action is so desirable even at the beginning. *The reader will consent to be concerned with setting and atmosphere, background, character traits, theme and philosophizing as fiction materials, only when*

[12] The writer will gain by describing his characters fully in separate analyses or summaries, keeping these descriptions by him for reference as notes, but not incorporating them bodily in his story.

[13] Once created, however, it can be continued by other means. Thus, in the falling action, it is sustained by our anticipation of the outcome—our desire to see the fulfillment of the plot.

these things have a significance outside themselves and in the action whereof they are the mere convoy. True, they may motivate this action, modify it, explain it, further it, hinder it—in brief, make it. Yet it is the action that gives them their vitality, significance, and function. Even character, which in an earlier division of this book we named as being closest to life itself in interest for the human mind, depends on action for dramatic presentation. For *not until the deed is done is the character back of it made manifest.* Hence the indirect opening of philosophical comment—an opening which both the theme and the character story find of frequent use—is to be adopted only when all these considerations have been carefully weighed anew with reference to the particular story in hand; and unless it clearly recommend itself because of its especial fitness and applicability in the particular case, it is to be rejected in favor of an opening surer to rouse a forward-looking attention and directly advance the true action of the story.

20. Attempting now a SUMMARY of essential facts about the opening as a division of the conte, we say: The function of the opening is, to seize interest, strike the keynote, introduce action, and convey exposition. Its materials must not merely have intrinsic interest, but must be so managed that they create suspense—anticipative desire. The surest means of creating suspense is the presentation of action, and action should, therefore, be introduced early, if not at the very first; dialogue is a form of action. The fiction elements which the opening may present, or out of which it may be built up, are action, character, setting, and theme (atmosphere is sought more mediately; it comes from accurate reporting). In well-

managed openings, several of the purposes of the opening
are accomplished at once.   Openings may be direct or indirect; immediate or mediate; dynamic or static (active or
passive); and may either distribute their information or
mass it.   The massed opening is generally of the indirect,
mediate, static type, and of the nature of formal introduction rather than of dramatic opening, and the immediate,
direct, dynamic type is to be preferred unless the conception, aim, tone, or plan of the story as a whole makes
such a beginning unsuitable.

21.   Finally, we should note that, when once the writer
has mastered the technique of his craft, he should thereafter—whether in the opening or elsewhere—allow his imagination and personality free play, subjecting the technique to his purposes rather than subjecting himself to
his technique.   *For after all, the technique is but the
means of securing adequate expression of that which the
man and artist conceives.*

XIX.   In the Body of the Story, the Chief Con-structional Problem is That of Sequence

1.   After the opening comes the body of the story.   In
some stories, it will be very clearly marked off from the
beginning.   There may even be a break between the two
parts—a stopping and a beginning over.   The story with a
philosophical opening is especially likely to be of this
sort.   But whether such a break is or is not desirable, is
a matter for particular rather than for general consideration.   *The general rule would be that the less obvious the
break, the better.   Yet sometimes the complete effectiveness
of the opening is gained by just such a breaking off and*

starting over; it sets the substance of the opening apart clearly by itself, giving it emphasis and significance. *In every case, the break must be one of form or of substance only, not of motif or theme.* The true function of the opening—whatever form it take—is to prepare for or add to the effectiveness of the drama. Hence if the opening is not in effect a presentation in some form or guise of the *motif*—of the vital central thought and purpose—if it does not in some essential way prepare us for or introduce us to the story so vitalized—it neither is nor can be a unified, homogeneous part of the narrative. In the larger number of stories, however, the writer is likely to find an easy transition rather than an obvious break. Often the opening is, to all effects and purposes, an inseparable part of the very body of the story.

2. These facts bring us to the question, how shall the materials, especially the material of incident, be grouped and ordered in the story?—the problem of sequence or groupings. How can we determine the arrangement of incidents, events, descriptive passages, passages of interpretive comment, and the like, so that their potency will best be realized toward the totality of effect at which our story aims? We will answer the less important part of the question first. This is the part that concerns descriptive, interpretive, and all other merely CONTRIBUTORY AND ANCILLARY PARTS. This amplifying, realizing, and concentrative material, as we have already seen, is indispensable, not so much to the plot, it is true, as to the totality of effect sought through both the plot and these its accessories.

3. Nevertheless, all material of this sort is adjunct material, introduced and employed as an auxiliary rather than as a principal factor—even though in fiction, as in

war, the auxiliaries it sometimes is, and not the main force, that wins success. But whether in war or in literature, the operation of the auxiliaries is, theoretically if not always actually, subordinate to the operations of the main force. We may, therefore, set down safely the principle, that *whatever material is contributory, ancillary, concentrative, or amplifying merely, is to be made subordinate and secondary to that which is primarily essential to the plot and its outcome.*

4. In practice, this will be found to mean either of two things: A, the actual minimizing of the contributing material by reducing it in amount or putting it in inconspicuous positions in the narrative; B, the emphasizing of the material, but only as an important element in some division or part of the larger narrative (this occurs, for illustration, when a description, characterization, or incident is made the opening of a stage, or "movement," of the narrative, in such a way that the development of the stage or movement depends on this opening and largely draws its significance therefrom). *Such employment of contributory material by making it important in the development of a division, scene, or stage of the story, actually has the effect of making it less prominent in the completed narrative;* for the stage, or movement, as a whole, is that which is prominent in the completed story, and the individual parts and contributory elements are subordinated and merged in the division of which they are but a part.

5. Recognizing the necessity of subordinating to the main effect all merely ancillary materials, we then come to the problems of grouping and ordering THE MAIN FACTS AND MATERIALS—the stages and movements, the incidents and events. The first fact on which we must insist is,

that *all narrative is fundamentally chronological,* for it relates action, and action begins at one moment, continues through a succession of moments, and ends at another moment. As a succession of acts, incidents, or groups of incidents, the short story occupies time from its beginning through its continuance to its conclusion; hence the logical (i.e., most easily comprehensible and most natural) order of presenting these incidents, is the time order. So far as incident is concerned, this is the governing principle of all fiction.

6. But as drama and dramatic narrative have a more important purpose than merely to present the events in their original, or historical, sequence, each of these two forms of *fiction is permitted to tamper with the time order so far as may be necessary to accomplish the dramatic purpose.* But no further; mere inversion and transposition of incident for no other reason than that events can be so dislocated and relocated, is neither good artistry nor good sense. Moreover, whatever the displacement of events that is made in the course of the narrative, *this displacement must at the end have completely disappeared; the narrative must at the last leave us with the feeling of a sequence unbroken and perfect from beginning through continuance to conclusion.* Only upon acceptance of these conditions is the writer warranted in tampering with the actual historical, or time, order of events. On no other terms can he attain the effect of actual history; lacking which effect, he must fail of verisimilitude and therefore of belief.

7. The true time order, therefore, is not lightly to be discarded. Now, what is the true time order? We have already described it: from cause, through phenomena, to

final effect. Let us state in more amplified terms what this means. Plot action begins as soon as any complicating influence makes itself felt. Then ensues a period in which one set of influences resist another set of influences, until comes a time when something gives one of these sets a lasting advantage over the other, and either then or later, a complete triumph. This is the natural plot sequence; the narrative sequence may and may not be the same. In all narratives in which the two sequences—plot and narrative—are the same (i.e., the order of time), we shall have *first, the complicating influence and the response of some of the persons thereto (initial response); second, the period of resistant delay, in which the episodes or stages of the conflict march along, each duly following those that belong before it in point of time; third, the act, incident, or other decisive fact that predetermines the final outcome; and fourth, the outcome itself, either alone or telescoped into and practically one with number three.*[14]

8. When now we seek definite schemes for thus dislocating and relocating blocks or divisions of the action, we find various possible arrangements. Disregarding the separate existence of an " opening," we can indicate some of these in outlines, as follows:

[14] Note that the period of resistant delay does not always end with the decisive fact. Sometimes, as in the story showing the tragic advance of fate, the critical period, being one of unsuccessful struggle to escape a foredoomed catastrophe, wholly follows the decisive fact. Indeed, the decisive fact may be a wholly antecedent fact and therefore belong, not to the action at all, but to the exposition. In stories which do not telescope the ending, continuance of conflict beyond the decisive moment accounts in part for the continuance of interest past this point.

Non-Chronological Order-Schemes.

A.

1. Incident or other material belonging to the period of resistant delay.
2. Complicating influence, and the initial response.
3. Further resistant-delay materials.
4. Decisive fact.
5. Consequent facts.
6. Outcome.

B.

1. Facts belonging to the period that follows the decisive fact (the grand climax, in whole or in part).
2. Precedent facts belonging to the period of resistant delay.
3. Discovery of the complicating fact, with initial response.
4. Decisive fact.
5. Outcome.

C.

1. Action or incident constituting the initial response.
2. Discovery of the nature of the complicating influence (may be postponed to follow No. 3 or come even later).
3. Incident and other fact belonging to the period of resistant delay.
4. Decisive fact.
5. Consequent facts (including climactic situation).
6. Outcome.

D.

1. Facts belonging to the period of resistant delay.
2. The complicating influence and the initial response.
3. The decisive fact.
4. Further fact belonging to the resistant delay.
5. Facts consequent upon the decisive fact (including climactic situation).
6. The outcome (grand climax may be included here instead of in No. 5).

E.

1. The outcome.
2. Facts belonging to the resistant delay.
3. The complicating fact and the initial response (No. 3 may change place with No. 2).
4. Decisive fact (may be either preceded or followed by No. 5).
5. Facts consequent on decisive fact.
6. The outcome.

9. The student is now warned explicitly that the schemes given above are (first) merely general and suggestive and (second) subject to further expansion and rearrangement. He will, therefore, please take them as they are meant to be taken—as hints, not as hard and fast sequences. In association with them, a few other significant matters may be mentioned. One is, that " outcome " is not necessarily the same as " ending "; the closing part of the story will be discussed later. Another is, that the entire body of facts belonging to any phase of the narrative—initial response, resistant delay, etc.—may be distributed. Although useful generally, this principle

is likely to be most observed in introducing facts that belong to the resistant delay or to the complicating influence. For instance, it is not uncommon to give just enough of the complicating influence in connection with the initial response to make this response intelligible, the remaining facts about the complication being revealed elsewhere, as they are needed.

10. We may here SUM UP the results of our consideration of sequence so far as we have advanced with it. The controlling order is always that of time (historical sequence); when the time order is not followed, the arrangement of the materials must be such as nevertheless to give the reader the feeling of historical sequence; and the time order is to be abandoned only when abandonment is necessary in order to attain a more impressive dramatic effect not possible with the plain historical sequence. Ancillary material is always to be kept subordinate, this implying either (a) actual inconspicuousness or else (b) actual prominence, but only in the development of some important phase, part, or movement of the story—the effect of the ancillary material being then realized, not directly, but indirectly, through the successful management of the movement which it helps to develop.

11. But all this is general and abstract, if not vague. What are the rules, put in plain, straightforward statement, that will enable one to tell HOW BEST TO ORDER INCIDENTS AND EVENTS, and group other materials of his story? That question I cannot answer very fully, nor have I found it very fully answered by others. Perhaps but one sentence of instruction can safely be written concerning the compositional construction of all stories equally, and that is, *Tell the story as you conceive it*. Study the story

in all its aspects; seek out its possibilities; consider the materials that are available; select those that are indispensable to your plot or the effect you intend; consider these materials in various groupings and combinations, estimating their effectiveness in all reasonable groupings; try out different ways of motivating, of characterizing, of indicating setting and atmosphere; weigh the effectiveness of different openings and various endings. Then—write.

12. *Clarify your conception and master your material. Then trust yourself.* Write the story as you conceive it, and rewrite it until it stands as you conceived it. If you are an artist, your conception once matured is of higher authority than all the formal rules of composition ever worded, and ultimately will override and subject them to its purpose instinctively. This is no counsel to a slap-dash, inspiration-of-the-moment method; for whether your conception spring full-grown and all equipped and panoplied from your Jovian brain, or whether (which is more probable) it be brought forth with long labor-pains and perfected only through infinite care and thought, does not matter. Matured it must be ere it can be transformed into a worthy story. And it is only you who can thus mature and thus transform it into the artist's product that will satisfy you and serve the world. The conclusion of the whole matter, then, is but a general commandment: Conceive your story clearly as a whole, then clearly plan and write it as you conceive it, both (a) as a whole and (b) in its parts. This done, the result is on the knees of the gods, who made you what you are: a literary genius or —something else.[15]

[15] Study of photoplays of the better class is recommended. True, the photoplay is almost always strictly chronological. But the

13. But there is one aim which the author will have in mind in all his efforts to find a satisfactory ordering of incident and situation: to *make each scene, when this is possible, " cue" the scene that is to follow.* If one movement, drawing to an end, has already brought forward persons and laid a stage of fact, whereon these persons will begin to enact the next scene, much has been gained in the way of smoothness and closeness of connection. What goes before introduces what next succeeds; one scene inducts the next; the close of one situation is the cue for the entrance of the next. *At times, however, such " cueing" may not be desirable. Emphasis, distinction, organization, may all gain if there be a curtain-fall between the scenes—if one conclude cleanly within itself, and the next begin sharply anew.* If each represents an important movement of the action, if they are managed well, and if they are logically grouped with reference to the main effect and plot, the mere fact that they are sharply defined

very skill with which the sequence is kept chronological will be illuminative. See the play several times, in order to become thoroughly familiar with it; it will pay to make a list of the scenes for study. Then rewrite the play as a short story. The plot, action, and total effect being already provided, the first attempt can confine itself to reproducing plot and action unchanged, merely (a) filling in setting and providing atmosphere material, (b) developing dialogue and indicating character, and (c) supplying connection and transition between scenes. As step two, rewrite more freely, adhering in the main to the picture story, but modifying, amplifying, compressing, and adding to, as may be necessary in order to produce a word narrative as fluent in its workmanship as was the photoplay in a different manner. Finally, rebuild the story completely, retaining the original plot-embryo, but otherwise departing from the photoplay presentation as much as possible. This will help to develop facility in adapting materials to varied methods.

one from the other in the body of the story will produce no incoherence. Rather, the emphasis and distinction gained by each through this independence will make their co-operative effect the stronger. The cueing of one scene by another, therefore, may not always be best.

14. Now, while incident and event are being grouped to create the movements which together constitute the body of the story, the other fiction elements must also be given place. Let us consider them. Suspense, we saw, is interest hurrying forward to be satisfied; and nothing draws interest on so much as ACTION. Significant action, therefore, is as important in the body of the story as in the opening. It need not proceed at a racing gallop; it may advance with the slow, steady finality of a great river, it may seethe and eddy like a strong tide in a cliff-bound cove, or it may ebb and flow with the regularity of the same tide on an open shore. But always it must be there, and even when it ebbs, he who in his reading barque has set out to sail in any of the waters of dramatic fiction must be able to perceive its current or feel its groundswell, and sense its returning flood. Whether the action be all compressed into one event, or whether it consist of episodes and stages, always the current of interest must be there, bearing on the anticipative reader. And to continue the metaphor, if it can carry him forward up to the very last, and then, with a final mighty sweep cast him upon the shore or point of outcome that he sought—why, so much the better.

15. CHARACTERIZATION affords an illustration of the impossibility of laying down universal principles for the exact placing of fiction materials. One might, for example, be tempted to advise that, in the case of important persons, the chief body of characterizing matter be given at once.

But often it would prove undesirable, if not impossible, thus to give at once either an epitome of the character traits or any considerable body of fact concerning single traits. Much of the interest, pleasure, and value of association with persons in fiction comes, not from receiving a sudden, sun-burst revelation of their character, but from getting acquainted with their character by degrees, as one gets acquainted with the character of the persons whom he knows in actual life.

16. But indeed, complete and immediate characterization is not always advisable even were it possible. For one thing, characterization is best accomplished through dialogue and action; and at once to introduce enough dialogue or action fully to set forth a character, even if it be the character of the principal person, might force us to abandon the original story merely to provide characterization in another form for the leading person. True, characterization by means of description remains; but the dramatic narrator is always cautious about introducing description, and wisely so. For a single person, portrayal through description might be satisfactory; but if several important persons must be introduced, each with his appropriate portion of character-description, the earlier part of the narrative may be crowded so full of this indirect matter as to resemble nothing as much as a fictional pouter-pigeon.

17. The best we can say, therefore, is this: *Unless the temporary concealment or suppression of character is necessary to the plan of the story, the introduction of each important person is usually well accompanied by characterization. This shall be more or less complete, and accomplished by one means or another, according to circum-*

stances. Ordinarily it is the dominant or decisive character trait that is shown; but for purposes of contrast, surprise, etc., an opposite or different trait may be first adduced. The italicized direction given just above we may supplement with another: *as persons without character are uninteresting, every important person must, on first presenting himself, give clear evidence that he possesses character.*[16] Otherwise we shall refuse to become interested in him and his doings, and that will be fatal to the story. We may, indeed, when we first meet an actor in the story, not realize what his character is; we may even be led to think it something different from what it is; but this one thing we must perceive quickly—that there is something significant in him, and that this significance will become manifest as the narrative proceeds.

18. The student will now perceive that characterizing material may be so ordered within the story that *the initial characterization will tend to be either (a) inclusive, and hence conclusive, or (b) incomplete and hence not necessarily conclusive.* If it be inclusive, it will summarize, or total up at once, the chief traits of the person, and put in encyclopedic or in epitomic form the leading facts that otherwise one could accumulate only in the process and progress of his reading. (Incidentally, we will note here

[16] Of course no one is without character; but character may be so weak or colorless as to seem uninteresting. Persons of such sort we are likely to describe as being without character. In doing so, we are wrong. They have character, and their character, if artfully reported or interpreted to us, will prove interesting. Here then, as always, we come back to the ability of the writer to see, report, and interpret, and our direction amounts only to a caution that the writer shall be especially careful in showing forth the significance of character in introducing his persons, especially if they be persons of the colorless, unimpressive sort.

that this method of placing characterization is, broadly speaking, typical of romantic rather than of realistic stories —romance being the deductive and realism the inductive method of fiction.)

19. Following such an introductory epitome, characterization is likely to be less prominent in the remaining presentation; for the author is likely to feel that, having given his reader a complete portrayal at the first, he need not develop it thereafter. He thereafter does his duty as character-showman by acting rather as demonstrator than as describer or expositor—by bringing forward from time to time, that is, references to or instances of characteristic traits already made known, thus merely illustrating them or recalling them to the reader's mind. In such instances, characterization may deteriorate into initial description and subsequent memory-tickling. We would not be understood as holding this method, well used, to be illegitimate or non-effective; but manifestly it has serious dangers and, for some purposes, serious weaknesses.

20. Having mentioned these, we ought also to mention a particular use that can sometimes be effectively made of the more inclusive initial portrayal—that of bringing forward at once the dominant character. Whatever initial description may lack as compared with action as a means of character presentation and as a suspense creator, it at least cannot fail to notify the reader that the person with which it is dealing so exhaustively is an important person in the action that is to follow; and the mind will quickly jump to the conclusion that the person so prominently brought forward at the first is the person on whom the story will center. Hence, as a device for focusing thought on this person, the full initial description is frequently useful.

If, therefore, the initial characterization can, by the introduction also of action elements, or in other wise, be made to produce in the reader a desire to see more of this important person, it justifies itself by success.

21. Of ENVIRONMENTAL FACTS, we must speak according as they constitute respectively setting or atmosphere material. The placing of facts that are primarily a part merely of the setting, is governed largely by one principle. As on the stage the rising of the curtain, followed soon if not immediately by action, reveals the stage already set, so in the conte the first of any action movement may well find the setting already indicated. *The essential facts about place, time, physical background, etc., are best indicated just before the action begins that is to take place in their setting, or when, the action having already been motivated or introduced, the setting becomes necessary to an understanding of the activity that is about to follow*— for example, when the two rivals have met and are about to fight; the nature of the fighting-place being important in the encounter, as when Bertram the Dauntless hurls the traitorous Count de Bun Quome from the beetling crag into a bevy of Hottentot maidens holding a sewing-circle character interment in the meadow far, far below.

22. The introduction into the narrative, however, of the setting just before the events are related that are to develop in it, is less effective than is the pre-provided stage set in the theater. For on the stage, the stage-set is actually before the eye throughout the action; when the hero's manly foot approaches the verge of the cliff, we then and there see the verge. We are not under the necessity of harking back and recalling that before him is an abyss that yawns. In narration, on the contrary, the setting must

be carried in memory; we must either recollect the yawning abyss, or the action must be stopped while the yawn is being explained to us—a thing mightily relaxing to suspense. *To overcome the consequent difficulties arising from this fact—the loss of vividness and of accurate realization of setting—narrative uses the method of distributed description.* Either (a) the items are mentioned only as they become immediately important in the action, or else (b) an inclusive outline of setting having been provided at some convenient place, its items are again referred to at the appropriate points in order to renew the suggestion of actuality and bring back the picture to us. These suggestions simply may recall facts already introduced, or they may go further, rementioning the principal facts of the setting already outlined, but adding further detail, thus not only vivifying the description, but also filling in and rounding out the original sketch.

23. The results that follow a successful introduction of the massed setting-statement (without or with the aid of distributed reinforcing statement) illustrate what can be done toward integration by subordinating and emphasizing materials at the same time (cf. XIX. 4). Integration means the working together into a homogeneous whole of all the varied materials that the author selects with which to tell his story and produce his effect. To introduce the setting-description just before the events for which it constitutes the stage, is to emphasize it by giving it prominence of place and space; if the narrative passage dealing with that group of facts with which this setting associates itself be reviewed, the setting parts will probably be found to stand forth prominently. The result of this prominence is important. First, it impresses the reader with an under-

standing of the locale of the action. But beyond this, it incorporates itself into the total effect of the story, because the feeling of this locale incorporates itself into the action. When, therefore, the action itself integrates with the larger story, this feeling—largely one of atmosphere—is carried with it and integrated also with the larger effect of the story. *By emphasizing indirect material in a subordinate relationship, we have both kept it subordinate to the narrative as a whole, and accomplished also the opposite thing and made it (but inobviously) prominent in due proportion in the effect of the story as a whole.* Thus all things do work together for good to them that love the artistically well-subdued and well-proportioned.

24. Dropping now the problem of mere setting, and taking up rather the problem of the placing of all atmosphere material, we find ourselves able to state no such absolute rules. But this will not surprise us when we recall that atmosphere is after all a flavor and impression, produced jointly and indifferently by the nature and quality of all the materials in the story together with the manner of treatment they receive from the author—a manner which itself is largely determined by the author's personality. Since there is no such thing, strictly speaking, as atmosphere material—or rather, since strictly speaking everything is atmosphere material—we cannot hope to analyze this material out and give separate rules for its separate management. As atmosphere is a quality found throughout the story, so the materials producing the impression of atmosphere are found in every part of the story. We must, therefore, confine ourselves to this one generalization. *Although whatever enters into the narrative should in some degree at least contribute to the impression of*

atmosphere, this impression should be especially emphasized in the opening and be well established and thoroughly confirmed by the time the narrative reaches its climactic height. Beyond the point of climax, any attempt to create an atmosphere not already felt will be unsuccessful in itself, and will in all probability break the other effects already produced. *The atmosphere should be felt early in the narrative, and fully realized in time to enter into and become a part of the climactic situation.*

25. We have now considered various particular devices, methods, and principles involved in the effective ordering of the incidents and events, and of the two other elements of dramatic narrative fiction—character and setting. Yet we find that the problem of the ordering and distribution of material remains specifically unsolved—that no arbitrary, universal set of directions exists by which these materials can always be assembled with the desired result. Even when we have been most dogmatic in wording statements, we have found ourselves compelled to refer these statements for final sanction to an object and purpose outside of the mere narrative sequence. *We have always to consider our narrative methods with a view to their final effect, the production through dramatic process of a dominant, single impression.*

26. Now out of this fact—the fact that the success of the conte centers in a single definite impression—comes another hint, and an important one, for the ordering of story materials. *This one dominant impression is the total effect of a body of lesser impressions, each pretty definitely made by itself, and all integrated into a larger, homogeneous whole. But at some point in the narrative one such contributing impression will be made that is*

deeper, that stirs and affects the reader more strongly, than any of the others, because it represents the culmination in a climactic situation—the height of suspense, interest, and emotion—of all the impressions that have preceded it.

27. This climactic height, or emotional acme, is that one situation toward which all the story moves (except possibly near the end—and then the movement is merely a quick, conclusive falling away from it, in so much of an ending as, and no more than, is necessary to bring the final stop). The importance of this climactic situation—already strongly emphasized—is the reason for stating the following important rule: *In any story, use that method of ordering and distribution which best prepares for, brings on, and strengthens the grand climax. For without an impressive climactic situation, there will be no strong impression from the story as a whole;* the unifying appliance will be missing from the machine—the parts will be assembled, but they will not be connected up. The further fact that usually those stories are most effective in which the grand climax is also the close, points clearly to the need of an arrangement by which *the climactic situation shall if possible be also the closing situation of the story as a whole.*

XX. THE ENDING, IF SEPARATE FROM THE CLIMACTIC
      MOMENT, EXISTS MERELY TO SUPPLEMENT AND
      CLOSE THE NARRATIVE

1. We have already indicated the most effective, and on the whole most desirable, form of ending—that which is involved in or closely follows upon the climactic moment. A few sentences more should, therefore, be enough

to dispose of this form of ending. But to prepare for them, we must first explain the function of the close. Stated in popular rather than in scientific terms, it is this: To *leave the reader with the feeling that the story has not only stopped, but actually is finished*—to produce the sense of a rounded-out completeness of events and consequences. It exists to prevent a restless after-feeling of " something left undone " when the story has been laid aside.

2. To leave the reader thus satisfied, is not necessarily to leave him satisfied with the outcome of the events; with this he may or may not be content. He may, for instance, be a believer in the " happy " ending, and, therefore, be disappointed with the story that has chosen to pursue the tragic workings of cause and effect to a logical unhappy ending, rather than to compose a less significant story of the " lived happy ever after " (so far as we choose to tell) sort. But if the story, whatever its individual nature, spirit, and outcome, leave the reader in full possession of the facts, with nothing reasonably to be asked further about the persons, action, or situation, it satisfies him in our sense of the term. He has seen the wheels go round that make up one tiny movement of the great timepiece of existence, and he has seen why these particular wheels go as they do; the purpose of the ending was to finish up this exhibition and explanation. Or, remembering that the short story, or conte, is but a fragmentary glimpse, a tiny cameo, representing in relief some single bit of life, we may say that the ending represents the last few gravings that bring up the relief into perfect clearness, which otherwise would have remained flat and obscure, making the gem appear poor and unfinished.

3. If now the climactic situation, together with what goes before and prepares for it, does not thus completely satisfy the curiosity of the reader to know thoroughly what (so long as it be material) actually befell in this isolated bit of life—if it does not constitute a complete close to its particular series of events, and leave him, moreover, in clear possession of the central thought of the story— then something must be added to provide this additional information or enforcement, in order that the reader shall lay aside the story with the full sense of interest satisfied. *The function of the separate ending is, to discharge whatever smaller parts remain unpaid of the debt of suspense when the climactic situation has been fully drawn upon.*

4. To make the grand climax likewise the satisfying close, two things will be necessary: First, an adequate revelation of the inevitable results of the conflict; second, a climactic situation which is in itself final and conclusive. The attainment of the first object—the revelation of the results inevitable upon the outcome—calls for what we may term *consequential exposition; that is, exposition of after-results as well as of initial situation,* a disclosure of what the after-situation will be as well as what the beginning situation was. The revelation of the inevitable consequences of the outcome is indispensable, for without it the narrative will be either ambiguous or else wholly obscure; the reader will be uncertain of the consequences involved in the conflict, and the conflict itself will, therefore, be deprived of definiteness and critical intensity. Watching a man struggling in the river, we shall feel great suspense if we know he is trying to save himself from drowning; and we shall feel some curious interest (suspense) if we know that he is merely an actor whose " stunt " is being

" filmed " for the " movies "; but we shall be troubled and irritated if we are left quite in doubt whether anything is wrong or not, and if anything is wrong, what it is. We say, therefore, that *although the conflict in dramatic narrative should keep us in doubt of the outcome; and although the outcome itself does not have to be inevitable, but only plausible and probable under the conditions supposed; yet the consequences that will follow the outcome must on the contrary be evident, definite, and sure, presenting themselves to us as inevitable.*

5. Sometimes this revelation of inevitable consequences dependent upon the outcome will be given by the disclosure of the complication and the development of the plot conflict. But not always; stories in which complication, conflict, and thoroughly interesting action exist are quite possible without an indication of the exact nature, the details, of the results that will follow the outcome. *It is only when the story is made fully to reveal these after-consequences, and to reveal them before the grand climax is reached, or at least before it is passed, that the climactic situation can conclusively end the story.* Coppée's *The Substitute* is a good example of the story in which this revelation is completed before and in the climactic situation. True, Coppée does add one sentence after the close of this situation: " Today he is at Cayenne, condemned for life as an incorrigible." But this sentence is not necessary. No reader but would understand from what has gone before that a further conviction of the ex-convict who is assuming another's guilt, will mean the terrific cumulation upon him of his earlier offenses and criminal record, unlightened by his later reformation. Possibly the words " for life " in the sentence quoted, add something

to our information—but not much; we knew before that it was colossal tragedy. And unless the reader is familiar with the horrible prison reputation of Cayenne already, the mention of Cayenne tells him nothing more; whereas if he knows it, he knows too that there men of the sort Jean François is supposed to be, are sent. We may, therefore, regard this sentence as superfluous; in which case Coppée's story ends absolutely with the closing words of the climactic situation: "Forward, bad lot!" and we know that Leturc's past has "got" him, tragically and ruinously.

6. When, however, the climactic situation does not in truth constitute a sufficient rounding out of the story, we have the distinct ending. This ending will be either of two things: interpretive or philosophical comment, or a passage in which is contained the revelation of the final results of the outcome. *The interpretive, or philosophical-comment ending, can be justified only when there is need of clinching the theme, express or implied, or of directing attention extraneously and pointedly to the effect intended.* This may be necessary when the story is written as a theme story, or when the nature of the material handled, or the point of view chosen, produces a somewhat more loosely-wrought narrative than is theoretically admirable. The ending of comment or interpretation is especially likely to occur in stories that open with philosophical or interpretive prelude. A particular form of this ending goes usually with narrative told from the viewpoint of spectator or participant; it is that in which the effect of the events or other elements in the narrative upon some person is reported. This person may be either a participant, a spectator, the narrator, or one of his supposed auditors. Example:

"Good God!" exclaimed Vansburgh, rising and looking about the café in horror. "That thing happened here?"

"At this very table."

Vansburgh gazed at the Lieutenant in a terrified fascination; he was white and trembling.

"Right there," continued the officer, pointing a slow steady finger at a place just beside the other.

Vansburgh's eyes dilated as he gazed—one would have said he saw the thing re-enact itself beside him. Then, with a gurgling cry, he reeled hastily to the door. A minute later we heard his big motor-car leap away from the curb in frantic haste.

The student will observe, however, that such an ending calls for an almost complete transfer of attention from the persons and action of the plot, to persons and action quite outside it—necessarily breaking the unity of narrative if not the unity of attention. It is, therefore, less artistic than an ending which closes at once the plot narrative and the story as a whole; but it may nevertheless be made necessary by the plan of narration chosen by the author. The lesson is this: do not without full consideration choose a plan of narration that requires such a break; respect the unity of action and of attention.

7. The ending is common which shows some person or persons belonging to the events, experiencing the after-results of the outcome. It may take the form of further narration—the persons appearing in action under the new set of conditions—or of dialogue, the persons by their conversation revealing what these results are. It may also take the form of direct statement by the narrator (see the sentence quoted in par. 5, which is an unusually short

ending of this class). Again, it may merge into that form of interpretive ending in which the story is interpreted by indicating the effect produced by it on particular individuals (see par. 6). We have already said that brevity is essential in the endings. But in one sort of story (e.g., *Xingu,* by Edith Wharton) the effect is got, not from the conflict, but from seeing the persons undergoing the results of the outcome. In such a story, the ending will be longer; or we might perhaps say that the plot outcome brings us merely to the exciting moment, so far as the total effect is concerned, and that the ending is in the nature of developing detail. In *Xingu,* which is satirical, the effect of the satire against pretentious ignorance in club-women is got by means of a long ending showing what occurred after the women discovered the hoax of which they had been the victims; this hoax is revealed comparatively early in the narrative. Some students may prefer to call this ending the falling action of the story—which indeed, from the viewpoint of plot theory, it is. The distinction is not, however, fundamentally important here, except as showing the possibility of constructing plots wherein (contrary to the customary fact) the effect is secured in and through the falling action.

XXI. A Preliminary Scheme of Important Compositional Facts Will Help the Author

1. The short story, or conte, is a dramatic report of some coherent bit of life. Therefore, as a report, it must cover the ground. To do so artistically and not merely as a chronicle, it must attend to a certain set of essential facts, assembling and managing all its materials with reference

to these facts; in looser but more familiar phrase, it must look out for certain points—attend to particular matters that will make or unmake the story. All of these " points " have been touched upon more or less specifically in the progress of our discussion; and here, therefore, we can set down a list of *matters which the writer should have clearly in mind* when he enters upon the actual composition of his story.[17] Most writers will gain time, definiteness, and effectiveness by using such a catalogue, filling it out completely in advance, consulting it during composition, and checking up the completed story by means of it.

2. This catalogue or scheme may take some form like that which follows.

In My Story

A. The theme is..................................
B. The working-plot is............................
C. The effect aimed at is.........................
D. The main complicating fact is..................
E. The dominant mood of the story is..............
F. The dominant person is.........................
G. The dominant character trait is................
H. The motivating facts are.......................
    ....
I. The decisive situation is......................
J. The climactic situation is.....................
K. The outcome is.................................

3. This scheme may be supplemented with another,

[17] The catalogue is revised from that given in Professor Pitkin's valuable book, *The Art and Business of Story Writing*.

listing further matters that, in any story, are likely to call for especial attention; namely—

L. The main setting is...........................
M. The atmosphere quality to be emphasized is.......
N. The foiling, balancing, or contrast elements are:
     (1) Persons and character.................
     (2) Setting ....
     (3) Situation ....
     (4) The anti-theme (theme denied, or in reverse) ....
O. The concentrative episodes are.................
P. The "identifying tags" are:
     (1) For the individual persons............
     (2) For atmosphere......................
     (3) For dialect:
          a. Ordinary speech...................
          b. Dialect ....
     (4) Occupation ....
     (5) Character trait......................
Q. The surprise lies in...........................

4. The supplementary list just given is not represented to be complete. It does give some of the commonest considerations that enter into the making of particular stories, or that belong to the more advanced stages of composition in any story. But every story involves peculiar elements which can be known only to the author as he works out its plot and plan; hence a scheme such as ours can be suggestive merely. Some such list should, however, be used; for in writing, as elsewhere, prevision and provision are worth any amount of patching up by hindsight.

CHAPTER IV

OTHER PROBLEMS OF FICTION-WRITING

XXII. Observance of Certain " Unities " Prevents
Dispersal of Effect

1. Approaching the short story from other points of
view, we find various other problems—such for instance
as choice of theme or of *motif,* choice and management of
particular materials and content, etc.—not all of them
strictly problems of technique or of the conte alone, but
all of them important in its final making. Some of these
we shall now consider, beginning with the problem of
unity.

2. The true short story (conte) is characterized, as
we have seen, by a single dominant effect. Some would
say, worthy effect; but the worthiness of the effect is not
essential so much to the artistic as to the ethical requirements of literature. It is possible so to construct a story,
and so to manipulate the materials and employ in the
narrative the devices of fiction, as to elevate an absolutely
trivial idea or emotion into the dignity of an effect. But
such an exalting of the trivial is a triumph of mere
technique; it is not informed with the high spirit of creative art; and the result is a toy, a curiosity, an interesting
yet useless by-product of the worker's skill, inspired
by vanity or idleness. It is like the models of ships,
complete sometimes in every detail, made by seafaring
gentlemen with a knack for tools and a fondness for the

sunny side of a water-butt, and landfaring ditto with too much time on their hands, owing to a similar fondness for the leeward side of a sun-touched wall.

3. Actual moral unworthiness we cannot, of course, afford. Nor are many artists found who indulge it, or show a tendency to do so. *All art, even of mediocre rank, seems in its serious efforts to have behind it a moral purpose, if not indeed to spring immediately from moral impulse. Earnest writers are animated by a desire for truth (even for* THE *truth, if it can be found by man)—and this very fact often accounts for their writing of things shocking to the great, laissez-faire public,* which any Lancelot Gobbo can see is sometimes, morally, stone-gravel blind. We need not insist on the matter here, but we shall be warranted in noting that time usually vindicates such writers, at last bringing a more plodding and dull-eyed world clumping flat-soled along the way which lighter-footed, keener-visioned men saw and traveled long before . . . grunting with satisfaction at having discovered it themselves; whereas they have merely chanced upon the trail broken by unappreciated pioneers whom they used to scorn. Another reason why we should not insist upon " moral aim," or whatever cant phrase may be in fashion at any time for the thing itself, is this: *the artistic conscience is not to be tampered with or constrained by outsiders; the deep-seeing, far-scanning artist (usually justified, as we have just remarked, by " the long results of time ") cannot do his work in the world with loyalty to either art or general welfare if he is to be bent to the constraints of anything but his own conscience, emotions, and judgment.*[1]

[1] " Emotions," because so great a part of human progress, law, and government, are founded upon feeling. The war between the

Nothing is more cruel, nothing more bigoted, nothing more blind to and destructive of the usefulness of art, than this imposition of stolid, stodgy, often stupid, standards by a generation educated just enough to believe in the value of morality, but not educated enough to comprehend the foundations of morality.

4. So much in digression about the worthiness, artistic and moral, of the impression at which the short story aims; now for consideration of that impression as the source of unity in the narrative. For *the unity of the narrative drama is to be judged solely by the unity, strength, and*

states was a war of emotions—and the after-results have shown that, so far as the merely reasoned arguments of the two sides are concerned, both were largely erroneous. Our war with Spain was emotional. At least two of the important political parties now existing are, or were at their founding, the outcome of deeply-felt emotion. The many so-termed reform measures now being enacted into law, and the innumerable humanitarian and philanthropic undertakings that characterize our times, are at bottom emotional. The analytical historian can thus trace some of the greatest movements of human development to the emotions as a source.

The fact that emotions play so great a part in our affairs, makes any sort of censorship unwholesome that attempts to interfere with the development or cultivation of the emotions, or with the direction of our feelings to particular ends. Such attempts cannot be prejudged, even by so great seers, prophets, and sages as police inspectors and commissioners. Their sole test is their successful or unsuccessful working out according to their own nature. Few of us would not prefer to live in a twentieth rather than in an eighteenth century—which fact may be taken as indicating in an empirical sort of way that on the whole the results of having things work out their own way are making a better world from generation to generation. Censorship of any sort is to be looked upon with suspicion; but censorship of art—attempts to interfere with the cultivation or direction of the emotions by the men whose whole business in life it is to see deep into and far over existence —is probably never warranted.

singleness of this effect. A story may violate all the canons of rhetorical unity, and yet (provided it be successfully motivated) triumphantly take its place among true short stories, if only it leave with the reader this strong single impression.

5. How shall this unity of impression be brought about?[2] We must still bear in mind the perpetual warning, that with the true artist all things are possible—that even the most absolute dogma of story-writing theory may at any time be upset by skilled achievement taking a different way. No principle can safely be declared universal. Therefore, although we now state the usual, we are not stating the universal when we say that *next to unity of action (par. 14), the surest way of providing for the single effect is to make one leading person the dominant person in the three phases of plot, action, and characterization.*[3] If the plot depends on and turns about a single person; if the main part of the action either is carried on by this person, or else, though carried on by others, yet keeps him rather than them in the front of attention; and if

[2] The all-inclusive answer to the question is this: *By attending carefully to all those matters which produce (a) verisimilitude, (b) convergence to a dramatic climax with a conclusive outcome, and (c) subjective coloring.* The paragraphs in the text aim merely to suggest particular means and devices by which this thorough integration may be achieved.

[3] He may be the dominant person in the plot-action without being the center of interest. Thus, in *The Hahnheimer Story* (by Arthur James Pegler, *Adventure*, March, 1914), the reporter, Singleton, is the dominant person, but the interest is in the group of men, all yellow journalists, with whom he stands in contrast. What he does is important only in providing a means of characterizing these others collectively.

this person, as the leading object of our interest, is more fully and individually characterized than the others;— then at the end we are almost sure to find that *the total impression, being thus gathered up in the fate of this person, is thoroughly unified.*

6. A few hints will be useful concerning the management of portrayal in order thus effectively to develop the full strength of the person in the drama. First of all, *the character (and sometimes the appearance) of the person must be fully conceived.* The writer must know this person's traits, habits, mannerisms of thought and action; otherwise he cannot depict him, but will at best turn out one who is only a type or a stock personage, not both a type and an individual. Second, *only the peculiarly usable characteristics must be portrayed.* For singleness of impression, these have to be kept few in number; *abundance and variety of trait and mannerism may be suggested, but the number actually presented must be few, and frequently the greatest concentration of effect is obtained by emphasizing one trait only*—the dominant one. Mannerisms of speech and action will naturally be chosen with a view to manifesting, explaining, and otherwise emphasizing the leading trait of character.

7. Third, *the characteristics of the person must be portrayed mainly through act and speech;* to present a character in a piece of dramatic fiction by means of description or expository comment is a mistake, provided the same facts can as well be presented by showing the persons in action. Similarly, for the narrator in his own person to present them descriptively is poor art, if he can portray them through the acts or speech of persons in the story. The author may tell us that Smith is a liar; but

this is not half so effective as to have Jones, a person in the story, say of his fellow-person: " Smith ?   Oh, he's a gold-medal liar."   That at once tickets both Smith and Jones ; moreover, it makes us feel as if we had heard Jones telling what he thinks of Smith—we *realize* it better. Fourth, *only the most impressive manifestation of a trait should be presented.*   Guarding always against sensationalism, the author should as far as possible present the most vivid, striking, and impressive deeds and speeches whereby the person manifests his character.

8.   Fifth, *although the various elements of the person's character ought to be enough suggested to prevent a sense of distortion, yet this part of the portrayal should be restricted as much as is consistent with just perspective.* Finally (and this comes near to summarizing the whole matter), *the person should always be shown in some activity that directly furthers the plot-action, in preference to that which will leave the plot unadvanced; but all that he does should, while advancing the plot-action, also reveal or explain his own character.*[4]

9.   The principles here stated are equally applicable in the case of less important persons, so long as the importance of these persons is kept subordinate to that of the leading actor.   About the portrayal of subordinate,

[4] Probably it is unnecessary to explain that the rule of plot utility just stated must be applied with judgment.   At times it may be worth while for the sake of characterization, theme enforcement, or atmosphere creation, to show the person in activity that does not *directly* further the plot.   *There may even be times when delay in or postponement of the plot-action will be desirable.* The author must use his judgment in determining how far he shall go in the employment of merely concentrative or amplifying material when presenting his leading person.

or secondary, persons, however, two facts should be noted. That the secondary person is less important to the final total effect, suggests that he should be portrayed with less fullness; accordingly, *the presentation of subordinate persons is, in comparison with the portrayal given leading persons, more sketchy and incomplete; and, whereas, the leading person is a type individualized, the subordinate person is likely to be merely the type or (possibly) merely the individual.* A fuller portrayal might result in disproportion in the completed narrative, and, even more unfortunately, in putting forward another person to compete with the dominant actor for our attention. The other fact to be noted is this: *Subordinate persons, especially when serving as foils and introduced primarily to offset or otherwise emphasize the dominant person, may sometimes be satisfactorily portrayed through expository description or comment where downright action would be used with the dominant person.* Such presentation enables rapid and summary portrayal to be made, thus preserving proportion and due subordination. It has too the advantage of permitting (by way of implied or directly stated contrast) comment upon and explanation of the dominant character, and of introducing this explanatory matter in the lower levels of suspense and the subordinate parts of the narrative, where it will not hinder or clog the action.

10. But although—excepting unity of action (par. 14) —unity of person (and, therefore, unity of character) is the commonest and on the whole the most dependable means for securing unity of narrative [5] and unity of impression,

[5] Emphatically, this assertion is not to be wrenched into commendation of the "history-of-a-life" or "from-the-cradle-to-the-

other means are often equally successful. There is, for example, *unity of time—the association of the events and persons so closely in time that they seem to belong naturally to the same body of fact and happening.* Turning this fact end-for-end, we may say this: when matters, even though otherwise closely associated, are widely separated in time, it becomes more difficult to think of them together. Therefore, *it is better that, for time unity, all the events be confined to a comparatively short and unbroken period.* What this period shall be is better left to the judgment of the writer when he comes to build his plot and determine the incidents of his story. (See par. 12.)

11. For indeed, whether this period shall be one of a few hours only, or one of years, depends much on the skill of the writer in *making all the facts depend upon one another so closely and so evidently that the lapse of a long time between cause and effect is either lost sight of or else is felt as an essential element of the situation.* Nevertheless, the general nature of the conte dictates that, *when the plot incidents are several and occur at widely separated intervals, the most significant of these shall be chosen as the chief, to produce the main situation, all the rest being reduced to complete subordination as mere expositional or ancillary fact.* The story then constitutes one main

grave" type of story. It is possible within a brief narrative to skeletonize the history of a courtship, a life, or any other series of events associated with a single person; it is even possible to make this skeleton history interesting (especially to immature readers of certain—and uncertain—ages); but seldom indeed is it possible so to unify such a concatenation of condensed episodes as to produce through them any single effect at all akin to that of the dramatic short narrative.

episode, incident, or event, supported by a body of secondary, explanatory matter.

12. It is evident, therefore, that the unity which depends strictly upon the time element is possible only when the chief incidents occur within a few hours or possibly days. *When the story material is distributed through long periods, the unity is that of action and motivation (or of character) rather than of time.* Thus, when the pope's mule, after seven years of waiting, kicks Védène zenithward in revenge for his scurvy trick of the earlier date, we feel no break in the action—in the operation, that is to say, of cause and effect. Nor in *The Necklace* do we feel any break in the continuity, the unity; and yet ten years pass between the motivating happenings and the revelation of the tragic outcome. We feel no break because there is no break; the moment the necklace is lost, that moment the outcome begins—cause begins to work effect, and skillfully condensed and rapid narration carry it forward, creating the illusion of long stretches of time, until the full catastrophe has been achieved and is ready for disclosure to the reader. We therefore say that, *when motivation is clear and adequate, unification results no matter how long the intervals between the initial operation of the cause and the final production of its effect.*[6]

13. Again, *a more or less satisfactory unity may result from the association of the events with a single place or set*

[6] The student is, of course, assumed to be familiar with the fundamentals of narration as a compositional process. He will appreciate, therefore, that in stories such as we have just been considering, the principle of continuity of advance (usually called movement) is especially important. The three means of retarded movement, accelerated movement, and emphasized transition, are here the writer's chief narrational dependences.

of surroundings. This we call unity of setting. Yet again, incidents otherwise unrelated may be akin in mood or tone —that is, in atmosphere quality—and therefore, brought together, may give us unity of atmosphere. Or yet again various distinct incidents may each illustrate and develop the same central thought or truth, in which case they produce, when assembled, unity of theme.

14. Yet another unity, however, is the unity most often urged by advisers upon undertakers of the short story—unity of action. *Unity of action results when the one definite single outcome is brought about by an unbroken sequence, or a completely interlocked set, of incidents.* We may without inaccuracy call it *unity of motivation,* provided that we understand the motivation to be directed to the production of a single outcome. *Unity of action is the necessary development of close-wrought plot;* and for this reason we need not discuss it in detail here. No plot incident needed for the unfolding and advancement of a close-wrought plot, will violate unity so long as it be kept within the bounds of proportion in its individual development. And lest this remark may seem perhaps to imply that all non-plot incidents violate unity, we will add that only such non-plot incidents as are episodic and digressive without being at the same time concentrative or intensifying, necessarily transgress the canon of unity of action. We have already made clear the function of the concentrative incident distinguished from the plot incident. To avoid a break in the unity of the action, therefore, the writer has only to guard against having more than a single final outcome to the story. There may be preliminary movements, of course, each having its own individual outcome. But before the story is ended, each and all of these

subordinate outcomes must have become incorporated in the action of the larger story, and made a contributing cause of the final outcome. *Unity of action, then, is secured by providing the necessary body of plot incidents to bring about the single final outcome of a close-wrought plot.* Its importance is so obvious that we need only to state it in order to emphasize it. It is alpha and omega among the unities.

15. As a closing word about the management of short story materials with a view to securing unity, we may set down yet another generalization. We can see that, in order to accomplish one purpose, the writer may be compelled to neglect other equally legitimate purposes which he might pursue by means of his dramatic narrative. In emphasizing theme, for example, he may find it necessary to pay less attention to characterization. But *no prudent writer will neglect any of the desirable ends of dramatic narrative at any time if he can serve them together without the sacrifice of his single dramatic effect at the end.* Unless compelled by inconquerable difficulties, he will not slight characterization in the story of theme or of action, nor atmosphere in the story which is to be effective through a surprise ending, nor action in the theme story. He will recognize that the more thoroughly he presents, at one and the same time, all the elements of fiction (all the time duly subordinating them to his dominating purpose), the more thoroughly will he succeed in his artistic aim. Our closing generalization is, therefore, this: *In any story, the fullest unity will usually depend upon the observance together of all the different sorts of unity—unity of person and character, of time, of place, of motivation and action, of atmosphere, and of theme. In proportion as these are*

*respected and utilized in the story, in still greater propor-
tion will that story at the end produce a completely unified
impression.*

XXIII. DECISION UPON PLOT AND SELECTION OF DE-
VELOPING MATERIAL MUST BE DETERMINED BY THE
AUTHOR'S DETAILED FAMILIARITY WITH THE FACTS
INVOLVED

1.   Young (that is, inexperienced) writers are notorious
for selecting themes and materials that they cannot handle.
Sometimes such a choice of unsuitable material arises only
from their lack of knowledge of what constitutes dramatic
value; sometimes it results more from a mere personal
dissatisfaction with life and environment—the writer assuming that because his vain imaginings of a life different from the sort he leads, satisfy him and solace his
restlessness, they are, of course, suited to entertain and impress other people.   The mistake is fatal.

2.   Mere personal dis-ease and ferment have seldom
made an artist.   They never did so unless the fermenting
person possessed in no inconsiderable amount artistic insight and judgment coupled with energy enough to make
him put his dramatic conceptions of better things into
finished, artistic form.   Even with the greatest, the attainment of some degree of settled conviction seems necessary to the production of the best work; the output of the
sturm-und-drang period—of the turbulent youthful days
when immaturity is kicking against the pricks and temperament and reason are seeking a working relationship
with the world—perhaps never reaches the excellence of
that which is put forth when the man has developed,

through questioning, impulse, and conflict, a more permanent and self-controlled attitude. The best work of any man is not that of his spiritual unrest, impulse, and rebellion. Schiller's *The Robbers* does not compare with his *Wallenstein;* Shakspere's earlier plays cannot compare with those written when he had come to a deeper, though a sadder, understanding with the world; Dante's *New Life* does not compare with *The Divine Comedy.*

3. Even with the masters, the storm-and-stress work is comparatively of inferior worth. The greatest art—with the individual artist as with the world's art—is positive, not negative, constructive, not destructive, fuller of faith than of ferment. It is *eager, not so much to protest as to see and know,* in order that it may report and interpret; and therefore, it does not cultivate itself as a solace and escape, but as a means to the expression of great conceptions sprung from great understandings of the world it has studied and experienced. Therefore again, it is always aware, not of merely the bare facts, but of the larger, deeper facts of which these things are solely outward signs and symbols. It has learned to stand aside and estimate the value of its possessor's knowledge and experience as material for presenting concretely the conceptions of life which take form in the mind of the artist. In this sense, it is detached, impersonal, coldly practical, and unimpassioned. It never makes the mistake of thinking that, because an author is irritated by a pebble in his shoe, he is, therefore, qualified to write a history of the journey of life.

4. It does not follow, however, that since the author accepts and rejects materials according to their value for his artistic purpose, only certain limited kinds of fact are

available to him. To the skillful artist, and under suitable conditions, any fact whatever is available. On this we will not linger; it is more to our purpose to note that the availability of any fact to a writer depends on himself much more than it does on the fact itself. If he lack dramatic instinct—if he have not the architectonic sense, the sense of the master-builder for form and method, whereby he discriminates justly between what at the moment will and what will not best body forth his conception, best serve his constructive and interpretive purpose by concretely expressing it,—he can scarcely use any facts effectively, no matter what they be. Without the dramatic sense, the constructive instinct for form and method, the master's judgment of the pliant suitability and expedient adaptability of certain facts over all others for his particular purpose—without these, the writer is a landlubber adrift on an uncharted sea, lacking, moreover, a compass and knowing not even the fixed stars.

5. The truth is, that *the value of any fact for dramatic narrative does not lie in the fact as a fact, but in its efficacy (direct or indirect) in bringing on an outcome that is significant.* Just what significance is, is hard to define. The veriest skit will sometimes interest us, lure us on to its conclusion, and satisfy us with its outcome, and yet have no outcome that drives home a serious truth, gives a philosophical view of life, or otherwise seems to be of permanent worth.[7] On the other hand, the most labored and serious narrative, ending in tragedy and ruin,

[7] Our satisfaction comes from having *realized* through the skit some aspect of life or feeling, even though but a trivial one—the presentation having in addition possessed the quality of being "interesting," as people are who can hold our attention pleasantly and escape boring us.

may fail to leave us with a sense of its being in any true way an interpretation of life (we usually describe it as " not convincing ").

6. Apparently, then, we must in the long run judge every conte [8] according to its outcome and effect. If it leave us with a sense of having been in touch with life as it is, or as it ought to be—if it interpret to us some person, motive, deed, environment, or truth, in such a way that we feel our time well spent in getting the interpretation— we are warranted in saying that the outcome has significance. *That outcome is significant which, helped out by the narrative, produces in us a better understanding of existence, the sense of having realized or of understanding life or men more fully, or a feeling of sympathy either with our fellows in general or with the individuals portrayed in the story; or which in some other way leaves us with the feeling that we have increased either our mental, our emotional, or our spiritual well-being or experience.* But for its fullness this assertion is identical with the briefer one that declares the purpose of fiction to be, either to divert and amuse, or to interpret life; but it has along with the disadvantages of length the advantage of setting forth a list of those matters which are the source of the diversion or the interpretation.

7. Now, *the man with the dramatic instinct is the man who can sense in a fact or a group of facts the potentiality of a situation and outcome that will thus divert or make real and interpret.* The facts suggest to him a situation, or a series of incidents and situations, that will either amuse us or make us think or feel more or less deeply;

[8] Equally applicable to the novel and other forms of fiction—but emphasizing " outcome " less.

they fall into organized relationships in his imagination, growing through a critical period to a climactic moment; he fore-visions this moment and its outcome, sensing its power to amuse or otherwise stir and stimulate people—he " sees a story " and an impressive outcome in them.   But the man who can thus fore-vision such a series of situations and perceive the effective outcome whereto they lead, is comparatively rare; he is the " born " story-teller, the " natural " dramatist, whose work will be of the highest dramatic quality.   A greater number of persons have this ability to a limited extent, and by assiduous training can develop in themselves a reasonable degree of skill in the conceiving and writing of stage or narrative drama; a still larger number have just enough of it to appreciate good artistry in play or story, but not enough ever themselves to become proficient playwrights or story-tellers.   These supply the " educated public " to whom the artist must look for anything like a just evaluation of his work; but unfortunately even they, lacking the creative gift, and owing their development largely to training based on the standards of preceding generations or past ages, are sometimes conservatively slow to recognize the merits of newer methods and newer embodiments of the eternal truths.

8.   There remain, however, all that part of the populace who have so little of the dramatic instinct, or have it so little developed, that they are incapable of discriminating the significant from the insignificant, and who, therefore, are not able to tell the worth-while from the worthless. Probably this part is larger than all the others combined. And yet most of the people belonging to it are to some extent readers—a fortunate thing, perhaps, since they afford a market for many writers who cannot reach higher

than the mediocre, and (a good deal more to the point) since their reading habit must in the end bring them to a higher standard and thus improve the popular standards generally. Yet always there will be a large reading public incapable of justly valuing stories, because lacking in dramatic and artistic instinct, insight, and sympathy; they cannot evaluate incidents or other materials of artistic presentation, cannot relate them justly to one another in their own minds, cannot comprehend them. Hence they are blind alike to significance or to lack of significance in the outcome itself. In thus discussing the public which reads, we are not in fact getting away from discussion of the author who writes, for, from what we have said, it is easy to return to the assertion, that the great writers of the short story must be born such before they can make themselves such, and that *only those with enough dramatic instinct to recognize the possible outcomes latent in any fact or group of facts, and the potential significance of such outcomes, can hope even for mediocre success in the writing of dramatic narrative.*

9. "But," the young writer with ideas of the "power" of literature will by this time be exclaiming—"But you have not said a thing about my view of life! Doesn't this cut any figure in my story writing? Am I not to choose great and noble and powerful themes, and then select my materials with reference to them? You speak as if I were to be merely a reporter, but I want to be in charge of an editorial page. I have a message for the world; I have something to say; I want to write in order to express my view of life!"

10. Perhaps the zealous young story writer who believes in the "influence" of literature is right in his conviction

that the author's view of life should determine, or at least help to determine, his choice of materials and his purpose. We will agree with him, provided that he and we can agree upon a definition of " view of life." To reach an understanding, let us talk over two or three matters. First of all, we have decided already that there is no reason in the nature of things why short stories cannot be written successfully as both contes and purpose stories. But at the same time we noted the greater difficulty of producing a thoroughly artistic story that should be also a purpose story. This difficulty should be a caution to the writer not to attempt the exploitation of his view of life unless his experience and skill assure him of ability to develop his chosen theme in a truly dramatic narrative—to embody it in a true short story, not merely to present some incidents and situations illustrative of the theme. And we have seen just above, that the only hope of producing a true short story lies in the possession of the dramatic instinct; we may have all the " views of life " that could be found in an epitome of the world's philosophies, and write stories about them from youth to old age, yet fail to produce even one true conte unless we have also this dramatic and artistic sense. And *if we have the artistic and dramatic sense, together with a seeing eye, we can write any number of short stories that will express a view of life, whether we have this end in mind or not. For (we repeat) a true report of any coherent portion of life cannot fail to embody a truth about life; the theme is there regardless of the writer. Life states and illustrates its own themes, and it interprets them itself.*

11. Hence, although the earnest young person's aspiration to be a writer of leading articles for the editorial

page of the great periodical of life is natural, it is often
dangerous to his success and usefulness, and almost always
unnecessary from any point of view. The editorial page
of the newspaper is valuable and necessary—but it is the
" big story " written by the good reporter and placed prominently on the front page, that mostly sells the paper. It
sells the paper because it is that wherein the reader finds
immediate contact with life and men; the editor gives him
a formal interpretation of men and events, but the reporter
(if he be a good reporter) comes far nearer to giving him
the men and the events themselves. And the men and the
events, not primarily the statement of their meaning, is the
thing of interest to the reader. According to his ability—
greater or less as the case may be—*the reader will find the
interpretation for himself if the report be adequate.* And
herein is more than a passing hint for the writer. As
it is primarily the news report and not the editorial article
that makes the newspaper, so *it is primarily the report
and not the interpretation that makes the drama, either
acted or narrated. The author can have no higher ideal
than the ideal of the great reporter—so accurately to report
the significant facts that their meaning is evident without
extraneous interpretation.* He will use not quite the same
reporting method, but he will aim at the same result. He
will tell the essential facts in such a way that they will
reveal their own meaning.

12. Yet inevitably every man—and the artist much
more than most other men—will have his individual view
of life, and this view of life will to no small degree color
and determine his report. He will not voluntarily permit
it to distort his report or falsify his presentation, but he
will not attempt to see things otherwise than as they appear

to him. To this extent, his view of life must and should enter into his writing. It is that which gives him a personal point of view, a body of standards, a set of tests, a touchstone, by which to estimate the significance of situations and events, of traits of character, of motives, of outcomes; in brief, the meanings of all those innumerable facts with which he has to deal. This means only (but very emphatically does mean) that the writer shall have thought over and studied the substance and materials of his art until he is thoroughly acquainted with them—until with the authoritative judgment of the expert he can formulate opinions well enough founded upon knowledge and professional experience to merit presentation in concrete form to the world. Only thus can he " write of the-thing-as-he-sees-it for the God of things-as-they-are."

13. By view of life, then, we shall agree not to mean a set of theories and hypotheses to be expounded and argumentatively established, albeit the great artist *can* expound and establish such theories by means of fiction. We mean, rather, that more or less consistent and unified set of personal opinions and feelings which determines the writer's attitude toward existence in the abstract—that is, existence separate and apart from him personally. This assertion, however, requires a little explanation. In saying that the writer's outlook is an outlook on existence in the abstract, we do not imply that this outlook shall not be affected by his personal experience of life. Were such an outlook possible—and it is not—it would be worthless; we had as well have seasickness described by a man who has lived all his life in the Sahara and never mounted a camel. What we imply is *an outlook generalized from the world's theory and practice in the light of personal observa-*

tion and personal experience. As thus generalized, the writer's view of life may be largely independent of and different from his individual practice of existence—from his individual morality, the "practical ethic" of his personal existence. Not infrequently, his individual practice will show many departures from the view of life —life as it is, or as it ought to be—embodied in his writings. This is inevitable. He lives his own life as he must and can; but upon life in general he looks with detachment, as a thing to be regarded removedly if not impersonally, and with scientific coldness. True, notable fiction has been written expressly to body forth personal experience, the emotional and spiritual history and views of the author as well as the external events of his life. But in much fiction of this sort, research shows, there has been extensive manipulation, modification, and idealization; the "autobiographical element" has been largely and freely altered, sometimes even transformed, in the treatment. Moreover, when this has not occurred, the world has usually found somewhat of weakness and inconclusiveness in the work. *The artist, we are compelled to acknowledge, is larger and more important than the man he inhabits,* and the artist's view of life is consequently larger, saner, more human, and more conclusive than the outlook merely of the man. And it is this broader outlook, this generalized opinion and conclusion about life, not to be expounded and exploited as theory, but to be bodied forth in the concrete form of imagined incident and character, at which the writer had better aim; for it is this view, rather than any more personal, emotional, and impulsive body of opinion, that can most helpfully enter into, inspire, stimulate, and give lasting interpretive value, to his work.

14. Here we may stop to answer a question that divides itself between the ethics of art and the demands of commercial success in writing; namely, whether the writer must always *believe or approve* the idea, or theme which can be found at the root of the story he writes? Must he so direct his story that the outcome presented, the thought exemplified, shall be one that he himself accepts, or is he at liberty—perhaps sometimes under obligation— to report life in such forms, under such combinations, and with such outcomes, as he would not have it, or feels that it does not, possess? Let us phrase this question in various ways. May he, with honesty to himself and his art, report life from any and all points of view? May he report it as the newspaper reporter presents his story of a murder, a seduction, a terrible accident, interpreting, making humanly comprehensible, without advocating the thing? As a literary creator and experimenter in human motives and behavior, must he confine himself to creation only of such characters and deeds and situations as he could approve of in actual life under the tests of his personal theory of morals, justice, social order, and the like? May he report what he knows to exist, even though it be in its nature contrary to his own moral standards? Is it allowable for him to study men and women, motive and act, character and life, by means of imagined facts, persons, and situations of a sort " beyond the law " of his own approval?

15. Stated in terms like these, the question loses a good deal of its seeming difficulty. *Not only is the artist a reporter, who therefore must cover his run; he is also a scientific observer and experimenter, studying and trying out life theoretically in many forms and under many conditions, and communicating the notes of his research to*

the world. As we have said repeatedly, he is under no obligation to assume the part of advocate. It needs no assertion, that the writer who could not conceive characters, incidents, and situations of a sort opposed to those of which he would himself approve, could not enter deeply into character or motive of any sort; his treatment of life would be superficial, because his understanding of it would be superficial—and superficial is an exceedingly weak word with which to designate the fact. The great duty of the fiction writer is to interpret life by reporting it accurately; half his possible usefulness would be made impossible if he were forbidden to report anything but that in which he himself believes.[9]

16. The moral difficulty of the question being thus removed, the commercial aspects demand consideration. The first of these is that involving the financial and worldly success of the author. Shall the artist brave inevitable misunderstanding, with consequent hostility, censorship, and persecution, because he has conceived a set of facts that do not square with the always-has-been or the what-I-think of a too-much-reading and too-little-thinking world? Mr. Arnold Bennett advocates the prudent horn of the

[9] True, a large part of the public cannot conceive how this is true. Lacking (as we have said) the dramatic instinct, analytical acumen, and consequently the ability to estimate values for themselves; unable to distinguish between exposition and advocacy; untrained to see effect in cause and cause in effect; accustomed and pleased to have their opinions supplied by others, since they cannot safely trust their own mental processes; and (one thing highly to their credit) possessed—though it be sometimes at second hand—of a strong conviction that right is right and wrong is wrong;—the contemporary public in any time is likely to protest with all the intensity of ignorant righteousness against examples of interpretation which are too much for its comprehension—provided that such ex-

dilemma; go as far as you safely can, is the substance of his advice—with the broad intimation that sometimes this will not be very far. Mr. Bernard Shaw exemplifies the go-as-far-as-you-like theory, but he exemplifies it only in the going. He has not escaped hostility and venomosity, although his brilliancy, independence, fearlessness, and various conditions that have aided him, have given him a success in facing down a censorious public that most of us could not expect. From the point of view of commercial success, Mr. Bennett gives good advice. Still more a matter of business is the second aspect of the commercial problem. If the writer is to supply a market, he must provide an adequate supply of goods. To do this, he will sometimes find himself obliged to make stories out of whatever materials are at hand. The mill must be kept grinding, and the miller cannot always wait until he gets a grist of good wheat. In all these questionings, the writer must decide his course of action for himself. But one may ask seriously whether the frequent construction of stories wherein his own conviction or point of view is set aside may not in the long run be likely to lessen

 amples happen to be brought to its attention sensationally enough to stir interest. Then we have the amusing situation of a well-meaning public raging against book, play, picture, or statue as "immoral," at the same time accepting without qualm or thought the "morality" of the melodramatic photoplay, of the slushy love-story found in women's magazines, of the inexpressibly stupid and vulgar "daily short story" of the newspaper, of the burlesque "show" of the theater, and other forms of rain-barrel or thunder-bird literature and drama poor enough or violent enough to gratify their primitive-era taste. Time, however, rectifies all these aberrations of that "amoosin' cuss," the public, and the interpretation that is accurate and true ultimately establishes itself in literature and performs its part in educating the world better to understand itself.

the strength and vigor of his earnestness. The good writer must obey the injunction of "put yourself in his place" when he portrays persons acting. To enter into the thoughts, feelings, and point of view of another for the purposes of artistic and spiritual comprehension is, however, one thing; to enter into them for the purpose of literary manufacture is another; and in art as in life, it is sometimes hard to tell where honorable association ends and virtual prostitution begins.

17. Here let us summarize. More is necessary to the writing of good short story (conte) or stage drama than the mere impulse to express personal ferment (or for that matter, enthusiasm). There must be in the author, supported and reinforced by an all-round literary sense, a true, well-developed sense of the dramatic—of significances distinguished from trivialities and non-significances, and of the relations of cause and effect (i.e., a sense for the motivation of situations truly illustrative or interpretive of life). This dramatic-literary instinct will find the most effective expression through accurate reporting based upon insight and the possession of the essential facts, such presentation being what gives effect even to stories that are frankly purpose stories. But for such reporting, a set of standards is necessary, and this set of standards is found in the writer's view of life, which guides him in seeing and presenting facts, and animates or gives spirit to his work. But his view of life need not stand in the way of his portraying themes, characters, or situations that are in opposition to it (especially when the presentation is objective). As a student of and experimenter with the facts and influences of human life, he is at liberty to make fictional report of things as he sees them, be they

what they are; and he may, therefore, portray that with which he lacks personal (but not artistic) sympathy, or that which is inconsistent with his personal (or with the usual worldly) view of life, provided that the spirit in which he makes the portrayal is that of the artist, and that he stop short if at any time he find himself making the portrayal in a way that violates his fundamental sense of propriety and truth.   The adjustment between personal and artistic conscience on the one hand and the presentation of uncongenial or uncommended or unaccepted *motifs,* themes, situations, and outcomes on the other, must be left to the individual writer.   Conscience, especially the true artistic conscience, will be his safest guide, and will, if he have it in sufficient degree, protect him from over-yielding to the temptations and constraints of the literary manufacturing industry.

18.   Giving all these considerations due weight, we come to that assertion which is of most practical importance to the student seeking knowledge that he can turn to use in the writing of stories.   This is, that *his decision upon a plot, and his selection of materials wherewith to develop his story, should be determined by his familiarity and lack of familiarity with the facts that will be involved in presenting the story so conceived and planned.*   The noblest conception, the most dramatic plot, the finest literary art in the construction and setting forth of the story, will be but as a mirage in the desert unless given substance and reality by adequate information.   The author must know what he is writing about—and the emphasis is here on KNOW and not on *what.*   No one can write effectively in any but a superficial and general way about that with which he is not familiar.   This sounds like a truism—and

it is. But people are often blind to the importance of
truisms, and the tendency of inexperienced writers to attempt incidents, plots, situations, settings, and characters
that are remote from their experience—about which they
in truth have only vague impressions and smattering information—is so strong that the danger lying in it calls for
emphatic presentation.

19. The reason why familiarity with the particular sort
of scene, persons, and acts to be depicted, is necessary to
the author—why he cannot depend merely on his general
knowledge of men and affairs—is plain. Because in his
story he must show forth life in appropriate concrete
forms, and because this cannot be done from merely general
knowledge, the writer must know his people and places
with an all-round knowledge that includes details as well
as general facts. Were story-writing but the finding of
a general human motive for action that is more or less
abstractly conceived, the story-dramatist could get along
with a general stock of information about human nature
and stock character traits. *But story-writing is no such
thing. It succeeds only when it bodies forth its conceptions
concretely and with variety of true detail. Therefore,
it must know with extreme intimacy and fullness the facts
with which it deals.* To base a story on the general fact
that men who are in love are likely to behave foolishly, it
must go beyond the general idea of " men in love "; it
must pass on to the concrete of " this man "—a particular,
individual man, millionaire, mechanic, or costermonger,
handsome or ugly, manly or effeminate, honorable or
treacherous, graceful or awkward, and so on. The millionaire in love will doubtless do just as foolish things as the
costermonger similarly deranged—but not always the

same kinds of thing. Nor will he do them in the same sort of surroundings, nor before the same class of people; neither will he and the people about him dress or speak as will the costermonger and his associates. A writer, therefore, whose knowledge of costermongers enabled him to do an excruciatingly humorous story of costermongers in love, might fail utterly in the same sort of story about millionaires in love, unless he knew millionaires as thoroughly as he knew costermongers.

20. Evidently, every part of the narrative must be worked out down to details, with a fullness proportioned to its importance; and *in all important parts of the narrative these details are always concrete particulars of such specific sort as makes them thoroughly representative of the persons, the kinds of character, the locale, the occupation and social rank, the habits, customs, mannerisms, speech, and thought, with which the story seeks to deal.* Unless the story be thus worked out in the concrete, it can scarcely be said to belong to fiction at all; and unless the concrete particulars are true to the life, persons, places, occupations, and atmosphere that they seek to present, they fail the writer as a means of giving plausible outward form to his conception. *Intimate familiarity with his materials, even down to minute detail, is indispensable in the production of consistent, convincing, and truly interpretive dramatic narrative.*

21. If from this the student does not realize the wisdom of getting out among men and mingling (though it be but as an observer) in their activities, we will not urge it on him; we will leave him to go on wondering why less studious, less scholarly, and less " educated " men, who do nothing but run about amongst folk, are " getting their

stuff over " so often! But we know the reason. The objectionable fellow who succeeds is rubbing elbows with life; he is getting " next " (Anglo-Saxon, " that which is closest to ") to life in the best way—by mingling with and becoming part of it. He is learning, not merely to look in from the outside, but to go inside and look out, and still more, to look about him while inside. Of course he can report life, for he knows it. When he wishes to give concrete form to any conception, he has an ever increasing store of observation and information from which to draw. The man of literary instincts who keeps himself " unspotted from the world " in his own study, can perhaps succeed as poet, philosopher, historian or essayist, but seldom indeed can he succeed as dramatist or fiction-writer. For to succeed, *he must have not only view-of-life, dramatic sense, and artistic impulse; he must have also such intimate and detailed knowledge of men and the world as will provide him concrete forms wherein to body life forth.* The story-writer who does not make himself intimately familiar with the life he would present, is unprepared either to conceive or to present it. Because he keeps himself unspotted from the world, he is more than likely to be unspotted by the world; for he cannot gain its attention by holding up before it what it wants to see —the concrete embodiment of itself in truly characteristic detail, imaginatively created by an artistic master.

XXIV. CHARACTERIZATION INVOLVES THE PRESENTING OF HUMAN TRAITS, CLASS ATTRIBUTES, AND PERSONAL TRAITS AND MANNERISMS

1. In turning again to the problems created by the presence of the character element in narrative, we will first

repeat certain assertions amplified in section X. These are:

A. Character is basic human nature shaped and modified into particular traits and tendencies that are manifested in the behavior and conduct of the person.

B. The second element in human character (human nature being the first) is temperament—the quality or disposition peculiar to the individual.

C. In the acts of men, which are that through which character becomes manifest, the element of reflective foresight is important—that quality wherein human action frequently differs from animal action. The existence of reflective foresight, releasing the person from purely automatic reactions, is what makes drama and fiction possible, for it is that which makes human motive possible and thus creates conflict and struggle. Fiction is interesting largely because it shows us man employing, or failing to employ, his reflective foresight in critical situations.[10]

D. Character in the individual is the sum of his moral, intellectual, and physical instincts, feelings, tendencies, qualities, and habits, resulting from the union in him of human nature and temperament.

To these we may now add:

E. Single acts and speeches are not sure revealers of character; neither is psychological analysis (or narration) of thought and motive (recounting events of the " stream of consciousness "). Single acts and speeches are seldom conclusive, although they may be very significant; they throw light on, but do not fully discover, character. *Char-*

[10] We must not understand that the *employment* of reflection is always necessary on the part of the person. His very failure to reflect may be the backbone of his comedy or tragedy.

acter is completely and conclusively revealed only by con-duct—the sum and outcome, under thoroughly testing conditions, of the person's reflection, emotion, impulse, and acts. Action not clearly the result of predominating traits and motives that will always produce like conduct under similar conditions, is inconclusive.

F. Single acts (or series of single acts) are produced by either (a) reason, (b) feeling, or (c) impulse. In (a) and (b), will is present; the person *chooses* his act through reason or through emotional influences. But in (c), the act is instinctive rather than determined.[11] As, however, conduct is the result and sum of single acts, the three sources of our acts are likewise the three sources of conduct. Therefore, conduct is either (a) reasoned or (b) not reasoned.

G. We can now proceed to another classification. *Acts that are—*

(a)   *indicative merely of human nature will always tend to be purely instinctive or emotional.*

(b)   *indicative of class characteristics will usually be instinctive or emotional,* growing out of settled class motives, customs, and feelings; but these may at times be reasoned upon more deliberately than those of basic human nature are likely to be.

(c)   *indicative of the individual temperament may be* either instinctive, or emotional, or reflective.

2. This last classification (G) brings us to the asser-

---

[11] Feeling is often the source of impulse. But as our classification is otherwise helpful, and as it works effectively for our purposes, we will be pragmatically satisfied with it, noting merely that feeling sometimes is subjected to reason and sometimes is impulsively obeyed.

tion that *the individual traits, qualities, and mannerisms are those which most prominently appear in characterization, and therefore call for the largest amount of direct attention from the writer.* These traits and habits must appear most prominently because, were it otherwise, the persons would be no more than stock persons, not individuals; and hence *the main value of characterization—showing life in its multitude of variations*—would be lost. Did a writer present a person in whose character only the basic elements of human nature showed, he would present an abstraction, and his fiction would therefore become an allegory, a mere piece of narrative exposition such as *Pilgrim's Progress* is. The same would be the case to almost as great an extent did he present us merely a type, or unindividualized representative, of the lawyer, the doctor, the cook, the priest, of the explorer, the home-stayer, the lover, the achiever, and so on through all the class categories. But the universal characteristics, or even the characteristics common to any particular class, are not those that primarily give life its endless daily interest through its variety and consequent uncertainty. The possession of individual traits and character qualities, of individual habits and mannerisms—this it is that makes men keep on interesting other men from day to day and generation to generation. To present a stock personage, a mere typeman, is not supremely difficult. But *to present a thoroughly individualized person under whose individuality is yet to be perceived the class and the race traits, is no easy task. And this is the task of the fiction writer.*

3. A further word of explanation may here be useful. The basic traits of human nature do not offer in themselves matters of sufficient interest for repeated presentation;

they are too few. The primary instincts and emotions make no extensive list. Hunger, sexual passion, fear, anger—a few categories such as these will cover all that is primarily an element in human nature. Even affection for offspring seems to be largely a developed instinct; so that, although we now regard it as fundamental among civilized peoples, it in fact represents a considerable stage of advancement; many tribes show it but sporadically, and possibly we shall not exaggerate greatly if we assert that among beasts the dam sometimes shows it more conclusively than do twentieth-century mothers (individual instances are of course what is meant). Such facts as these, by the way, illustrate our thought, that *it is the individual variations rather than the fundamental nature that produces the uncertainty and immediate interest of life*. The same generalizations are true about class characteristics: [12] the distinctive class traits are few, and were it not that many men of many temperaments possess them in common, would afford little more than a formula for the writer—an unchanging pattern on which all his characters would of necessity be shaped. What life actually affords, however, is countless characters founded upon human nature and more or less also upon class traits, but showing forth innumerable variations of this human nature and class attribute brought about by the innumerable variations in the conditions of environment and in the many other natural causes that are productive of individual

[12] The student will observe that class traits represent individualizing influences operating upon entire groups alike. The group thus becomes individualized from the rest of mankind, and therefore, after this has occurred, the individual traits of its individual members stand in the same relation to the collective traits of the class as to basic human nature.

temper. Hence, *it is only when the character portrayed is true, first to human nature, then to class form,*[13] *and finally, to a clearly conceived individual temperament such as is logically produced by the determining causes of variation, that we get individuality, or personality, the quality so indispensable to complete characterization.* And again, therefore, we must point out the necessity of knowing not only man, but men; for nothing else will supply that store of understanding out of which the author can conceive characters that not only are true to race and class, but also show infinite human variety.

4. We come then to this counsel. *In characterizing, think rather negatively than positively of race and group traits, but very positively of individual traits; make certain that the materials selected do not violate the fundamental truth of human nature and class attribute, but make equally certain that the materials selected do present a clearly conceived and clearly individualized person having a personality, a character, all his own.* This, of

[13] In actual writing, the author not infrequently finds that class attribute may be safely disregarded; only at times does class characteristic become important. There are, for instance, many situations that can as well be worked out with a preacher or a gambler as the central person, as with a lawyer or an engineer. The conte is less likely than the longer forms of narrative fiction to give extended attention to class trait, because its space precludes much portrayal of character purely for the sake of portrayal. Even in the most concentrated short-story treatment, however, the preacher and the gambler must be true to type except in those cases in which the story arises wholly or in part from their being untrue to type—and then class trait is presented in contrast merely. The point of this comment is, then, that class attribute cannot be undertaken solely for its own sake in the short story, except in cases of special character aim and purpose, when the story itself depends on the class character.

course, advises no actual disregard of the more general and basic characteristics, but suggests rather the proportionate emphasis that each should receive; for *it is unlikely that any conception of individual character, if true to life in the elements that give it individuality, will be untrue to life in fundamentals.* The single character imagined from intimate and accurate observation of the motives, acts, and action of men, can scarcely fail to be true to the more basic facts of human nature. Accurate reporting will take care of this. Yet lest these assertions result even yet in misapprehension, let us set down again that the merely individual character—that failing in its individuality also to represent mankind and class—is scarcely worth depicting; at best, it can be but one of the curiosities of literary portraiture, a member of the gallery of freaks, and it is still more likely to be merely a nullity and "nixnutz." [14]

5. Before considering specifically some of the means of presenting character, we may speak briefly of the attitude taken by the author toward the person he is depicting. Two attitudes are possible: the author may assume an attitude of personal judgment and interpretation toward his creation, or he may merely put it forth, then leave it to get understanding and win favor or dislike from the reader for itself. *In letting appear his own feeling toward or judgment of the character, he will find disadvantage along with advantage.* Perhaps the advantage lies chiefly in two things. By letting his opinion of the

[14] When the author's purpose is, to portray the class, not the individual—to make the person a personification of a type, or the embodiment of some general trait—the procedure is reversed. The individuality of the character is then minimized, and the person transformed into a symbolical or allegorical figure by emphasis of the general traits.

character be seen, the author can readily indicate his view of life; yet just for this reason, authors—young authors especially—laboring under the belief that their " message " must be conveyed directly and obviously, are likely to over-do their approval or disapproval—as are older writers also who are more fired with zealotry than possessed by an artistic appreciation of life, or who permit themselves to become enamored of or displeased by the persons of their story. Second, by distinctly notifying the reader how the author regards the person, the author gives incompetent understandings a push in the direction he wishes them to take.

6. But probably most readers prefer to appreciate the character for themselves; certainly this is true of the more cultured reader, unless the author's exposition of the character be redeemed by some extrinsic quality, such for instance as Thackeray's genial sarcasm. The reader gets interest out of reaching an understanding of the person by employing his own faculties and judgment, and there is loss of zest when he finds himself served with a meal of predigested character breakfast-food. Moreover, when the attitude of the author becomes sentimentally admiring or antagonistically bitter, readers are likely to feel down-right dissatisfaction—the more so because often in such instances the author's ability in character portrayal proves less than his facility in maudlin approval or intolerant condemnation.

7. Finally, we must reflect that *in the conte the space allowable for direct or explicit expression of the author's point of view, is small indeed. Unless he can indicate his attitude by means of quick epithet, of adjectives, adverbs, and phrases of characterization that imply rather*

*than assert opinion, giving it by subjective coloring rather
than by any obvious means—in brief, unless by suggestion
he can convey without obtrusiveness the view he holds, he
can seldom with safety attempt such an expression in the
short story.*   In the novel he could do it and, if his attitude and philosophy proved worth while, command attention thereby.   But the limitations of the short story in this
respect are far stricter than are those of the novel.   Yet
the short-story writer is not without means even for
direct presentation of character estimates.   *He can make
the persons in his story express, by both word and deed,
their judgment of their fellow-persons.*   By this means and
by skillful suggestion otherwise, the skillful author will be
fully able to embody in his narrative his personal estimate
of any character without at all thrusting himself into the
story to do it.   But even when all is said, *the facts, accurately reported, remain the best means of revealing the
beauty or ugliness, the worthiness or unworthiness, of any
character, and no adequately portrayed person in fiction
will be seriously misjudged by competent readers, even
though the author's attitude toward him be left wholly
unrevealed.*

XXV. "CHARACTER" IMPLIES AN ORIGINAL CONCEP-
    TION OF A PERSON HAVING DEFINITE INDIVIDUALITY;
    ITS TRAITS BEING PORTRAYED BY DESCRIPTION,
    ANALYSIS, PSYCHOLOGICAL NARRATION, AND ESPE-
    CIALLY ACT AND SPEECH

    1. How is an individual character created in fiction?
Is it copied from the character of some person—a repro-
duction of an original?   Many persons, even critics who

might know better, seem to think so; for we find endless attempts going on to identify the "original" of this or that noted person of fiction. Yet even when there in fact is an original, the copying is always so free—the suppression of traits that are present in the original, the addition of traits not present in the original, and the placing of emphasis upon certain traits in preference to others—all this is so common, as to make most copies nothing but highly idealized derivatives of the original character. When scientific biography gets to work upon these "copies," it nearly always proves that the most which the fictional presentation accomplishes is, to give a suggestive, but not an accurate, portrayal—to show what the person copied might have been, but not what he was. *Art, in fiction or out of it, cannot produce copies of actual things; it must adapt, modify, and indeed build entirely anew.*

2. Yet the conte is better adapted to the copying of actual character than is the novel. The short story must confine itself to some dominant trait, or at most to a few prominent traits; all beyond this it must either exclude or merely hint at and suggest. True, *in the best artistry, this hinting will be so managed as to give the reader the impression of character completeness; it will make him see the character in perspective,* with the least possible amount of that distortion which must follow the emphasizing of but a single trait or small group of traits. Even so, however, it cannot attain to complete character presentation. But because one of its legitimate and necessary methods is, thus to select out and deal with some dominant element of character, relegating the many modifying and accompanying elements to relative obscurity, the short story can upon occasion more successfully base itself thus upon

some prominent trait in an actual person, than can the ampler novel; and by selecting also the environment and incident appertaining to this person in actual life, it can thus produce a " copy " of the " original " that will be effective. *Yet even the short story, in making this repro-duction of an actual character, must omit, tone down, tone up, and otherwise manipulate, modify, and idealize* the facts in accordance with the requirements of dramatic plot and artistic impression. Moreover, because the presenta-tion of the actual person so made will emphasize but a single element of his character, it will, even when more suggestive than that given by the novel, be if anything even less complete and broadly adequate as a true presentation of the actual man. We are forced to concede, therefore, that *in fiction the creation of a character can not be ac-complished through the copying of characters actually known in individual men and women.*

3. This, however, is fortunate, not only for the author, but for the world that depends—more perhaps than it suspects—upon the interpretations of literature for an understanding of men and character. For although every character in literature is, in some degree at least, a con-crete, individual character belonging to a distinct, individ-ual person; yet in that character every element and trait is an element and trait that belongs to human nature and human temperament, and is to be found somewhere in the characters of actual men and women. But these ele-ments will not be found always in the same groupings, or in the same degrees, or in the same circumstances; and *it is the opportunity and task of fiction to know these manifold characteristics of men and man, to bring them to light, and to exhibit them in their inherent quality.*

Further, to effect new combinations of them in imagined characters, to try their effect upon men and the affairs of men in different degrees and different combinations and different circumstances, falls also to the fiction-writer. Whereas copying would restrict him to the mere setting forth of character elements in only that degree, those combinations and circumstances, in which he might have a chance to observe them actually existent in actual persons, character creation on the other hand calls upon him to do a far more pleasant and far more profitable thing. In character creation, he is to handle the elements and traits of character with the freedom of an experimenter charged with the duty of finding new proportions, new combinations, new conditions, and new results, by means of his expert knowledge and expert skill. He works as the chemist works in seeking new and useful compounds and products, or as the botanist works in seeking to produce new varieties and determine the behavior of plants in widely variant conditions, or as the practical philanthropist works who seeks to bring about in individual men a new combination and proportion of qualities, and an adjustment of surroundings, in order that he may create a new character in the individual man.

4. *Character creation, therefore, consists (1) in the selection and combination in due proportion of certain traits, elements, or qualities of human character; (2) in making these consistent with basic human nature and class character; (3) in making them also significant of some particular phase or phases of human nature (and perhaps of class character); and (4) in addition to this, in embodying them in concrete acts, mannerisms, speech, and conduct that will impress the reader as belonging to a*

distinct and individual personality. The actual process of this selection and combination may go on in different ways. One may (A) begin by determining the particular phase or quality of human nature that he wishes to interpret. He then seeks acts, conduct, situations, and speech, together with appropriate setting and other environment, such as best agree with and express this phase and quality. Or he may (B) begin with certain mannerisms, acts, or behavior, and from these determine the aspect of human nature, and conceive the character, that his story must present; his principal task thereafter being, to provide a sufficient body of such acts, conduct, and speech adequately to display this aspect. Or again, he may (C) begin with the conception of a particular setting, environment, atmosphere, or situation, deciding from this upon that aspect of human nature and those qualities of personality which he must present, and upon the concrete acts, conduct, and speech necessary to this presentation.[15] There may be other ways of determining character, and the means of expressing it; but the three here mentioned are the commonest.

5. *The conception, therefore, of the character to be portrayed, may often determine the choice of persons to appear in and carry on the action.* For we need know the world but moderately well to know that types of character frequently associate themselves with types of individual. Brutality is characteristic of ignorance; gross luxury and barbaric display are associated with the self-sculptured person who is an artist only in the rough and

[15] Setting and environment, but especially setting, are more likely to influence the selection of class than they are to enter into the determination of character in other respects.

has devoted more attention to the multiplication of riches than to the polishing off of his self-hewn character; bigotry accompanies membership in any class educated through dogmatic precept and not through development of the reason—which fact accounts for the frequency with which literature has coupled intolerance with certain scholastic, legal, and clerical types of person. On the other hand, there are qualities of human nature and temperament that cannot be associated with any particular type of person, but are widely distributed among all types, and perhaps are universal. Pity is found in the rich and the poor, the coarse and the refined; hatred and affection characterize every class; honor and treachery may be found in the soldier, the priest, the merchant, the prostitute; there are stupid professors and lightning-witted ditchers. The more deeply the quality is rooted in basic nature, the more universal it will be. We conclude, therefore, that *although our choice of actors in the story may sometimes be guided or even determined by the character type to be portrayed, yet nevertheless the more the character quality belongs to fundamental nature and the less it is adventitious—the result of special modifying and conditioning circumstances —the less surely will it associate itself exclusively with any particular type of person.* The basic traits of man are to be found in every type and every individual.

6. We have already emphasized the necessity of the fiction-writer's dealing with materials that are within his experience, avoiding scene, situation, person, character, and action, with which he is not familiar. But this necessity should be urged again here. *Nowhere is ignorance— lack of intimate information—more fatal than in the attempt to present persons in character,* and nowhere is

such ignorance so impossible of concealment. Without knowing man and men, the writer can never create persons who will move and live. Yet the frequency with which we find inadequate equipment in this indispensable qualification for dramatic narrative, is surprising. It is surprising because a writer needs not to know all the world and its " cities of men "—needs not to have traveled widely, to have lived a life of thrill, change, adventure, or far-extending activity himself. He will without this have sufficient opportunity for studying and learning men. We are forced to conclude, therefore, that many of the wish-I-were writers have not exercised their powers of observation and sympathetic understanding, or indeed lack such powers; so wofully do they fail in comprehension and representation of human trait and mannerism.

7. One of the most common manifestations of this hopeless lack of equipment is found in those stories that go far away from home—far outside the writer's range of experience—for person, plot, or incident. The ambitious college girl, whose broad experience perhaps includes life in her home town in Maine, Iowa, or Colorado, and in the little " city " where the state university or woman's college is, with (perhaps) a flying visit to Boston or Chicago and one supreme occasion when she was guest at a " junior prom " in some man's college—this little lady must attempt a story of the Riviera, of St. Petersburg (Russia, not Florida!), of Hongkong or Mandalay; must undertake to show us Siberian exiles, Japanese naval officers, the inhabitants of some (largely imaginary) Chinatown; must try to build a plot of vast financial or political intrigue, of domestic infelicity in " high life," or adventure on the " high " seas. All of which is pitifully an exhibition of

poor judgment. For though it is true that the basic traits of human nature are the same always and everywhere, it is not true that the customs, manners, and mannerisms, the social conventions, the setting—all the endless range of those externals through which characterization must be achieved—it is not true that these things can be intuitively realized. The externals must be known, and known familiarly, if they are to be reported convincingly, and *even a genius must be intimately acquainted with that multiplicity of accompanying detail through which alone the characteristic individuality of character, of setting, and of incident, can be established.*

8. Perhaps the college girl who has lived her twenty years with open eyes and interpreting heart can—if blessed of the gods—write a passable story of the things that might happen in her home town, or in the college. But she knows nothing of the habitués of the Riviera, of Russian grand dukes and princesses, of Siberian exiles, of Japanese naval officers, of the " four hundred "—nothing except that they are men and women. And lacking knowledge of them, she lacks the first essential to adequate reporting. It is inadequacy of information that gives us the stock Englishman who is an Englishman only because he litters up the floor with H's that he ought to be more careful of, and can't keep his monocle in his eye; the stock cowboy who is a cowboy because he yells whoopee! swills whisky, and shoots up the town whenever he steps outdoors; the " darky " who is a darky because he says " Gorrymighty, massa " at every opportunity; and other wooden-man creations that have no individuality and about the same amount of human nature. The writer with an understanding of the nature of true characterization, will shun these stock

persons as he would the plague; and the writer with a just sense of the possible and impossible in characterization will undertake to present no character that calls for such setting, environment, incident, or other accompanying material as he is not sufficiently familiar with to report with convincing accuracy of detail.

9. We have in the preceding paragraphs spoken of character and of the person possessing the character, as if they were identical. And this, for most practical purposes, they are. Hence in the succeeding paragraphs, wherein we now consider the means by which character traits are presented to the reader, we shall continue to speak of the character and the person as one. We pass, then, to this consideration. Our first observation is, that *physical description of the person may be utilized to suggest character.* This function, indeed, is the main function that description of persons can lay claim to in fiction. There is, to be sure, a limited interest merely in knowing that the hero is tall and dark and has curly hair, that the heroine is petite and " walks with a grace all her own," and even that the old farmer is lean and angular. But such information is too often of the unimportant-if-true sort, and with discriminating readers is scarcely of interest at all—certainly not when it represents only the callow writer's conception of her own appearance or the appearance of her wished-for sweetheart, as they might be if things were different. There must be a more commanding reason for describing the person; and this justifying reason is found in *some relation that always exists between personal appearance and essential character.* This relation may be that of resemblance, or that of contrast; the outward aspect may be an index of the spirit within, or it

may be one of those always startling physical incongruities reminding us that noble spirits may house in ignoble bodies, and fair bodies incase foul souls.

10. Of the two relations, that based upon *incongruity of the outer and the inner man* is the less common and on the whole the less frequently available. Indeed, it is usable at all only because the other relationship, that of correspondence between the inner and the outer, is the rule. The fact that, even aside from conventional conceptions, the outer man so often bewrays the inner, gives an added effectiveness to characterizations in which the exception is presented. Incongruity thus becomes the method of delineations where sharply engraved outlines are desired— the effect of keen contrasts, with the resulting effect of pathos and tragedy or of humor, satire, or burlesque. The fat man full of sentimental love, the deformed woman full of deep and passionate affection for the man who loves the physically perfect in woman—figures like these, presented adequately, must always move us deeply. But from the nature of the method, we find it best reserved for stories in which the effect of strong contrast is especially sought.

11. But *similarity between the inner and the outer* is common enough in actual life, and has established itself so thoroughly in the technical conventions of art as to become the rule. When, therefore, contrast is not sought, the depicting of the outer man as corresponding with the inner is the natural method. The shrewd man has sharp features and small, sharp eyes; the prying person has a thin, pointed nose; the good-humored person has many little wrinkles at the corners of mouth and eyes; the big and leering mouth is the sign of foolishness; shifting eyes

betray the shifty spirit; fingers that are never quiet speak
of nerves that are never at rest; a swinging gait means
independence—perhaps the independence of resolution and
courage, perhaps the independence of carelessness and irre-
sponsibility. There is truth in the popular song, " Every
little movement has a meaning of its own." So has every
line and attitude. He is indeed fortunate who has observed men and women to such purpose that their character is revealed to him by trivial, yet all-significant,
externals—to whom the significant external signs present
themselves surely and naturally when he conceives a trait
and portrays a character. For these things are not matters
of downright invention, cannot be thought up or manu-
factured. They lie in the natural relations existing between man's body and his character. The outer bodies
forth the inner.

12. Description of the person of an actor, therefore—
of his appearance, his mannerisms of physical expression
and act; of the outward man that so suggestively cor-
responds to the man within—can frequently be used effectively toward characterizing the individual. Such
description may be massed (but not without the disadvantages that attend massed description), or it may be distributed; it may be given by the author directly, or be
placed by him on the lips of some person in the story—
even those of the person himself who is being characterized; it may include only details, or it may include also
a summarizing description that gathers up the details in
a general estimate. Illustrations of direct description can
be found everywhere; the books on rhetoric, narration,
description, and fiction-writing abound with them. A
single example must serve here:

Tall, he was, and queerly suggestive of a spinning-top turned upside down and fitted with legs; for his head was small and pointed, and hinted, moreover, of being as hard as the iron peg of the top; and the loose and modish topcoat in which he had encased himself, hung on narrow shoulders, but below flared out with the brazen independence of fad-bold styles. Had Ranger been less colossal in height and diameter, he would have resembled an overgrown gnome, tubby and rotund in the middle, making his uncertain way on teetering legs. Yet there was physical strength in the man notwithstanding his ill proportions. The long arms looked as if they had been practiced in reaching out and seizing, or in giving tremendous blows. The bulbous body looked as if it were able to remain inert against great pressure, giving stability to the uncertain legs, and the head looked as if by sheer repeated pecking it might pierce a way through stone-wall obstacles. Only when you looked into the eye—which was hard to catch—did you see that the dwindling legs and the pindling cranium might be truer indexes of the man's character than were his fusiform globularity, his mass, his height, his prehensible arms and hammer fists, and his head with its shape of the steel-nosed bullet.

13. *Another direct means of characterizing is that of frank analysis.* Analysis, however, is closely akin to expository writing; and to say this is enough to warn the tempted writer that forbearance is better than indulgence when he entertains any doubt about the advisability of employing this method. Further, since exposition grows disproportionately obvious as it grows longer, passages of analysis must needs be short—particularly so in the

conte. It is better to break the passage up into smaller portions of analysis or explanation, and distribute these at opportune places in the story, than to permit the analysis to grow unwieldy in a single longer passage. What is here said, however, does not imply that one shall fail to *give a key to the character early in the presentation,* even though many of the doors to full appreciation of it be left for later unlocking. Neither does it imply that occasions will not arise where outright analysis will not be, all things considered, the best method—as when a person must be shown in action without sufficient precedent opportunity to develop by other means that trait of character which must be understood in order to understand the motive with which he is now to act, or when subordinate persons must be characterized whose importance is too slight to justify the more dramatic methods of presenting their character. We scarcely need add that, *when either description or analysis seems to be required in mass, the best places for it are the points of lowered interest in the narrative*—the troughs between the wave-crests of action. To break into the action-movement, stopping it in order to describe or analyze, is crude and often fatal malpractice. A brief passage of analysis is here given, to illustrate concretely this method of direct characterization:

His was a soul that thrived upon black tempers followed by hysterical melancholy. Between these black storm periods, with their sequence of penitential rains, he was blithe, indifferent, chirpy, moody, active, quiescent, as chance decreed. But these intervening moods were merely the fortuitous variations of his spiritual year, and had no fixed relations with his full seasons; sullen rage and equi-

noctial remorse were his spring, summer, autumn, and
winter of emotion, and swayed all lesser periods, as spring,
summer, autumn, and winter dominate all the minor epochs
of the solar year.

14. Yet *neither description nor analysis is the writer's
best dependence. On act and deed only—on the action of
the individual—can be founded dramatic characterization.*
Description and analysis are but accessories and aids to
this higher method. We best perceive that a man is quick-
tempered when we see him " fly off the handle " and do
something in hasty anger. We need no explanation to
make us know that a woman is treacherous if we see her
wantonly betraying a friend. The clerk seen appropriat-
ing a package from the shelves is classified by his act; the
boy who takes a thrashing to save a weaker lad from too
severe punishment, wears a Carnegie medal to our eyes
without its being pinned on him by an analysis of his
courage and sympathy. The man whom we find sitting in
his club, telling unclean stories—we know the fullness of
his heart from the speech of his mouth, as we do that of
his brother the other loafer who tells the same stories in
the country store. The patient response of a husband to
the nagging of his wife, characterizes him as much as her
nagging speeches characterize her. All this but says that
*act and speech dramatically reveal character as nothing
else can do.* Therefore, the writer has endless opportunity
to achieve varied dramatic characterization; for as the
variations of character and temper, and the number of
convincing combinations of them, is infinite, so *the number
and kinds of act and speech through which character can be
portrayed, are infinite.* The act and the manner of the act,

whether one drive a dagger to his enemy's heart or flick a fly from his own bald head, are the best revelation of character—and I do not know that any degree-pursuing research enthusiast has yet had the brilliantly barren impulse to look up just how many ways there are of doing either.

15. We cannot close this section without speaking of one other means of indicating, more or less directly, the character of the actor—*psychological narration*. Psychological narration is found most extensively in the so-called psychological story, but it is likely to be useful anywhere, the danger of employing it lying in the ease with which internal action can displace external action in the narrative. Psychological narration sometimes is hard to discriminate from psychological analysis, but it is, in its clearest forms, distinctly separate. *It consists in narrating, or recounting, mental and spiritual operations, and its justification lies in the fact that no external act can intelligibly express some of the significant operations of intellect, impulse, mood, and spirit through which acts and conduct are determined.* Unless, therefore, the psychological events be narrated that constitute these operations, they cannot be presented in any dramatic or even pseudo-dramatic way. To narrate thus the incidents that make up the stream of consciousness, is to reveal motive by revealing the hidden springs whose release sets going outward events. Hence it reveals character, at least indirectly, since motive results from character. The beginning writer, however, should use no more psychological narration than he finds himself compelled to use, and should admit it only in short and well-distributed passages.[16]

[16] Naturally, the longer the story, the longer the passages of description, analysis, psychological narration, and the like, that can be introduced.

XXVI. Dialogue Lightens the Narrative, Contributes to Exposition and Intensification, Furthers Action, and Characterizes

1. In contemporary short fiction, dialogue is prominent; sometimes it displaces all the other means of presentation, and the story becomes still more nearly a play—conversation constituting all the story and suggesting even the " business " of the actors. The increasing prominence of dialogue has been an accompaniment of the general improvement of narrative method; for dialogue has been found not only to have a function particularly its own in fictional narrative, but also an ancillary function, relieving the heaviness and monotony sometimes attending narration even when concerned immediately with action. Experience has demonstrated *the usefulness of dialogue in lightening the narrative, contributing expository or intensifying detail, advancing the action, and indicating the character of the persons.*

2. The usefulness of conversation in lightening the narrative is evident. A steady flow of purely historical assertion must sooner or later grow monotonous, and readers of fiction find this especially true. Probably there is, consciously or unconsciously, the reasoning that in life itself men speak freely about themselves and their affairs, and that fiction ought to represent them as they are in life—the more so as the ebb and flow of converse in actual life goes so far toward making it interesting and explaining the motives and character of men to one another. *The occurrence, therefore, of passages of dialogue in a fiction narrative makes the presentation seem more*

dramatic (in both senses of the word), breaks up long historical statement into livelier and briefer form, makes reading easier to the eye, makes the humanity of the fictional persons more apparent, enables the reader to get illuminating glimpses of character without the need of wallowing through explanatory mud puddles, and—in a word—brings the story closer in form, method, and matter to the realities of life.

3. Yet numerous good stories are told without the employment of dialogue; for to some narratives it is not essential, and some successful authors have no gift in dialogue. We are to remember that there is no hard-and-fast rule of fiction-writing—that the author's conception and the material which it calls on him to present may at any time produce a new set of conditions, to meet which he may have to do even the exact opposite of the rule, and that his success will be determined by the significance of the conception and the skill with which he meets the conditions created by it. Good stories are written in which dialogue is not required at all, or in which it is avoided. But this does not lessen the importance of the counsel: *when the speech of persons needs to be reported at all, it is usually best reported in direct dialogue form, not as indirect discourse; and for the sake of variety, vigor, and naturalness in the narrative, effort should be made to include dialogue whenever its presence will not interfere with more important ends.* This can be summed up in the advice to use dialogue freely when the requirements of the story will permit it.

4. The utility of conversation as a means of indicating the premises on which the plot depends—that is, of present-

ing exposition [17]—is very great in the hands of a competent story-teller and dramatist. In the hands of the unskilled, it is a doubtful means. Exposition given through dialogue, is almost of necessity distributed, not massed; very seldom does a long passage of expository dialogue succeed.[18] At its best, it is usually not better than massed direct exposition would be, and as conversation it wants naturalness, spontaneity, and lightness—is not true to the nature of ordinary conversation, which seldom goes back of the present moment or attempts a massed résumé such as the massed exposition must be. But *if care be exercised to keep the speeches from growing too long, to keep the conversation from monotonously over-dwelling on the expository facts, and in such way to couple the statement of the expository facts with the situation and incidents of the moment that the reader feels a situation to be developing in the present and at the same time revealing to him the past out of which it springs—then dialogue becomes a thoroughly satisfactory vehicle of exposition.*

5. Exposition of the results of the outcome—consequential exposition—can likewise be given, either directly or by suggestion, through dialogue. When Hotspur, al-

---

[17] Presentation of setting and environment, and indeed many of the effects of atmosphere, can be worked through dialogue. Setting and environment may at this point be regarded (for practical purposes) as included in exposition. The employment of dialogue for the creation of atmosphere scarcely permits of separate treatment. The effect of atmosphere will result from the subjective coloring found no less in the substance and manner of dialogue than in the other elements of the story.

[18] For a long speech of exposition that does succeed, see the opening of Coppée's *The Substitute*. But note that the manner of the speech is not notably successful; the expression is over-sophisticated and over-mature for a mere boy.

luding to something else just said about the hazard of
certain action that is as full of risk as crossing a torrent
" on the uncertain footing of a spear," bursts forth with
the vivid comment, " If he fall off, good night! " his
speech amounts to consequential exposition; the failure
of this undertaking will mean ruin.   Consequential exposition, however, is less likely to appear, for the simple reason
that most plots reveal sufficiently, without explanation,
what the after-results of their outcome will be—although
in comedy the fun may sometimes be intensified by allusion
to these results.   Indeed, either comedy effect or tragic suspense can be heightened by such allusions, provided that
they are introduced in such manner as not to anticipate
the outcome itself.   As comprehension of the consequential
results is necessary to appreciation of the complication and
crisis, and as in the management of the story they associate
themselves naturally with the complication rather than
with the outcome that would produce them, the skillful
writer can accomplish this revelation successfully without
letting the reader know prematurely how the struggle is to
turn.   And dialogue is one means to this end.

6. Again, *dialogue is useful as a means of intensifying
mood-impression or emphasizing important facts.*   In so
using it, however, caution is necessary.   Conversation
cannot be utilized merely by flinging it into the narrative;
it must be rooted deep in the incident, must take place
because at the moment nothing but the breaking into
speech will so adequately agree with the situation.   It
never does to say, " I will now use some dialogue to lighten
things up and throw emphasis on these few facts."   If
the dialogue does not spring naturally from the situation,
it is not to be admitted; and if it grows long without in

some way aiding the progress of the story, it must be excluded, even though its concentrative effect is good. If this seem too strong an assertion, let us say that *concentrative, or amplifying, dialogue must never be permitted to interfere with advance in the movement of the story.*

7. And the sentence with which we have just closed the preceding paragraph recalls what must always be, from the viewpoint of dramatic construction, the main object of the story: advance. The story must always march forward, with only those halts and campings that are necessary for recuperation and survey of route before another advance. *In the furthering of the action which is thus described, dialogue may have an important part.* Study of stories in which conversation is prominent will quickly make evident what is meant by advancing the story through dialogue. At the close of the dialogue passage, a motive has been settled, a complication revealed or resolved, a determination reached, or some other condition established, without which the incidents could not proceed at all, or could not proceed so directly, toward the decisive moment, the climactic height, or the outcome.

8. As intimated already, there are situations of which only dialogue is the natural expression and resolution; the action has come to a point where the persons must speak—must express themselves, their character, their mood, their motives, their determinations, by words. Speech is one form of action—a form in which motive, character, will, cause and effect, the final and decisive play of the motivating forces, are often seen in rapid and conclusive working. Thus in *Markheim,* most of the action is in the dialogue (psychological narration); "Anthony Hope" made the *Dolly Dialogues* mainly out of

dialogue—so much so that they seem almost stage-drama instead of narrative drama. Examples of dialogue (single speeches or interchange of speech) that constitutes or furthers action can be found in many stories; the student has only to look over the short fiction in the current magazines, but specific citations of standard stories are: Barrie's *The Courting of T'Now-head's Bell,* Mérimée's *Mateo Falcone;* Stevenson's *A Lodging for the Night;* Daudet's *The Pope's Mule;* and Kipling's *Without Benefit of Clergy.* (Kipling and O. Henry are among the authors who employ dialogue easily and much.)

9. All the functions or employments of dialogue yet mentioned, however, are at least partly contributory; the dialogue is used as a device or means to some end not directly dependent on it, is accessory, ancillary, subordinate. It is, for example, useful in advancing the action, but is thus useful merely as a narrative and dramatic device, not primarily for its own sake. Has dialogue then no function that is distinctly and primarily its own? Must it always be employed as a servant of servants, never rising itself to the rank of a principal officer in the household? And if it indeed has some function that is eminently its own, what is that function? *It has such a special function, the function is exceedingly important, and dialogue often performs it as it could be performed by no other narrative or dramatic agent. The function is, characterization.*

10. Character can be laid before the reader in three ways; by outright explanation, by acts and deeds, and by speech—a form of action, but important enough to be considered by itself. *Only those manifestations of character which are made through act or speech are truly dra-*

matic. *Therefore, dialogue is one of the two sole methods by which inner character and motive can be made concrete and outwardly manifest.* And as even the lightest and most inconsequential fiction, if it rises to worth in its own class, is based upon character as a premise—whether the story emphasize character or not—dialogue becomes one of the most important dependencies of the fiction writer. As such we will now consider it.

11. " Out of the fullness of the heart the mouth speaketh." That is the foundation principle of dialogue as a means of characterization. And it holds universally. For even if the words uttered are false, the course of events in the story (which herein surely rises superior to actual life) will make their falseness manifest, and thus show the fullness of heart out of which they are spoken to be falsehood. Speech, therefore, associated with act and deed, should in fiction infallibly reveal character. And from this fact we draw two immediately applicable rules of practice for the writing of dialogue: A. *Conceive with clearness the character that is to be presented, its essential traits and qualities.* B. *Build the dialogue directly upon this conception, putting such speech (and on the whole* [19]

[19] The restriction is far more important in short than in long fiction. In short fiction, only the " high lights " can be presented; the selective process has to be carried much further, and exclusion made much more strict, than in long narratives. The novel has time for bringing out what the photographer knows as detail. The metaphor is helpful. The conte is a snapshot; it can catch only the strongest outlines of the picture. But the novel is a time exposure, and can be so regulated as to get the detail that lies in shadow. Again, speed and a large lens aperture go with the snapshot, and this means lack of " depth "; but the time exposure, using a small, intensifying, perspectifying aperture, dwells more seeingly and lingeringly on the subject, and has not only outline

only such speech) into the mouth of the person as springs from these traits and qualities, and serves, along with his acts, to reveal them clearly.

12. For the creation of dialogue based upon character as moral quality, explicit directions (of course) cannot be given. How to perceive what substance and manner of speech will accord with any particular character trait and quality, is no more susceptible of being taught than is the process by which the author shall conceive the character itself. These are things that must depend on his powers of observation, his knowledge of men, and his sense of inner correspondences. The teacher can do no more than impress on the student the vital necessity that *the speech of the person shall be consistent with, and more than that, shall be highly indicative of, the character with which that person has been endowed*. When, however, we regard dialogue in its outward aspects—in its linguistic and not its moral or symbolical guise—we can state at least some general principles definitely enough to be laid hold on practically.

13. Among these, the main or guiding principle is but shade and tone, background and depth, with many gradations of distinctness in the half and quarter lights and the shades. Yet again, in the development, the best that can be expected from the snapshot plate is such *suggestion* of full detail as prevents the negative from being merely a skeleton outline in which the shadows and their content show only as thin or bare spots. But in developing the time-exposed plate, such manipulation is possible as will coax up the shadows and bring forth a rich abundance of softening and contributory detail. In like degree, *the short story (conte) may and should* **suggest** *the softening half-lights and shadow, with their accessory detail; but it cannot aim to develop these out in any degree of fullness*. It has its own artistic aim, which is different from that of the timed picture; and it must confine itself to what that aim involves.

that of individualized language—language made to fit the individual who uses it, and the moment and situation when it is used. We begin with this in its most general sense, and say that *speech must be fitted to represent the type of character and person with which it is associated.* Frivolous character will produce frivolous speech; religious character, conversation that is tinged with religion; rugged character, speech that is itself rugged. In like manner, different classes of person use different manners of speech. The lawyer is likely to have a speech that is involved and periodic, from the study of forms and books and from pleading before judges, or a more colloquial and plausible (and sometimes overbearing) manner, from questioning witnesses and addressing juries. There is—at least conventionally—a speech characteristic of the farmer; the Hebrew cloaks-and-suits manufacturer certainly has his own style of expression, if Mr. Montague Glass's stories of Abe and Mawruss are to be taken as accurate. True, many of the " types " familiar to us are conventional; true also that many influences are strongly at work to break down the differences in speech between class and class; and true yet again that the classifications overlap, grow confused, and become both arbitrary and indistinct. Even so, however, we find numerous quite apparent manners, or if you wish, dialects, characteristic of distinct groups. The Yankee villager, the Southern Cracker, the ranchman of the West, the seaman—mention of these is sufficient to convince us that there are manners of speech broadly belonging to one class or group of persons and not to any other. It is not necessary here to enumerate these classes; but when we come to write, *it emphatically is necessary that we realize what form of speech is appropriate*

*to the type of person whom we are portraying, and place
language in his mouth accordingly.*

14. Yet many things besides merely his membership
in some more or less clearly distinct group will modify
and determine the speech of any individual. The educated
man (to illustrate) may be lawyer, clergyman, merchant,
scientist, or mechanic; the mechanic may be Yankee,
Southerner, French-Canadian, German-American; the
German-American may be grocer or editor; the editor may
be college bred or the product of life in a country town
plus a scramble upward from the job of printers' devil.
A thousand influences may shape language as spoken by the
individual, modifying it and making it to vary from the
type-language of his class; and *the fiction-writer, in portraying person and character, must thus individualize the
speech that he causes his persons to speak, just as he
must individualize those persons themselves.* Here again
his safest—indeed, his only safe—guide must be, close
observation and acquaintance with varied types and individuals. Nevertheless, we can catalogue some of the influences that help to determine the language of the
individual person.

15. First, *a man's past is always perceptible in his
speech.* The farm-boy may become the city man, rising to
eminence as journalist, banker, or lawyer; yet a few at
least of the traces of an unlettered boyhood will always
remain; he is likely to mispronounce a few words that
he mislearned, and to employ now and then some turn of
phrase more notable for rusticity than for grammatical
correctness or rhetorical purity; the very care and precision
with which he handles his later language is reminiscent of

days when he spoke with less finish and care; and in a larger sense, his language will be colored by his past through the fund of rural figure and illustration with which his early life has supplied him. A " Bowery Boy " —albeit " there ain't no sich annymile " now—though risen to be political master of a state, will yet speak much in the dialect of his origins. Even as early as the age of ten or twelve, the lad who has been acquainted intimately with books will have a finish and correctness of speech that will not wholly disappear, even should later circumstances turn him into foreman of a street-gang (though, if he have the quality of survival, he is likely then to acquire for practical purposes a language far from bookish!).

16. Offsetting this, *a man's present also affects his speech.* Thus, his occupation surely and persistently influences his language, supplying him subjects of conversation, determining the matter and direction of his thought, insinuating into his vocabulary the terms and cant of his business, and otherwise making him speak after its own manner. Occupation, however, is merely one aspect of environment; and to greater or less extent, environment inevitably constrains the speaker's speech. If he be in surroundings that are natural and easy to him, he speaks in the main the language peculiar to that environment; if it be unnatural or uneasy to him, his natural form of speech will feel the constraint and suffer from it; but always he speaks the speech in no small part as it is taught him by molding circumstances. Again, the speaker's mood, be it temporary or more deep-seated, will color and shape his expression. The angry bricklayer does

not speak as does the bricklayer in good humor; the morose man, embittered against his work, the people about him, or the world in general, will reveal his bitterness in his words, his sentences, his conversations.

17. Manifestly, then, a varied assortment of influences enter into the making of individual speech, and all these influences must be recognized by the writer when he undertakes to create appreciation of character and trait through dialogue. We say "when." For dialogue is not always to be worked to the hardest with a view to characterization. It must always be consistent with the character, but it may in certain circumstances be over-emphasized if its characterizing value alone be thought of. A less definitely individualized speech, for instance, will be assigned to minor persons in the story than is worked out for the leading person. Just as the subordinate persons are less minutely specialized in character (so that they shall not divide character interest with the central persons), so their manner of expression may be less minutely individualized; they can without danger speak a more standardized language than can the leading person. So, too, when dialogue is not required to serve the particular purposes of local color, its dialectal and linguistic peculiarities, especially in the speech of minor persons, will be less emphasized. Even so, however, the dialogue must still be kept true to the character, the person, the situation, the environment, the mood, and the action; and to keep it true to person and character, the writer must definitely realize all the influences that have affected the character or worked upon the speech of the persons as that person has been conceived.

XXVII. The Main Practical Problems of Dialogue are, to Make Sure of Essential Truthfulness and Produce Verisimilitude

1. We have seen that dialogue must be true to the person, the situation, and the character. This means that it must faithfully represent the person, not merely as a member of a class group, but also as an individual; must faithfully represent his character in (a) its outward traits and (b) its inner springs and motives; and must faithfully represent also the mood in which it is spoken, and the mood and spirit of the situation and action of which it constitutes a part. That is, *dialogue must be essentially true.* All this has been dwelt upon in the preceding section. We need here, then, note only what the elements of dialogue are in which this essential truthfulness will be found. In this, the universal principles of expression guide us. *Truthfulness lies in the substance and the manner of the dialogue.* According as the thoughts, ideas, and feelings that it embodies are thoughts and feelings of the sort that would be thought or felt by the individual member of a certain class, possessing the character with which the author's conception has endowed him, and finding himself in the definite situation now created by the action—to the same degree the speech will be essentially true, provided that its manner be likewise such as accords with the person, with his character, and with the situation and mood. Assuming that the author has as definite a conception as he should have of his type, person, character, and situation, he needs then, to secure essential truthfulness, but to follow the good old rule for judging people in actual life; *put yourself in his place. What would be thought and*

felt in such circumstances, what should be said, and what the particular person would say, will then become apparent.

2. But—at least in its substance—dialogue may be essentially true, yet not appear to be so; it may lack verisimilitude. And with the attempt to produce verisimilitude, most of the problems usually discussed in connection with the practical management of dialogue usually associate themselves. Assuming essential truthfulness in the substance of the dialogue, let us now consider how essential true-seeming can be produced. We may begin by saying that *verisimilitude in dialogue is the effect of plausibility created by the skillful management of conversational details.* The aim of this plausibility is, to make the reader feel that the person and his character are actual, and that the person is speaking as naturally he would speak in the same circumstances did they actually surround him.

3. This aim recognized, *dialogue finds itself shut off from all forms of expression that suggest self-consciousness,* except in the instances in which the author purposely shows the speaker forth as self-conscious. On its prohibitive side, this fact will be seen to bar the employment of long, intricate, periodic, or otherwise bookish, oratorical, or affected sentences when they do not owe their quality to the intentional representation of corresponding character-traits in the speaker. Normal conversation is neither stilted nor pedantic, is not a constant struggle for " style "; it is downright and direct, the colloquial expression of thought, simple in proportion to its matter, colored and either heightened or lowered by the circumstances of the moment. And *normal conversation must be the standard for the choice of words and the form of sentences employed in reporting dialogue. All departures from this norm*

must be justified by the individuality of the character and person or by particular circumstances in the mood or situation.

4. Yet *dialogue cannot be merely the reporting verbatim of speech* such as the persons would employ were they conversing in actual life. Were it this, it would in print prove prolix, redundant, grammatically faulty, and tedious. *Normal conversation cannot be carried over unchanged into print and continue to appear normal.* Reading of biographies in which the conversations of great men, reputed to be interesting talkers, are reported with that inaccuracy that comes from too close adherence to actualities, should be sufficient to convince one of this fact—and "realistic dialogue" in fiction should be more than enough. All artistic effect is the result of discriminative selection of impressive aspects for presentation; and in conversation reported for artistic purpose, this is as true as it is elsewhere. In making this selection, we *choose the significant portions and manner of representative talk by the persons at particular moments when situation, mood, action, or character gives this talk especial value.*

5. We may assume here that the substance of the conversation reported has interest—that it associates itself vitally with matters that, from the nature of the story, are significant. But it must do not this only; for verisimilitude, it must also compress its substance into relatively limited compass. This compression is the result largely of the pruning away of verbal excrescences, of immaterial facts, of redundancies, and all the mass of conversational underbrush, watersprouts, and dead wood, usually found in actual talk. The main trunk and limbs of the thought, and no more, are ordinarily to be left. Only that remains

which is of importance in suggesting or outrightly saying what, by means of the conversation, we desire to convey. *Compression, therefore, in our sense of the term, results from simplification and rejection; it is the process of concentrating and intensifying speech until it becomes charged with significance and interpretive effect.*

6.   We are, however, not yet done with the term " representative speech." Is idealized speech—the natural language thus pruned, shorn, and denatured—representative speech? Do we not falsify by thus improving? We do not. For *verisimilitude in dialogue results only when some degree of improving manipulation is exercised upon speech in its natural form;* the raw material must undergo treatment before the necessary results are produced. The language of the blasphemer cannot be as blasphemous in fiction as it often is—and with less effect—in actual life; the language of the bookworm cannot be so pedantic, the dialect of the woodsman cannot be so illiterate.[20] There is, when the best effects are attained, nearly always a toning down or a toning up from the actual into the idealized; and language thus idealized may, through its suggestive power—the very product of this modifying process—carry the desired impression home more truly than would verbatim repeating.

7.   There are, then, pitfalls in the way of the tyro when he undertakes to report dialogue for fictional effect. Some of these have already been hinted at; he may, for instance, fall into *the error of choosing words that the person he has conceived would be unlikely ever to use, and of neglecting words that would be exceedingly natural to*

[20] " Cannot be," yet they frequently are; for not a few writers depend upon exaggeration, not adjustment, in dialogue.

the same person.   Or he may throw the speech into a sentence-form that is unnatural or untrue, forgetting that normal speech—the standard he must keep in mind—is usually uttered in comparatively short sentences composed of comparatively simple and familiar words.   On the other hand, he may forget that, *though ordinary conversation shifts rapidly and irrelevantly from topic to topic, fiction dialogue must be so directed that its stages accomplish each a definite purpose*—the expression of a mood, the advancement of an incident, the presentation of a theme, and so on.   Actual conversation may and does meander, but dialogue in fiction must, even when it seems to linger and stray, drive forward to a point, and its substance and its manner must each be determined with this point in mind.

8. Other pitfalls, too, there are.   One of the widest, deepest, and least suspected of these is that of attempted brilliancy.   The writer fancies that it is his opportunity and his duty to supply " scintillating coruscations " of fine phrasing and wonderful repartee for the delight of enraptured readers; whereas, it is his business to find out how groceryman John Jones and schoolteacher Sally Smith will speak in the circumstances in which he has imagined them, and to report their words with the least amount of " improvement " that is consistent with giving them the appearance of truth to life.   *In the conte especially is there small opportunity for that egoistic, or egotistic, exploitation of the author's conversational brilliancy which to the apprentice seems so desirable.*   For the short story does not exist as a vehicle for the author's public parade of his own wit and philosophy; it exists solely to body forth a single conception of certain persons acting

out a certain set of incidents until they reach a conclusive outcome.   Act or speech that does not clearly aid in bodying forth this coherent and climactic passage from life, has no place in the conte.   Whether it has a place in the novel is quite another matter; it may have, and it may not.

9.   Another pitfall, that of over-accuracy in the reporting of speech, has already been explained.   *Truth to conversational effect is not attained by stenographic transcripts of what the persons say; it is attained rather by omitting the large amount of irrelevant, redundant, and verbose detail which they ordinarily speak, and heightening and simplifying the part of their speech that remains.   Effective dialogue, therefore, seems like actual conversation, but is indeed merely its substance and manner idealized.*   Yet another pitfall, that of attempted self-revelation, gapes just along the pitfall of attempted brilliancy.   Emphatically, the "message" that the young writer feels he has for the world does not call for preachment; not often is his philosophy of life important to the telling of his story except in so far as he owes to it his point of view.   Rather, *it will reach the world most impressively through the characters he conceives, the persons he presents, the scenes he chooses to set forth, and the atmosphere that he creates from all these materials.*   Any other "message" is secondary in importance to that which his story, unclouded by accompanying philosophizing or sermonizing not vitally involved in its own narration, will carry to the reader.   And moreover, though in long fiction there is sometimes a place for extraneous matter of this sort, in the conte there is no separate place for it.   If it cannot be packed into the substance of the story, it cannot be taken along at all;

it is excess baggage, and as such should be packed and transported separately.[21]

10. Particular hints on the management of speech in dialogue need not be further multiplied. The beginner, however, will be bothered by the problem of " he said " and like expressions. He should try to avoid the necessity of oft-repeated " saids " by casting the dialogue in such form that the identity of the speaker will be plain without specific indication. When verbs of utterance are necessary, they should be varied from speech to speech. This prevents monotonous repetition, and affords an opportunity to characterize the speech by indicating its quality; thus " drawled " will be full of characterization when " said " or " remarked " will be colorless. Long lists of synonyms for " said," " remarked," etc., will be found in books and periodicals upon writing and composition. The question which evidently has no purpose except to afford an opening for explanation or answering speech, is baldly inartistic; as, " What did you do then ? " Devices for indicating broken or hesitating speech, and the like, are almost entirely mechanical. If the dialogue calls for such speeches, means of indicating the desired effect will suggest themselves. They should always be simple—a dash, a line of leaders (. . . . .), and the like.

11. The question, Dialect or no dialect, and if dialect, how much ? may be raised here. The dialect story is not in as great favor as it was at one time. It was a form of the local-color story, and this too has fallen off in popularity, although it has by no means disappeared, nor

---

[21] But distributed comment may be effectively used, introduced in association with dialogue by means of commenting words placed before or after the speech.

will. A story strong in dialect may prove a pleasant variation, affording new opportunity to show the underlying
nature of man working out the course of human life in
new surroundings—for when dialect is important in a
story, the persons, setting, and environment are usually
also somewhat different from the formal standard. A
story calling for much New England dialect, for example,
is likely to be a story cast and staged to show New England
village life, New England seacoast life, New England
lumbering life, or the like—the life of some more or less
separate and distinct, if not isolated, social group in its
characteristic environment. There is, of course, no reason
why the speaker of any dialect cannot be brought into the
most familiar and usual surroundings, and there portrayed,
provided that his introduction into and continuance in this
alien environment be made plausible.

12. In managing dialect, one great danger is, that the
dialect will be overdone. Both speech and spelling can be
made extreme. *Merely a salting of dialect terms, and a
restrained employment of dialect spellings, will be more
successful* than the building up of freakish speech such as
never was on sea or land. In indicating speech intended to
have a foreign tang—the language of foreigners attempting
English, or the English rendering of a foreign tongue—the
introduction of foreign words in large numbers should be
avoided; instead, employ a fairly literal translation of
the foreign idiom over into English. And no historical,
foreign, or other dialect verisimilitude ever resulted from
the mechanical employment of titles, names, and phrases
that are merely formal and conventional devices—the gad-
zooks, 'sbloods, and car-r-rambas of brummagem imitation.

13. The foundation of successful dialogue-reporting is

now plain—the same foundation as that of successful portrayal of character and individual action. The writer must know his people, his society, and their environment. He must know not merely what people in general talk about, and what they say; he must know, also, what persons of the particular class with which he is dealing talk about, and what they say, and how they say it. Thus we come back yet again to the counsel that cannot too often be emphasized for those who wish to write fiction: *get out among people; learn men, their ways, their thought, and their speech. No writer who was even moderately skillful in the use of his pen, ever had insurmountable difficulty in presenting either dialogue or deed, incident or motive, who knew his people, their ways, and their world.*

THE QUESTION ANSWERED

A number of the questions often asked by beginners in short-story writing are here set down and answered briefly by themselves, although most of them are answered, at least by implication, in the preceding pages.

What is climax? Climax is the rise of the plot and interest to its heights of suspense and emotion. Really the term covers all the period in which this rising effect is evident; but it is often used to indicate merely the height of the climax.

What is suspense, and how is it produced? Suspense is a stirring of present interest coupled with a strong sense that we are approaching some climactic situation or incident, the nature of which we strongly wish to learn. This interest is produced by selecting significant material and combining it gradually in such a way that the reader perceives a steady increase in its total importance, and thus is led to follow the action through until the outcome is revealed. Suspense is greatest at the climactic height, but its accompanying interest does not cease until the outcome is made clear. But in order that the interest shall continue, the outcome should not be too long postponed after the climactic height is passed.

Shall I try to forecast the outcome to the reader? Not if you must betray the outcome to do so. But if the forecasting so hints the outcome as to stimulate interest, raising a doubt or an expectation even while seeming almost to settle it, the effect is good. This is one means of creating suspense; the facts, incidents, or hints make us expect an outcome of significance. (But in a story that shows the steady advance of fate, the effect is produced largely by the sense that the struggle is futile; therefore, the forecasting may be plainer.)

Is it advisable to introduce opposed atmosphere or tone elements? They may be introduced for the sake of contrast, and in longer stories different movements may have each a different atmosphere or tone. But the final effect must be one of unity, not of incongruity.

How can I be "original"? By having energy and thoughtfulness enough to create a viewpoint of your own in you, and then by daring to see the world from your point of view. Originality implies independence, observation, knowledge, and power of expression. Perhaps it is largely a matter of temperament, and therefore a gift of the gods; yet it can be encouraged by means of resolute and discriminating independence of view, and it can be destroyed by submitting to influences that produce blind acceptance of stock ideas. Systems of education that constrain all pupils to the same kind, quality, and extent of achievement, have been charged with destroying originality. The accusation may not be without foundation.

What must I do to attain " compression "? Employ the fewest possible means for establishing the fact and creating the effect that you are concerned with (economy of detail); suppress inessentials; reject materials that but moderately serve your purpose, and choose those that are pre-eminently effective. But do not think that compression means the complete stripping of the narrative to the bone; write all you need to write—managing your presentation skillfully —to accomplish your purpose.

You strike out so much of my detail; isn't it necessary to motivate and explain the various things that happen? It is necessary to motivate everything, but not to explain the motivation. For illustration: A person in your story is on one side of the street; it becomes necessary to have him on the other side. You need not explain how he comes to cross; it is immaterial whether he crossed to look into a show window or to flirt with a young woman. All that is necessary is, that it seem reasonable to have him on the other side. People cross the street for every sort of reason and no reason: why explain? In a word, then, explain only when explanation is unescapable; otherwise, make certain that the thing is reasonable and plausible, and let it explain itself. In the main, well-managed motivation requires no explanation; it requires only presentation.

Must the motivation make the outcome of my plot

inevitable? No; otherwise, where would there be any conflict? Ordinarily, there are two equally possible outcomes up to the decisive moment; only then does one outcome become inevitable and the other impossible.

Does the problem story have an outcome? Not always; see *The Lady or the Tiger?* If it have any outcome, this outcome will be of such character that it merely emphasizes the problem raised by the preceding facts.

Can I tell a story within a story? You can, but you had better not. Even in novels the story within a story is often pretty awkward; in the conte there is little place and less reason for it. Probably ninety-nine of every hundred story-within-a-story narratives could be remodeled to avoid this awkward method.

How can I get thoroughly familiar with the persons in my story? Before beginning the story, write the biography of each person; show him up to yourself in this history, so that you have a record of his past, his characteristics, and know him better than he knows himself. Then you won't have to stop so often to ponder whether his action is according to his character or not—quite likely deciding upon inconsistencies through this fragmentary method of creating your persons.

Is the document form of narration good for the short story? Any form is good that works, but the management of letters, notes, telegrams, diaries, and the like, calls for well-developed selective judgment, extreme skill in condensation of language, much skill in suggesting incidents from the documents, and a light, sketchy manner of composition.

How long ought the beginning to be? Make it as short as you can without losing its effect. Keep it in proportion with the narrative proper. Of course, when the action begins with the beginning, we can scarcely say that the story has a separate division called the opening.

Ought I to revise much? Of course you ought, and to rewrite too. Not infrequently a complete recasting of plot and narrative is necessary.

Are poetic words out of place? Not if they fit themselves to a poetic thought and this thought fits the tone, purpose, and subject of the story. Otherwise, they are out of place.

How can I acquire style? Don't try to—directly. Strive rather to report accurately what you observe and think and feel. Study words and language only with a view to becoming more able thus to set down truly and adequately what you have in mind. If you can do this, you will have style in abundance—provided what you have in mind is of value. In other words, don't struggle for " style "; struggle for thought, imagination, sympathy, understanding, and the power to utter what is in you. In any other sense, " style " is a snare and a betrayer.

Why do so many writers speak of the labor of authorship? Because authorship, seriously pursued, is laborious. Don't get the idea that, when you take up the writing profession, you are going for a picnic lunch in the cool of the evening. If you want an easy job, take up farming instead.

What short-story writer should I take as a model? All—and then none. Every writer who has done well enough to get a story into a reputable periodical is likely to show you something from which you can profit. But don't copy models; learn principles and apply them. It is *you* that will make your story worth reading if anybody does so.

But won't imitating help me? It may, at least in your earlier apprenticeship. Some persons can benefit materially from imitating, merely for practice purposes. But this is a sort of inductive study, exactly as is the copying of a great master by a student of painting; he copies in order to discover (a) just what the effect is that the master worked, and (b) just how he managed things—his principles and devices—to work that effect.

Who is the best short-story writer? The man who observes most, understands best, sympathizes deepest, most masterfully creates new persons and situations out of what he knows, and most clearly embodies in language the fruits of an abounding imagination.

Why do you strike out my descriptive beginnings? Frequently because they are not openings. A true opening does more than merely stand before the story; it " belongs "; it does something that the telling of the story calls for, and calls for at that place. Besides, your description keeps getting in the way of the action. Why describe when dramatic action is waiting impatiently for a chance to begin? And—you make them too flowery; your story often raises the suspicion that you wrote it just for a chance to work in the description.

How shall one block out the plot? After getting the working-plot and synopsis clearly in mind, make an action-plot or a scenario. Study the method of writing scenarios or action-plots for photoplays, and frankly follow that.

Where can I study motivation? In the great novels, short stories, and plays, and on the stage. The better class of photo-dramas sometimes afford excellent studies in motivation—but keep away from most of the European films, the melodrama, and the slapstick comedy. Photo-dramas written expressly for the screen show motivation better than do adaptations of plays, novels, etc.

Tell me how to learn to write dialogue. Listen to others, watch their tones, pronunciations, mannerisms, peculiarities of inflection, and vocabulary, etc., etc. Then practice; write out talks that sound true. Keep it up. You can get some practice, too, by writing out dialogue to accompany scenes from photoplays. Imitate; talk in the character of the person whose conversation you are trying to reproduce. Remember, successful fiction writing requires you to put yourself in the place of the person—and do in imagination what he would do.

How can I put my personal beliefs into a story? Don't; write a sermon—maybe someone would care for them there.

I see plenty of stories but can't discover a theme for them. You write the story; let the reader find the theme. 'Twill be there if you really have a story.

I can think of plenty of themes, but I can't find stories. Quit; or if you go on, drop the themes and think of nothing but plots, people, and stories.

Ought one to write about horrible subjects? Sometimes; sometimes not. As long as the painful, the repulsive, and the horrible, are part of life, art will be under the impulse and the obligation to interpret them. But too much horror destroys the pleasurable esthetic emotion that art is supposed to aim at. Commercially, the answer depends on your reading public. There is a steady market, of a certain sort, for " thrillers "; but if one does not wish to specialize in this border-line sort of stuff, he had better keep the horrible in a subordinate relationship to his other materials. Unpleasant stories are not desired by the magazines that " cater " to the " average " reader, and even the best magazines will seldom handle stories, even of power and literary excellence, that stir the emotions too strongly with intense motifs productive of a depressing or unpleasant reaction. Naturally, the artist, when he has such a story to write, will write it, and the God of Things as They Are will recognize the labor even though the gods of things-as-we-doctor-them-up can't really follow Him that far, don't you know.

Why are a good many of the most noted short stories based on intense motifs? Because the short story (conte), like the lyric, is especially adapted to presenting situations strong in feeling. We hear that " the short story gives us only a crisis,"—an assertion that is not strictly accurate, but that emphasizes an important tendency of the short story. And as we all know, emotion concentrates and breaks at the height of the crisis. Like this climactic height, the intensity of this emotion is transitory. We do not remain in a transport of feeling long at a time. Hence the short story, developing some brief situation, is peculiarly suitable for presenting those situations in which horror, grief, and other intense emotions, are uppermost.

The short story is so inadequate; one can't present the universal in it. Can't one? Can he present it even in a novel? If you mean that one can present only a bit of a fraction of the universal, we won't dispute. Presenting the universal merely means, when interpreted, selecting incidents and persons and situations that are representative of life, and handling them in such a way that they suggest a broad range of other situations in which similar conditions exist. Does not Ameera, in *Without Benefit of Clergy,* clearly and inescapably suggest the universal fact of woman's love and mother-devotion? After all, " presenting the universal " is just one of our cant phrases; nobody knows the universal truth; the best we can do is to seize upon some aspect of it, and set it forth so that others shall see it too. And any artist—short-story writer or other—can do that.

What is social characterization? It is the making clear of social conditions such as enter into the story. Anything that shows general facts about the society and life surrounding the persons and incident of a story, accomplishes social characterization. Study Mérimée's Corsican stories *Mateo Falcone* and *Colomba,* and Maupassant's *A Piece of String,* for passages in which the society appertaining to the central persons and incident is characterized. Many of Barrie's stories can be called social characterizations, because they interpret Scotch conditions so clearly; a similar thing could be said of Mrs. Freeman's New England stories. Stevenson's *A Lodging for the Night* is strong in social atmosphere, or characterization. Social characterization may sometimes give background *(The Piece of String, Without Benefit of Clergy),* and sometimes explain motive and act *(Falcone;* Morrison's *On the Stairs).*

Is it good practice to divide the story by means of asterisks or chapter numbers? Some books say it is not. Good writers do it. As the narrative drama often consists of separate movements, scenes, or situations, it seems nonsensical not to mark these off when they become long or are distinctly separated in the structural plan.

Can the short story interpret national character? What else do Barrie's Thrums stories do? Is not this what is done in part in Kipling's *An Habitation Enforced?*

What are character hints? Acts, words, etc., that give

us a suggestion of the character from which they spring. What sort of man has his room decorated with pictures of bathing-girls? What sort uses perfume? or walks two miles to the post office to trade a spoiled postcard for a good one? or buys twenty-five-cent cigarettes and takes his wife candy at twenty cents the pound? Similarly, there are picture hints, mood hints, and incident hints. Picture hint: A rugged, long-faced, slender old man, with his mouth even wider open than his eyes.—Mood hint: Penny Rod grabbed for his hat, and not getting it, danced a howling anger-dance at the feet of the bean-pole sixth-former.—Incident hint: Grimes went about methodically bandaging his hand in arnica-soaked strips of old flour-sacks. "Hit something?" asked Davis. Grimes's jaw set. "Hard," he answered laconically. After a pause, he added: "They had the doctor."

Why do my descriptions seem so vague? Because they are vague. You don't visualize, or you at least visualize but dimly. You explain a scene or an act, instead of seeing it in your mind's eye "just as real as real" and then writing down what you see. Train your imagination to picture things to you so that you clearly see them. Clear visualization is one chief explanation of Shakspere's greatness.

My first scene will be good, and then I run down. What's the cause of that? Lack of staying power and impatience to get the story in writing. You get a workable idea and think out a scene to begin with; then you are in such a hurry to see how the story will sound that you slap down the rest of your narrative without waiting to work it out incident by incident and detail by detail. You want your cake before it is done, or you haven't the endurance to stay with the job long enough to do it properly.

What are the important elements of a setting? Show me the setting and I will try to tell you. There are as many kinds of setting as there are kinds of bores. A setting may be material or psychological, moral or immoral, picturesque or commonplace, colorless or full of color, silent or noisy, quiet or full of action, clean or dirty, depressing or animating, and so on, and on again. The important elements of any setting are those things that make it especially useful for your action, theme impression, etc. Find out what that needs, and then study the setting for the right qualities to meet the requirements.

What books do you recommend? The book of life. After that, any that will broaden your mind, better your taste, develop your sympathies, inspire you with the spirit of words.

I want to write romance, but all my material seems so commonplace. You are blind on the romance side, and are holding your hand over the realistic eye. Give yourself a good long opportunity to discover romance in the common things of life, and if you fail, take up the writing of an Advice to Girls column in a newspaper. Honestly, can't you see the romance in that love affair between Billy, the hardworking clerk in the drugstore, and Grace, in at Miss Beeson's shop? Nor in young lawyer Kane's fight to keep Younger the hardware man from getting control of the coal supply of your village? Look again.

In getting material to adapt in new stories, how far back ought one to begin in the magazines? About six thousand years. If he wants really to be honest as well as safe, he ought not to " adapt " anything published later than the year one before the creation.   One may find hints and suggestions of new plots, new themes, new stories, anywhere; but there is an uglier word that means the same as " adapting."

How can I criticise my own work?   That is difficult to do, but if you are serious you will find a way.   But self-criticism presupposes dramatic and literary insight—the gift of perceiving when a piece of writing is well achieved or the opposite; if you lack this qualification, even earnestness will not help you.   You must also cultivate an impersonal attitude toward your completed work; so that you shall be able to regard it as unconcernedly as if it were your neighbor's.   Few persons can criticise their writings to advantage while the composition is still recent; hence the excellent advice so often given, that stories be laid aside and allowed to " cool " before criticism is attempted.

My friends say——.   Pray to be delivered from your friends.   Supposing them to be otherwise qualified, they are prejudiced by their friendship for you.   Some won't wish to offend you; others will think what you write good because you wrote it; others will be flattered by the chance to commend or disapprove a " real author."

How long shall I wait before inquiring about a manuscript submitted to an editor?   Be careful not to submit to doubtful periodicals; then give the editor all the time he seems to want up to six months.   The longer he keeps your story, the better the chance that he is pleased with it. If you wish to make certain that the MS. is delivered, enclose a postcard with it in this form:

...............19......

Receipt acknowledged of MS..............,
submitted to this magazine at owner's risk.

....
By........

Such a card is not necessary, but most offices will fill it out
without grumbling. Above all, when you do make inquiry,
don't do so in a complaining, grouch-begotten manner. Be
courteous and business-like.

Are market-notes in the writers' magazines accurate?
Many of them are as accurate as circumstances permit.
But often they are no more so than is a news item in a trade
journal, telling of the existence of a market, but indicating
absolutely nothing of the responsibility of the firm. Don't
send MSS. hit or miss on the basis of such information.
Some publishing firms so reported are little better than
fly-by-nights.

Can I copyright my story in advance of publication?
No. Our copyright law leaves the writer without any
protection from dishonest publishers, who can print his
work, copyright it themselves, and refuse to make settle-
ment in any way. Such publishers are usually law-proof.

INDEX

INDEX

FORENOTE

To instructors and students: Stimulus and helpful suggestion result from open discussion and free exchange of ideas. So far as possible, therefore, all exercises should be presented before the class or section—of course not omitting individual conference and criticism when advisable. Sometimes it proves feasible to place the students' exercises in the library or the seminar-room for reading and study by all the class. When this is done, the critical and suggestive reports from the members of the class will usually prove more carefully considered and more specific than are the opinions formed merely from hearing the narratives read aloud.

Every instructor must of course determine for himself whether he will lay out the time of the course on the basis of a large proportion of written work, with the textbook study collateral, or on the basis of textbook study, with writing and the other exercises merely supplementary thereto.

CHAPTER I

THEORY OF THE SHORT-STORY TYPE

Section I

1. *Reading-survey; the purpose of fiction.*—Make a rapid survey of short fiction in the current magazines, observing the emphasis of the stories upon *life* or upon *entertainment*. (Outside study-time for two or three recitations can well be devoted to this survey, followed by one period of class-room report and discussion. Large classes can be sectioned and the reading apportioned among the sections; and if the time be limited, the reading can be further apportioned to individuals. It will be better, however, for all students to read the same magazines, including those of the interpretive and those of the diversional tendency.)

In the following list, the more accessible and representative magazines are grouped, roughly, according to a general resemblance, or tendency, to be found in the stories they seem to prefer.

Group 1   The Little Review.
           The Atlantic Monthly.

———

           The Century.
           Harper's Magazine.
           Scribner's Magazine.
           The Touchstone.

Group 2   American Magazine.
             McClure's Magazine.
             Everybody's Magazine.

Group 3   Adventure.
             Argosy.
             All-Story Weekly.
             People's Favorite Magazine.
             Popular Magazine.
             Top-Notch Magazine.
             Detective-Story Magazine.
             Black Cat.

Group 4   Saturday Evening Post.
             Collier's Weekly.
               (Leslie's Weekly.)
             ———
             (Metropolitan Magazine.)
             ———
             Red Book Magazine.

Group 5   Ainslee's Magazine.
             Smith's Magazine.
             Munsey's Magazine.
             ———
             Blue Book Magazine.
             Green Book Magazine.

Group 6   Smart Set.
             Cosmopolitan.
             Hearst's.
             Live Stories.

Snappy Stories.
Parisienne.
Young's Magazine.
Saucy Stories.
Breezy Stories.
Telling Tales.

Group 7   Ladies' Home Journal.
Delineator.
Designer.
Good Housekeeping.
Harper's Bazar.
McCall's Magazine.
Pictorial Review.
Woman's Home Companion.

Group 8   Youth's Companion.
St. Nicholas.
Christian Endeavor World.
American Boy.
Boy's Life.
Open Road.

Book Group   Today's Short Stories Analyzed.
Best Short Stories of (current year).
This is the annual collection made by
Mr. E. J. O'Brien. It tends, however, to select stories of a specialized
manner and mainly of interpretive
spirit.

2. *Writing.*—In an expository or philosophical form,
state and explain some truth or principle of human

life.   Then write out a narrative or descriptive incident in which this truth is embodied in concrete acts, conduct, or speech.   (Make what is done and said show forth the abstract conception.)

3. *Writing.*—(Par. 14).   Write a sketch or incident in which you use familiar surroundings and persons as raw material, but work them into a product that differs noticeably from the originals.

4. *Writing.*—(Par. 15.)   Out of your own experience and knowledge, write an incident or sketch, or present a situation, that shall be the product of your own insight and understanding expressed in an original creation by your own imagination.   Length from 600 to 1500 words.

Sections II–III

5. Examine the stories read in connection with exercise 1.   Which ones are a development of loose-wrought plot, and which ones have a close-wrought plot?   (See sec. III.)

6. Continue the examination of the stories, classifying them according to their general structure, as sketches, tales, scenarios, etc.   (See sec. II, par. 3.)

7. *Writing.*—Work out a set of incidents for an original narrative of the loose-plot class.

8. *Writing.*—Work out a set of incidents for an original narrative of the close-wrought type of plot.   (If you can adapt to this exercise the incidents used in doing exercise 7, so much the better.)

Section IV

9. *Writing.*—Plan out and state a situation that depends on character (i.e., one that, when developed, will be

dramatic in the sense of par. 1, sec. IV). Do not attempt anything too complicated for comparatively brief development.

10. *Writing.*—Work out the set of incidents necessary to present and develop this situation. (Keep par. 6 in mind.)

11. *Writing.*—Write out the narrative that you have planned in exercises 9-10.

Section V

12. Review the narratives read in doing exercise 1, or read others that may be assigned in *Today's Short Stories Analyzed* or from magazines. Which of them present the situation in its most critical period only? Which of them present not only the critical period, but also tend to dwell on antecedent matters out of which the crisis grows?

13. Continue exercise 12. Is the critical period long or short in most of these stories? How long or short?

14. Consider the narrative written for exercise 11. Is the situation presented in its most critical period only, or does the narrative tend to dwell more or less on preliminary matters also, or otherwise to spread over more than the crisis?

Section VI

15. Return to the narratives read under exercise 1, or read others assigned by the Instructor from magazines or *Today's Short Stories Analyzed*. In a single sentence (when possible), state the dominant impression, or effect, produced. Have any of the stories a loose or general interest rather than a single, concentrated, dominant impression? Note how many of the loose-interest narratives are

narratives that develop the situation at its crisis only.
Are the narratives that devote themselves especially to the
crisis of the situation, loose or general in their interest,
or do they tend to be concentrated in effect? What conclusions do you draw from the examination?

16. *Writing.*—List ten definite, single impressions, or
effects, each of which might be taken satisfactorily as the
object of a story.

17. *Writing.*—Endeavor in limited space—as much
under 100 words as possible—to create a definite, pre-
planned impression. (Probably you will adopt the anecdote form, but not necessarily so.)—Repeat the exercise,
using a different form of presentation.

Section VII

18. Examine the narratives read under exercise 1, or
others that may be assigned from the magazines or from
Today's Short Stories Analyzed, etc. Note (a) those in
which the effect of the story is owed to the plot, and (b)
those in which it is owed to elements other than the plot.

19. Continuing the examination, determine concerning
each story whether its effect is that of (a) theme, (b) character, (c) incident and action, or (d) atmosphere. (See
par. 4.)

Section VIII

20. *Writing.*—Lay out a theme-story, setting down the
preparatory summary, or specifications, of it in writing.
(Pars. 10-11.)

21. *Writing.*—Write the narrative laid out in exercise 20.

22. *Writing.*—As in exercise 20. Lay out a purpose theme-story.

23. *Writing.*—As in exercise 20. Lay out a theme-story that presents a problem.

24. *Writing.*—Develop the forecast of No. 22 into a completed narrative.

25. *Writing.*—Do the same with No. 23.

Section IX

26. Examine narratives of the plot type, noting the parts that have to do respectively with (a) action, (b) incident, and (c) activity. (Plot stories are frequent in group 3, exercise 1, with group 4 and then group 2 probably following next in order.)

27. Continue exercise 26. Note which narratives especially belong to the ingenious-complication type, and which to the action type.

28. Find good instances of the mystery-story; of the surprise-plot.

29. *Writing.*—Lay out a story of the ingenious-plot type, and write the preparatory summary, or forecast.

30. *Writing.*—As in No. 29, but an action-plot story.

31. *Writing.*—As in No. 29, but a mystery story (cf. par. 9).

32. *Writing.*—As in No. 29; a surprise-plot story (unless one has already been laid out in one of the exercises just preceding this).

33. ⎫
34. ⎬ Write the story laid out in exercise ⎰ 29.
35. ⎪   ⎱ 30.
36. ⎭   31.
                                                32.

Section X

37. Cite stories that concern the dealings of men (a) with the physical world, (b) with other men, and (c) with moral or spiritual matters. Let some of the illustrations be drawn from contemporary sources. Note especially any story in which the physical, the social-human (men with men), and the spiritual are involved together.

38. Set down a catalogue of the fundamental elements or traits of human nature, or character (cf. pars. 8 and 11).

39. Pass in review before your mind five persons whom you know intimately. Catalogue the individualizing traits and tendencies of each (par. 9).

40. Continue your analysis of character in two or more of the five acquaintances. What individual traits of each can be traced to temperament, and what is the temperament of the individual involved? So far as you can judge, how has this particular temperament been produced in the person who has it? (See pars. 12-13.) To what causes do you ascribe the remaining individual traits?

41. *Writing.*—Conceive an imaginary character (a person and his or her traits). As concisely as possible, describe the character of this person in a direct expository statement or analysis. (Aim at a natural conception rather than at one of the exaggerated, bizarre, or sensational sort.)

42. *Writing.*—Using as a guide the character-statement just prepared, produce a character-sketch (not more than 1200 words). So far as possible, accomplish the presentation by recounting speech, acts, and conduct, rather than by direct explanation or mere explanatory description.

Section XI

43. In *Today's Short Stories Analyzed,* or other recent collection of short fiction, or in current magazines, find good examples of narratives that emphasize atmosphere, or subjective coloring.

44. *Writing.*—By means of narration, of description, or of the two combined, present a setting that is strong in atmosphere, or subjective coloring.

Note: In Nos. 44-48, seek the atmosphere in the thing itself; do not arbitrarily determine it. See No. 49.

45. *Writing.*—As in No. 44, but employing environment other than setting (see par. 8).

46. *Writing.*—As in No. 44, but employing subjective details (see par. 6, with note 21, and cf. sec. X, par. 15).

47. *Writing.*—Probably one or more of the exercises above (44-46) will possess mainly an objective atmosphere (see par. 6, note 21). Endeavor now so to treat its materials as to give it the atmosphere of mood or tone (subjective atmosphere) instead of that of material fact (objective atmosphere).

48. *Writing.*—As in No. 47, but endeavoring to change subjective atmosphere over to objective atmosphere.

49. *Writing.*—Determine in advance a mood or tone the impression of which you wish to give. Then present setting, environment, person, character, or situation in such a way as to create this impression. (This exercise may well be repeated, with variations of the impression planned for, of the length of the narrative, and of the means of creating the impression.)

CHAPTER II

THEORY AND PRACTICE OF THE PLOT

Section XII

50. *Writing.*—Work out and submit a plot-abstract for a dramatic conte. After consultation with the instructor, revise it.

51. *Writing.*—In from 20 to 75 words, characterize each of the persons, setting forth only those traits which are essential to the narrative. (Par. 2, A., B.)

52. *Writing.*—Make a summary of each of the incidents necessarily involved in producing the intended outcome. (Par. 2, C., D.)

53. *Writing.*—Give a statement of the reaction or threatened reaction of these incidents upon the persons. (Par. 2, E.)

54. *Writing.*—A statement showing the mutually opposed conditions or influences that create the complication. Then briefly indicate the progress of the conflict up to and including the crisis; and then on to the outcome.

55. *Writing.*—State the person's motive in each significant act or action wherein he has part. Do this for all the persons. (Par. 3, A.)

56. *Writing.*—State the effective cause or causes of each significant incident or development. (Par. 3, A.) This carries one further than does No. 55; the latter involves no causes other than individual motive in the persons.

56A. *Writing.*—For the moment, lay aside the plot on which you have been working, and devote yourself to producing a brief dramatic narrative after the general plan of *What the Vandals Leave* (but possibly a bit longer) or *The Song.* (See *Today's Short Stories Analyzed,* pp. 3 and 6.)

57. *Writing.*—Endeavor so to treat *Anchors Aweigh* (*Today's Short Stories Analyzed,* pp. 10 and 12), as to turn it into a dramatically plotted narrative. (Other episodes, sketches, tales, etc., of the non-dramatic type, will afford material for similar practice.)

Section XIII

58. *Writing.*—Returning to the plot taken in hand in Nos. 50 to 55, set down a summary of the situation, covering all important facts as they exist at the beginning of the action (i.e., summarize the matters belonging to the exposition).

Section XIV

59. *Writing.*—State what constitutes the exciting moment in your plot (Nos. 50-55 and 58); the generating circumstances. Then present the narrative completed as far as the beginning of the development. (This of course will not be possible in case your narrative opens with action belonging to the development of the plot.)

60. At this point, a review may be made of the various plots on which the class members have been at work, to test the complication and generating circumstance for naturalness, congruity, and plausibility. Pars. 5-14.

Sections XV–XVI

61. *Writing.*—Continuing the development of the plot worked out in Nos. 50-55, 58-59, write out the first stage [1] of the rising action from the point where the narrative was left by exercise 59.

62. *Writing.*—Produce the next stage [1] or stages of development, up to and including the decisive moment. (Note whether this is also the climactic height of your narrative.)

63. *Writing.*—Complete the narrative, unless it reached completeness with and in the decisive moment. If your narrative includes falling action, consider whether it gains or loses thereby, and whether, by readjustment, the stage of falling action cannot be avoided with benefit to the artistic effect.

64. Study the completed narrative with reference to the kind of interest belonging to its incidents (see sec. XV, pars. 19-22).

Are the matters introduced interesting in themselves?

If not, do they become interesting because of their importance in the action?

Are they sensational or melodramatic? Necessarily so? Displeasingly so? Implausibly so?

Are they conventional, hackneyed, dull?

Are they true to human nature? to class trait? to individual character? to experience?

To what extent are they drawn from ordinary life, persons, and affairs?

---

[1] The term may here be regarded as including single incidents that advance the action, with such contributory matter as coheres with them in the natural process of narrating.

If there is failure of interest, is it caused by unsympathetic treatment or lack of imagination in the presentation? by lack of command of style and expression? by over-detailed or under-developed presentation?

What means can you suggest by which interest may be created or intensified in the narrative as a whole, or in any of its parts or incidents?

65. Study the narratives with reference to the presence in them of intensifying, or concentrative, material (sec. XV., pars. 30-42).

Is this material helpful to its narrative?

In what way?—to create mood or tone? to intensify environment or setting effects? to gain other atmosphere effects? to emphasize character or person? to emphasize theme? to increase the impression of activity?

Is it well selected to accomplish its purpose?

Is it well presented, especially with regard to its purpose? In what respects?

Is it skilfully " integrated " with, or worked into, the narrative?

Is there too much of it? Is any of it too much amplified or otherwise made over-prominent?

Does it agree with the narrative, in view of the latter's motif, or basic theme and purpose? Or does any of it seem incongruous?

66. *Writing.*—Thoroughly revise, and if necessary entirely reconstruct, your narrative in accordance with the increased realizations of its problems and possibilities that you have gained.

CHAPTER III

The Compositional Construction of the Story

Sections XVII–XVIII

67. *Writing.*—Work out another plot. Develop it to the scenario stage.

68. *Writing.*—See pars. 1 and 4, the tables. Write an opening for the story outlined in No. 67; let it begin the action.

69. *Writing.*—Write another opening for the same story. Let this one emphasize character.

70. *Writing.*—Write yet another opening for the story. This time let it especially create atmosphere.

71. *Writing.*—Write a fourth opening, this time bringing forth the theme.

72. Study the individual effectiveness, merely in themselves, of each of the four openings.

73. Study the four openings with reference to their effectiveness in introducing, or starting off, the story. Which evidently gives this narrative the best start? Which seem less well adapted to introducing this particular narrative and its body of materials?

74. *Writing.*—Write a fifth opening, in which you endeavor to accomplish together all the various purposes aimed at separately in the four previous openings. Compare its effectiveness with that of the others.

75. *Writing.*—Finally, write the opening that you feel is the right opening for its own sake—that is, an opening

that seems to you most artistically and satisfactorily to accord with what is said in sec. XVII, par. 21, and sec. XVIII, par. 21, regardless of the experimental forms already prepared. In this last draft, freely follow your own instinct and feeling.

Sections XIX–XXI

76. *Writing.*—Complete the telling of your story from the point at which you left it in one of the openings constructed in exercises 68-71, keeping the narrative adjusted to this beginning. (See No. 80.)

77. Writing.—Complete the telling of your story as you prepared for it in exercise 75. Let this version represent freely and thoroughly your own conception and method.

78. Submit your personal version (exercise 77) for criticism by the class and the instructor with reference to:

Basic conception and motif.

Plotting and motivation.

Management of incident and action.

Conception and presentation of persons and character.

Interest and suspense.

Integration of materials.

Degree and effectiveness of atmosphere.

Esthetic and artistic qualities—imagination, emotional appeal, style, etc.

Ultimate impression—its strength, effectiveness, truth to experience and probability, spiritual value, etc.

79. *Writing.*—Make all the betterment that you can in the story; then submit it (typewritten) to the most

probable market. In case of rejection, submit the MS. in turn to three or more other markets.

80. Examine the version of your story prepared in exercise 76. Has the telling been hampered or otherwise affected disadvantageously by the form of opening employed? What means can you see for making this version more effective as a whole, though still adhering to its original plan? Could the opening be beneficially rewritten, retaining however its original purpose? From what point of view, if any, might the telling of the story in this form be advisable?

CHAPTER IV

Other Problems of Fiction-Writing

Section XXII

81. *Writing.*—Lay out a narrative in which one person unmistakably dominates the whole (it may be possible to have but this one person in the story). Tell the story.

82. Examine the completed narrative, noting the presence or absence in it of the unities mentioned in pars. 10-15.

83. *Writing.*—Lay out a narrative in which the leading person appears in both childhood and maturity, but in which the central action concerns that person only as a grown-up.

84. *Writing.*—Lay out and write a story in which an interval of several years falls in between important stages of the central action. Pay especial attention to the management of the transition, so that the existence of this time-break may not interfere with the reader's sense of unbroken continuity and single unity in the story as a whole.

85. *Writing.*—Lay out and write a narrative in which part of the essential action takes place at a remote distance from the scene of the rest. Especially try to give a sense of relation and connection existing between the separated locations, thus preventing, if possible, the effect of break and strangeness, with the consequent necessity of readjustment of the reader's imagination. (Sound motivation will

require that the double location be essential to the plot.)

86. *Writing.*—Try the experiment of writing a narrative in which the single ultimate impression is produced merely by the fact that the incidents introduced all take place in the same setting (or the same setting and environment). Study the completed narrative with a view to finding means of strengthening it in interconnectedness and otherwise increasing the sense of unity in it. (Par. 13.)

87. *Writing.*—Try a similar experiment, aiming especially at atmosphere effect from assembling several individual incidents of like impression-quality. (Par. 13.)

88. *Writing.*—Try a third experiment, aiming at theme presentation from incidents not closely associated with one another otherwise than by the fact that they illustrate the same idea. (Par. 13.)

89. Study the narratives produced by the experiments of exercises 86-88. What degree of unity seems likely to result from the employment of the plan of structure, or kind of plot-structure, depended on in these narratives?

Section XXIII

90. *Writing.*—State 5 plot-germs.

91. *Writing.*—Selecting one of the 5, adjust and develop it into a working-plot of (A) theme; (B) character; (C) atmosphere; (D) action.

92. *Writing.*—Taking one of the working-plots stated in accordance with exercise 91, set down a list of incidents and other materials adapted to its effective development. Submit the " layout " for criticism and suggestion.

93. *Writing.*—Another, as in No. 92.

94. *Writing.*—Another, as in No. 92.

95. State the outcome of each of the working-plots (exercise 91), and determine whether or not it promises enough "significance" (interest or interpretation) to justify your completing the narrative. (Par. 5.)

96. Are the conceptions and materials of the working-plots (exercise 91) such as the writer who proposes them is, by reason of familiarity with them, probably qualified to treat?

97. Study the proposed working-plots (No. 91) with reference to their natural fitness for story purposes—i.e., their "dramatic availability" as that term is explained in par. 7.

98. *Writing.*—Having revised the most promising of your working-plots, write the story from it.

99. Read three or more of these stories (in *Today's Short Stories Analyzed*), and decide whether or not, by their reporting of life, they present some definite view of or attitude toward life; (see pars. 10-13):

In the Matter of Distance.
A Ragtime Lady.
Little Sunbeam.
The Last Rose of Summer.
An Epilogue.
The Defective.
That Hahnheimer Story.

Is this view or attitude stated explicitly, or is it merely implied in the situations and details reported? (The same test can also be made upon narratives appearing in the current magazines.)

Sections XXIV–XXV

100. In *Today's Short Stories Analyzed* or other collections, or in current magazine narratives, find good examples of characterization. Bring them to class for discussion.

101. *Writing.*—Narrate an anecdote, incident, or episode that reveals miserliness in its central person.

102. *Writing.*—Repeat the exercises of No. 101, exemplifying such character-qualities or traits as:

A. Hopefulness.
B. Courage.
C. Gluttony.
D. Bashfulness.
E. Faith.
F. Generosity.
G. Vengefulness.
H. Flippancy.
I. Cruelty.
J. Deceitfulness.
K. Stupidity.
L. Grossness of taste.
M. Imaginativeness.
N. Sympathy.
O. Slovenliness.
P. Fickleness of purpose.
Q. Irresoluteness.
R. Bullheadedness.
S. Love of children.
T. Luxuriousness.
Etc., etc.

103. *Writing.*—Following the instructor's directions, develop some of these "studies" into character-sketches. Aim at narrational and dramatic presentation so far as it is possible.

104. *Writing.*—Make an observational study of persons engaged in the same occupation or otherwise belonging to a distinct, clearly distinguishable class. By means of sketch, incident, etc., portray a member of this class, as such. The following list of class-subjects is suggestive merely:

The Swedish farm-laborer, the Hungarian miner or steel-worker, etc.

The Polish housemaid.

The rural or the urban school-ma'am or school-master.

The stenographer (man; woman).

The young army officer.

The floor-walker, the male department-store "clerk," etc.

The newly-prosperous, society-aspiring, small-town woman of humble past.

The blacksmith, the plumber, the painter, etc.

The preacher.

The chauffeur, the taxi-driver, etc.

The idle or coddled son or daughter of well-to-do parents.

The village politician.

The city or the small-town "bum."

The person of aristocratic instincts (look up the meaning of "aristocrat.")

The person of intellectual or of non-intellectual instincts.

The person of imaginative mind.
The literal-minded person; the bigot; the prude.
Etc., etc.

105. *Writing.*—Make an observational study of some particular race or nationality. By means of sketch, incident, etc., portray a person or a group of persons of this race or nationality, putting emphasis on the race or national characteristics.

106. *Writing.*—Lay out and complete a narrative in which one set of national or race traits is in conflict with another set in the same person. This might (for example) be the case in a person of mingled Negro and White blood, or in one of German family but American or English or French or Italian culture.

107. *Writing.*—By means of sketch, incident, etc., portray two persons of widely different class, yet in whom the same basic traits of character assert themselves. (One illustration can be found in *In the Matter of Distance,* in *Today's Short Stories Analyzed.*)

Sections XXVI–XXVII

108. Make an observational study of the manner of speech of several persons of the same degree of education and similar social status.

109. Study the differences in manner of speech between the men and the women of this group.

110. *Writing.*—Write a few short conversations representative of the manner of speech of these persons. If the conversations are made to arise out of and develop a situation, so much the better.

111. Study the speech of other groups and classes; as, that of:

New Englanders.

Ohio Valley residents.

City dwellers, villagers, and country folk in the same region.

Natives of particular localities, states, or sections; as, the Pennsylvania German districts; Kentucky, Arkansas, Iowa, Montana, Quebec, British Columbia, etc.

112. As opportunity offers, study more extreme dialect peculiarities—the vocabulary, pronunciation, sentence-structure, etc., of persons of foreign national or provincial language, or of occupation, environment, or status productive of dialectal peculiarities; etc. For example:

Italians, Armenians, Japanese.

Sailors, miners, farmers; lawyers and policemen; youths of slum breeding; etc.

Lowlanders of the Blue Ridge region.

Mountaineers of the Blue Ridge region.

Venetian Italians and Calabrian Italians.

Educated Parisians and Parisians of the streets.

(The causes producing peculiarities and divergences of speech are many. When an author is faced with the necessity of introducing dialect, he may have to make a special study of the speech of the class of persons he is presenting.)

113. *Writing.*—Continue the practice-writing of conversation and dialect, as outlined in No. 110.

114. *Writing.*—Carefully attend on chance conversations within your hearing; then endeavor to reproduce them *verbatim.*

115. *Writing.*—Endeavor to turn the conversations reported *verbatim* in No. 114, into a form that would be usable in fiction or stage pieces.

116. *Writing.*—Reproduce conversation of some precise, restrained, colorless talker.

117. *Writing.*—Reproduce conversation of a vivid, animated, imaginative talker. (Setting off the two speakers of 116 and 117 will afford practice in contrast.)

118. *Writing.*—Do a character-sketch that depends principally upon conversation as the means of portrayal.

119. *Writing.*—Lay out and write a narrative that is developed largely by means of dialogue.

SUPPLEMENTARY PRACTICE

The exercises that follow provide practice in various contributory processes important in fiction-writing.

120. *Writing.*—Study 10 persons. Adequately picture each in a compact descriptive characterization of from 10 to 30 words.

121. *Writing.*—Study 10 rooms, interiors, buildings (any sort), etc., and picture each forth in its leading aspects or impression, in from 15 to 40 (at most 50) words.

122. *Writing.*—As in the two preceding exercises, endeavor in the fewest adequate words to make the reader realize:

A. The characteristic movement or motion of 10 different things, animate or inanimate.

B. Ten experiences, or sensations, of sound (separate or in medley).

C. Five sensations of touch or contact.

D. Five sensations of taste.

E. Five odors or smells.

F. Five different psychological or nervous states or reactions, depending on either physical or mental cause or provocation (as, that resulting from a sudden blow; the experience of "coming out" from the influence of an anesthetic; the feeling that accompanies joy, grief, surprise, etc., etc.).

123. *Writing.*—Using but a sentence or two for each, indicate or suggest (but do not tell outright) the mood of 5 persons, the mood in each instance being different from the others. (If possible, observe actual persons under the influence of a mood, and base these mood-hints upon the behavior so noted.)

124. *Writing.*—Moneyless Miss Carman has her cap set for the wealthy but blundering and sensitive Professor Nimmo. Offering her refreshments, he has just spoiled her one good evening gown by upsetting coffee over it. Reveal, in a few words, her feelings. Afterward, endeavor by means of other hints to reveal the same thing in four other forms.

125. *Writing.*—Set forth another situation such as would produce a mood, and by recounting behavior and similar signs reveal the mood so produced—but without naming it. Do the same twice more, but for other moods.

126. *Writing.*—Continue exercise 125 as directed or as time permits. In some of the work, do not set forth the situation, but make what you write reveal not only the mood, but the circumstances producing it. Let some of this practice be based on immediate observation, and some of it be imaginative.

127. *Writing.*—Describe a scene (as, persons at a town meeting or a political rally, at a religious revival, at worship, at the theater, in the home, etc.) wherein mood or moods are noticeably present. (Good practice is obtained by observing actual gatherings and accurately reporting them descriptively, then changing the report into a description that aims at artistic rather than at fact presentation.)

128. *Writing.*—Do a narrative-descriptive sketch in

which you portray the feelings of a person undergoing for the first time what to him are unfamiliar experiences; as, a city boy or girl in the country, a landsman taking his first sail on the salt water, a timid tourist lost in the slums, etc., etc.

129. *Writing.*—Something is taking place outside the reach of your direct observation; but a group of persons whom you can see are in turn observing that which is going on—the capsizing of a boat, the slaughter of "bourgeois" prisoners by the bolsheviki, the spanking of an offensive child by its mother, a rescue from a burning house, a burial. So describe the behavior of these persons, their attitude, movements, expressions, etc., that we shall understand what is taking place and share their feelings.

Note.—Artistic suggestion is accomplished largely by the employment of details and diction that make what is dealt with seem vivid, real, and even actual. It involves *visualization,* or the ability to see things clearly, in the concrete, and as it were with imaginative background. To say that "The swimmer was a large, fat man who must have weighed more than 300 pounds," is to be merely matter-of-fact. But to say that "The swimmer was a blubberous leviathan of a man, whom any old whaling-captain would have estimated at a glance as capable of trying out whole barrels of oil"—that is to set forth a picture that goes far beyond the matter-of-fact in imaginative stimulus and interest. (Visualization extends to everything that can in any way be perceived by senses or mind. Thus, odor is suggestively visualized if we say, "As the Pole's big fist flourished itself under Harold's nose, it struck his dainty nostrils with a smell as if the man had been pulling onions since childhood and had never washed his hands in all that time." A state of mind is visualized for us by such a sentence as this: "He could measure his own terror in the cold contraction of his heart and the strained staring of his eyes.")——The following group of exercises will afford the student opportunity both to test and to increase his power of visualization and his skill in artistic suggestion.

130. *Writing.*—Put before us Christmas day in a Jewish family; in a New England or other native American family.

131. *Writing.*—Tell of foods or eating in such a way as to make the reader's mouth water.

132. *Writing.*—Visualize to yourself some favorite place of childhood. Set it before the reader in language that will make him feel the charm it had for you. (Very likely you will idealize it somewhat—a legitimate thing in seeking artistic effect.)

133. *Writing.*—Similarly, make the reader realize some spot or place that you dislike.

134. *Writing.*—It is New Year's morning. Make the reader feel like it.

135. *Writing.*—Begin with the words, "The slender tree bent with her weight." Then put before us an incident in which a girl or woman has been treed by a dangerous animal—anything from a man to a skunk. The situation can be anything from the ridiculous to the tragic.

136. *Writing.*—Visit a slaughter-house, packing-house, soap-factory, tannery, or the like, and describe the place with reference especially to its odors, individual, cumulative, and collective.

137. *Writing.*—Observe a sunrise and visualize it for the reader. Avoid the trite, conventional, and bromidic. (Practice in visualizing aspects of nature can be continued indefinitely, observing the same things under different conditions, thus learning their endless variations—sunsets, rains, snow-storms, winds, cyclones, dry weather, heat, cold, trees and woods, fields and pastures, etc., etc.)

138. *Writing.*—Visualize for the reader:

A. A dog-fight.

B. A bull-fight (not necessarily the Spanish kind).

C. A fight between stallions.

D. A man-fight.

E. A fight between women.

F. A cock-fight.

G. A fight between bee-martins and a hawk.

H. The struggles of a hooked fish.

I. The struggles of an animal taken in a trap.

Etc., etc.

139. *Writing.*—Visualize for the reader a family scene in a happy home; then one in an unhappy home.

140. *Writing.*—Visualize for the reader the reversal of conditions in these two scenes (No. 139) through the sudden receipt of bad or good news.

141. *Writing.*—Visualize for the reader a crowd in which numerous diverse types are mingled.

142. *Writing.*—News of a great national defeat has been received. Visualize for the reader your home community under its effect.

143. *Writing.*—Visualize for the reader 10 prominent persons in your community. Aim less at mere fact-precision than at artistic realization, or " suggestive selection and intensification of details."

144. *Writing.*—Visualize for the reader the pens of a large stockyards, or some other place where cattle are assembled in large numbers.

145. *Writing.*—Visualize for the reader the behavior of a dog that has just been whipped.

146. *Writing.*—Visualize a flourishing poultry-yard, devoting half your space to a hen that has just laid her daily egg.

147. *Writing.*—Visualize a cat or group of cats characteristically occupied.

148. *Writing.*—Visualize a hospital or sick-room scene.

149. *Writing.*—Build a narrative in which Betsy Billings (who fits the name) and Kathleen Knowles, are set off against each other, contrast playing an important part in producing the effect of the story.

150. *Writing.*—Edwin Sayres, intellectual and studious, is the son of the " rich " family of the town. The family have no sympathy with learning and dislike his intellectual aspirations. In Joe Forbes, a blacksmith, he finds a congenial friend, well and on the whole soundly read. Sayres decides that Forbes's life is happier and his ideals higher than those of the Sayres family, and apprentices himself to the trade. Write this out. The force of the story will lie in the contrast between the opposed points of view, ideals, living-conditions, and conduct of the Sayres family and the blacksmith. (If a love element be introduced, keep it subordinate to the main purpose of the narrative.)

151. *Writing.*—Write a story based on the complete contrast between the outer life of the central person, and his (or her) deepest inner desires and longings. (Example, the " fighting terror " of the police force,

whose greatest, though secret, ambition is, to own a little green-house and grow violets.)

---

152. *Writing.*—Build a story out of this situation: Rural environment; people largely ignorant and credulous; religious sect among them, preaching the last trump and end of the world to come within the next two years; sweetheart of young woman convert dies; in order not to be separated from him at the last day, she takes up a constant vigil at his grave.

153. *Writing.*—In several negatives of outdoor scenes, a kodaker finds the same face appearing among the flowers or foliage. Build up a story from this beginning idea.

154. *Writing.*—The husband has at last discovered that his young wife cannot cook well, and probably will never learn. He has also discovered that his attractive sister-in-law has a natural gift for such things. Carry husband and wife through the domestic crisis without sacrificing probability or wrecking the marriage.

155. *Writing.*—Build a story that, in character and class traits, customs, language, occupations, etc., is definitely localized (as, for instance, on a North Dakota wheat farm or in a Short Creek lead-and-zinc-mining town).

156. *Writing.*—Lay out and write a narrative in which a poisonous snake has an important part. Avoid the exaggerated and sensational.

157. *Writing.*—Hammell's chickens keep getting into Brown's yard and injuring the garden. Build into a story the history of the tragedy (or comedy) that develops.

158. *Writing.*—State working-plots for stories to bear the following titles:

A. Squab Pie.
B. The Suffragette Parrot.
C. The Patched Window-Pane.
D. Folding Doors.
E. Purple Asters.
F. Sorrow Shack.
G. McCarthy, Moving and Trucking.
H. Subway Guard 098277.
J. Something You Wish, Madame?
K. I'll take the Check.

159. *Writing.*—No. 158 continued:
L. I ka' klo' (I cash clothes; i.e., pay cash for old clothes.)
M. Umbrellas to Mend.
N. "Returned—No Funds."
O. One Chinese Cash.
P. A Time-Table on the Z.R.
Q. Pink Glasses.
R. One Flight Up.
S. Next Station is Ellumville.
T. Skimmed Milk.
U. Mulcahey's "Old Master."
V. Crab-Apple Jell.
W. Middle Age—and Millie.
X. On Approval.
Y. A Mistress of Arts.
Z. Mis' Pellew's Old Quilt.

160. *Writing.*—As opportunity permits, develop the working-plots to the scenario stage (Nos. 158-159).

161. *Writing.*—As opportunity permits, complete the stories (Nos. 158-160).

162. *Writing.*—Submit 20 titles of your own creation for consideration.

163. Begin a note-book or other file for preserving plot-ideas; for preserving memoranda concerning character traits, appearance of persons, peculiarities of speech, notable settings and environment, incidents and situations of dramatic promise, suggestive titles, etc., etc. (This record should be kept up and steadily enlarged.)